Thomas Carpenter

**The Scholar's Spelling Assistant**

Thomas Carpenter

**The Scholar's Spelling Assistant**

ISBN/EAN: 9783337306779

Printed in Europe, USA, Canada, Australia, Japan

Cover: Foto ©Paul-Georg Meister /pixelio.de

More available books at **www.hansebooks.com**

THE SCHOLAR'S
# SPELLING ASSISTANT;

WHEREIN

## THE WORDS

ARE

## ARRANGED ON AN IMPROVED PLAN,

ACCORDING TO THEIR RESPECTIVE

## PRINCIPLES OF ACCENTUATION.

IN A MANNER

CALCULATED TO FAMILIARIZE THE ART OF SPELLING AND PRONUNCIATION, TO REMOVE DIFFICULTIES, AND TO FACILITATE GENERAL IMPROVEMENT

INTENDED

## FOR THE USE OF SCHOOLS AND PRIVATE TUITION

---

### BY THOMAS CARPENTER
MASTER OF THE ACADEMY, ILFORD ESSEX.

---

*Thirtieth Edition, corrected, and the Appendix enlarged and improved.*

---

Charleston, S. C.
PUBLISHED BY McCARTER & DAWSON,
CORNER OF MEETING AND PICKNEY STREETS.
1861.

Entered according to Act of Congress, in the year 1835,
By PHILIP HOFF,
in the Clerk's Office of the District Court of the United States, for the District of South Carolina.

## ADVERTISEMENT.

The first and second American Editions of "The Scholar's Spelling Assistant" having been more generally adopted by Seminaries of Learning, than was originally anticipated, has induced the publisher to offer a Seventh Edition, Revised.

In the *Appendix* to this, English derivation is extensively considered. The prepositive and terminational particles are critically explained and illustrated. It is hoped, that the view of the Greek and Latin prepositions may prove useful to all classes of learners in determining, in many cases, independent of usage, the English prepositions which ought to *follow* particular words.

As an inducement to the study of derivation, it may in general be said that many words are derivatives of but a single root, and may therefore be defined by joining the meaning of the root with those of the modifying particles. Ignorance of derivation and its converse operation is undoubtedly a principal reason that children never have a stock of words commensurate with their combination of ideas. Hence they can hardly commence this study too early. They should in deed be put to it as soon as they can read and have learned to distinguish nouns, adjectives, verbs, and participles; and be exercised in reducing words to their primitives; in defining them by joining the meanings of the modifying particles first to the primitives, and then to the meanings of the primitives; and finally, in the converse operation, that of determining the words from their definitions. It is by this last exercise chiefly that they can increase their stock of words, and be prepared for the important study of the synonymes and general usage of words.

The body of the work is still printed page for page with the former Editions, and the corrections made so as not to prevent the different impressions being used in the same class.

# PREFACE.

The design of the following work is to furnish young persons with an easy guide to Spelling, and to combine utility with cheapness. In treating the subject, the Author has not only been attentive to the usual classification of words according to alphabetical order and their number of syllables; but he has likewise taken care to arrange the words in separate divisions, according to their respective modes of accentuation, which he considers as an additional, and very material improvement; as the uncertainty of placing the accent, which appears to be the most general difficulty to the young scholar in pronouncing his language, is successfully obviated by this method of arrangement.

As an additional help to ascertain the proper pronunciation of particular words, the equivocal sounds of the letters *c, s,* and *g,* are carefully distinguished in an easy and compendious method. Thus the learner will observe that the letter ç with this mark annexed to it, always bears a soft sound like the letter *s,* as in cell (*sell;*) and if marked thus ç it is sounded like *ts,* as in çhaff (*tshaff:*) ᶻs denotes the sound of z as in wiᶻse (*wize:*) ʲg represents the sound of j, as in 'gem (*jem;*) and G with the cedille affixed, has a similar sound. When such marks are not affixed to these letters, they must be understood to retain their natural and more general sound, as in the words *call, house, get.* It must be observed likewise that in words where *h* is printed in the Italic character, it is not aspirated; and wherever any other letter occurs in that character, its sound is dropped. A circumflex over a vowel denotes a *long* sound, as in bôlt. Where difficulties or irregularities arise, which cannot be thus easily obviated, the scholar is referred to the bottom of the page for a correct pronunciation. The plan itself is doubtless extremely simple. But when the circumstances of those for whom it is professedly designed are considered, this simplicity itself will probably be esteemed a recommendation.

The Author regards the rapid circulation of the preceding editions of this little work as bearing testimony of an extensive approbation among the educators of youth; and he flatters himself that this approbation is founded on a general experience of the utility for the purposes which it professes to serve.

The authorities here principally followed, with regard to orthography, accentuation, and the occasional documents of pronunciation, are the dictionaries of Johnson, Walker, Sheridan, and Bailey. As to the explanatory matter, that of Bailey, with some exceptions, has been selected but where a concise or satisfactory exposition of a word could not be obtained, the Author has introduced one of his own.

To the spelling lessons he has added a few particulars necessary for the learner to be acquainted with; such as a table of Grammatical Terms, with their Marks and Explanations; another Table of the Contractions of Abbreviations commonly used in print or in writing.

He has likewise subjoined a catalogue of words apparently synonymous; but which are distinguished on a closer view, sometimes by minute, and sometimes by very striking shades of difference. It is not pretended that the distinct significations of these apparent synonymes are ascertained in every instance with etymological propriety or critical exactness. They are frequently exhibited merely according to their popular acceptation, and in a manner which, it is hoped, is accommodated to the ideas and capacities of those persons for whose use the book is particularly intended.

And to render it more unexceptionable to youth of both sexes, the greatest care has been taken to omit words of an impure and immoral tendency; as the minds of youth cannot be too circumspectly guarded against the admission of improper ideas.

On the whole, therefore, it has been his ardent endeavour or render the *Scholar's Spelling Assistant* as extensively useful as the prescribed limits of the undertaking would permit; and no less acceptable to teachers, than to those for whom it is peculiarly appropriated

# THE
# SCHOLAR'S SPELLING ASSISTANT.

*a.* for Adjective; *s.* for Substantive; *v.* for Verb; *part.* for **participle** *pro.* for Pronoun; *ad.* for Adverb; *prep.* for Preposition; *conj.* for Conjunction; *intj.* for Interjection; *pr.* for Pronounced.

## WORDS OF ONE SYLLABLE.

Parts of Speech.

### A.

*s.* ACHE, *pain*
*s.* Adze,* *a cooper's axe*
*s.* Arch,† *part of a circle*
*v.* Ate, *did eat*
*s.* Auln, *a measure*

\* When any letter or letters in a word are printed in Italics, the sound is dropped in pronunciation.
† *Ch* with the cross affixed to the Ç sounds like *tsh*, without this mark it must be understood to have the sound of *k*.

Parts of Speech.

*s.* Awe, *dread*
*ad.* Aye, *yes*

### B.

*s.* Babe, *an infant*
*s.* Balm, *an herb*
*v.* Balk, *to disappoint*
*s.* Batch,§ *a quantity*

§ ç with the cedille subjoined, has the soft sound of *s*.

s. Beak, *a bird's bill*
s. Blaze, *a flame*
v. Bleaçh, *to whiten*
a. Bleak, *raw, cold*
a. Blithe, *merry*
s. Blood, *the red fluid in animals*
s. Bloom, *blossom*
s. Blotch, *a pimple*
v. Bôast,* *to brag*
v. Boil,† *to bubble up*
s. Bôlt, *for a door*
s. Bomb, *a globe of iron containing combustibles, &c.*
s. Booth, *a tent*
v. Botçh, *to patch*
part. Bought, *purchased*
s. Braçe, *a couple*
s. Brain, *of the head*
s. Brawl, *a quarrel*
s. Breaçh, *a broken place*
s. Breadth, *width*
s. Breast, *the bosom*
v. Breathe, *to give air*
s. Breeze, *a gentle wind*
s. Bridjge,‡ *a passage*

a. Brief, *short*
s. Brine, *dissolved salt*
s. Broaçh, *to tap*
v. Brôgue, *corrupt speech*
s. Bronze, *brass*
s. Brooçh, *a jewel*
part. Brought, *of the verb to bring*
v. Brow$^z$se, *to feed*
s. Brui$^z$se,§ *a hurt*
v. Budjge, *to move*
v. Build, *to erect house*
s. Bulb, *a round root*
v. Buzz, *to hum*

C.

s. Calf, *young of a cow*
a. Calm, *quiet*
s. Calx, *hard cinder*
s. Caph, *a liquid measure*
v. Catçh, *to seize*
part. Caught, *seized*
v. Caulk, *to stop leaks*
s. Çhaff, *husks of corn*
s. Çhair, *a seat*
s. Çhai$^z$se, *a carriage*
s. Çhalk, *a white substance*
s. Çha$^z$sm, *a gap*
a. Çhief, *principal*
v. Çhirp, *to sing*
s. Çhoir,‖ *a band of singers*
s. Çhord,¶ *a line in geometry*

* ô. This mark over a vowel gives it a *long* sound.

† It is highly improper to pronounce this, or any other word that has the dipthong *oi*, such as boil, toil, soil as if written *bile, tile, sile*.

‡ The soft sound of *g* is here distinguished by a small *j* before the letter, thus jg, and the capital letters by a cedille G, which obviates the necessity of any directions in the way of notes, and when pointed out properly to the young learner, will be equally intelligible. Without these distinctions the *g* must be considered as having a hard sound as *gay, gum*.

§ zs. When *s* occurs with this mark to it, it sounds like *z*.

‖ *pr.* Kwire.

¶ *pr.* Kord. In words derived from the Greek, *ch* takes the sound of *k*; as *chorus, choir*.

# SPELLING ASSISTANT. 9

s. Chyle,* *stomach juice*
v. Clean²se, *to scour*
v. Cleave, *to stick : to split*
s. Cleft, *a crevice*
s. Cliff, *a rock*
s. Clòak, *a garment*
v. Clòthe, *to dress*
s. Clutch, *grasp*
s. Coin, *money stamped*
s. Coomb, *a corn measure*
s. Core, *the heart of an apple or pear: the inner part of fruit containing the kernel*
s. Corpse, *a dead body*
s. Couch, *a seat of ease*
s. Cough,† *a convulsion of the lungs*
s. Còurt, *a seat of justice, &c.*
v. Crawl, *to creep*
s. Crease, *a plait or fold*
s. Crew, *a ship's company*
v. Crinʲge, *to fawn*
v. Cròak, *to cry like a frog*
v. Cruiᶻse, *to sail in quest of an enemy*
s. Crutch, *a support*

s. Dart, *a weapon thrown by the hand*
v. Daub, *to smear*
v. Daunt, *to discourage*
s, Dawn, *break of day*
a. Deaf, *void of hearing*
s. Dearth, *a scarcity*
s. Death, *mortality*
v. Deem, *to think*
a. Deep, *low*
v. Deign,‡ *to vouchsafe*

\* *pr.* Kile.   † *pr.* Cauf.   ‡ *pr.* Dane.

v. Delve, *to dig*
a. Dense, *thick*
s. Depth, *deepness*
s. Desk, *a writing table*
s. Dirʲge, *a funeral song*
s. Disk, *face of the sun or moon*
s. Ditch, *a trench*
v. Dodʲge, *to shift place*
s. Dome, *a cupola or arched roof*
s. Doom, *fate*
s. Door, *of a house*
v. Doze, *to slumber*
s. Drain, *a water course*
v. Drawl, *to speak lazily*
s. Dread, *fear, terror*
s. Dream, *thoughts in sleep*
s. Dredʲge, *an oyster net*
s. Dross, *scum of metals*
v. Drudʲge, *to labour hard*
s. Dwarf, *a little person*
v. Dwell, *to live in*

## E.

s. Earl, *title of nobility next to marquis*
v. Earn, *to gain*
s. Earth, *land, mould*
s. East, *where the sun rises*
s. Eaves, *edges of buildings*
s. Edʲge, *a brink*
s. Eight,§ *a number*

## F

s. Fact, *truth : deed*
v. Fadʲge, *to agree*
v. Fail, *to do amiss*
s. Farce, *a mock comedy*
s. Fault, *an offence*
v. Fawn, *to flatter*
s. Feast, *a treat*

§ *pr.* Ate

v. Fetch, *to bring*
s. Feud,* *a quarrel*
s. Fief,† *a manor*
s. Field, *a meadow: the ground of battle, &c.*
a. Fierce, *furious*
s. Fight, *a battle*
v. Filch, *to steal*
s. Film, *a thin skin*
s. Filth, *nastiness*
v. Flaunt, *to strut about*
s. Flaw, *a defect*
s. Fleece, *wool of a sheep*
s. Fleet, *a company of ships*
s. Flight, *a running away*
v. Flinch, *to shrink back*
v. Flirt, *to move with quickness*
v. Float, *to swim*
s. Flock, *a crowd*
s. Flood, *a deluge*
s. Flour, *ground corn*
v. Flounce, *to toss about*
part. Flown, *gone off*
v. Foam, *to froth*
v. Foil, *to overcome*
s. Forge, *a smith's fire-place*
part. Fought,‡ *of the verb of fight*
a. Frank, *free, unreserved*
s. Fraud, *deceit, artifice*
a. Fraught, *filled with*
s. Freak, *a whim*
s. Friend, *a companion*
s. Fright, *terror*
s. Fringe, *a trimming*
v. Frisk, *to skip*
s. Frock, *a child's gown*
v. Frown, *to look sour*

\* *pr.* Fude.
† *pr.* Feef. The diphthongs *ie, ei,* and *ea,* generally take the sound of *ee,* as in *beak, b'each, bleak, defeat, grievance, receive.* ‡ *pr.* Faut.

s. Fruit, *plums, pears, &c.*
v. Furl, *to wrap up*
s. Furze, *a prickly shrub*

### G.

s. Gall, *bile: malignity*
s. Gaol, Jail } *a prison*
s. Garb, *dress, outside appearance*
v. Gasp, *to gape for breath*
v. Gauge, *to measure casks*
a. Gaunt, *lean, meager*
s. Gauze, *thin silk*
v. Gaze, *to stare*
s. Germ, *a bud*
s. Ghost, *a spirit*
v. Gild, *to adorn*
v. Gird, *to tie round*
s. Girth, *a girdle*
s. Gleam, *a streak of light*
v. Glean, *to gather up*
s. Glebe, *soil, turf*
s. Glimpse, *a short view*
s. Globe, *a round ball, a sphere*
s. Gloom, *darkness*
s. Gloss, *brightness*
s. Glue, *a sticky substance*
v. Glut, *to cloy*
v. Gnash,§ *to grind the teeth*
s. Gnat, *an insect*
v. Gnaw, *to nibble*
v. Goad, *to spur on*
s. Goat, *a beast*
s. Goose, *a fowl*
s. Gore, *clotted blood*
v. Gorge, *to glut*
s. Gourd, *a plant resembling a melon*
s. Gout, *a disease*
s. Gown, *a long garment*

§ *G* is always mute before *n.*

v. Grasp, *to seize hard*
a. Gray, *a colour*
v. Graze, *to feed on grass*
s. Grease, *fat*
s. Grief, *sorrow*
v. Grieve, *to mourn*
s. Groan, *a deep sigh*
s. Groom, *one who has the care of horses*
a. Gross, *bulky, fat*
s. Ground, *land, first principle*
s. Group,* *a cluster*
v. Growl, *to snarl*
v. Grudge, *to envy*
s. Guard, *protector*
v. Guess, *to conjecture*
s. Guest, *a visiter*
s. Guide, *a director*
s. Guile, *fraud, deceit*
s. Gulf, *a bay*
s. Gurge, *a whirlpool*

### H.

s. Half, *one part of two*
v. Halve, *to divide*
a. Harsh, *severe*
v. Hatch, *to breed young*
s. Haunch, *the thigh*
v. Haunt, *to frequent*
s. Hawk, *a bird of prey*
s. Health, *soundness of body*
s. Heap, *a pile*
s. Hearse, *a carriage for the dead*
s. Hearth, *a fire place*
s. Heath, *a small shrub : a place where it grows*
s. Hedge, *a bushy fence*
s. Height, *tallness*
s. Helm, *the rudder*
s. Herb, *a plant*

* *pr* Groop.

a. High, *lofty*
s. Hinge, *of a door*
s. Hire, *wages, fare*
s. Hoard, *a secret store*
a. Hoarse, *having a rough voice*
s. Hoe, *a garden tool*
v. Hoist, *to lift up*
s. Horse, *an animal*
v. Howl, *to cry aloud*
s. Husk, *the coat of corn, &c.*
s. Hutch, *a corn chest : a rabbit box*

### I. J.

s. Inch, *a measure*
s. Ire, *anger*
s. Jaunt, *a ramble*
s. Joint, *a joining*
s. Joist, *a small beam*
s. Judge, *a chief justice*
s. Juice, *gravy*

### K.

s. Keel, *the bottom of a ship*
a. Keen, *sharp*
v. Knab,† *to bite*
s. Knack, *trick, habit*
s. Knee, *of the body*
v. Kneel, *to bend the knee*
s. Knell,‡ *the toll of a bell*
s. Knife, *a cutting instrument*
s. Knob, *a knot*
v. Knock, *to hit*

† The sound of *k* before *n* in the same syllable, is slight and almost imperceptible.
‡ It is worthy of observation that *l* at the end of monosyllables is always doubled, except where a dipthong precedes it : for example, in the word before us, *knell*, there is only *one* vowel : but, in the foregoing, *kneel*, there are *two*, which constitutes a dipthong.

## L.

v. Lapse, *to slip or fall*
s. Latch, *a door-catch*
s. Lath, *a slip of wood*
v. Launch, *to put in the water*
s. Lawn, *fine linen: a plain between woods*
s. League, *treaty: three miles*
v. Learn, *to improve*
s. Lease, *a tenure*
s. Leash, *three creatures of a sort*
s. Leech, *an insect*
v. Leer, *to look archly*
s. Length, *distance*
v. Lie, *to lie down*
a. Liege, *trusty*
s. Lieu, *instead of*
s. Light, *illumination*
s. Load, *a burden*
s. Loaf, *a mass of bread or sugar, &c.*
v. Loathe, *to detest*
s. Loam, *a rich earth*
s. Loan, *any thing lent*
s. Loom, *a weaver's frame*
a. Loose, *not tight, lax*
s. Loss, *a losing*
a. Loud, *noisy, clamorous*
v. Lounge, *to loiter*
s. Lunch, *a meal*
v. Lurk, *to lie hid*
s. Lyre,* *a harp*

## M.

v. Maim, *to wound*
s. Malt,† *a preparation from barley*
s. Match, *for kindling*
v. Maul, *to beat soundly*

\* *pr.* Lire.
† It is Barley steeped, fermented, and dried.

s. Maze, *a labyrinth*
s. Mead, *a liquor: a meadow*
s. Mess, *a portion of food*
s. Mire, *dirt, mud*
s. Mirth, *joy, cheerfulness*
s. Moat, *a ditch*
s. Mode, *a fashion*
a. Moist, *wet, damp*
s. Month, *four weeks*
s. Mosque, *a Turkish temple*
s. Mound, *a bank*
v. Mourn, *to grieve*
s. Mouth, *part of the head*
s. Muff, *a case for the hands*
s. Mulct, *a forfeit, a pecuniary fine*
s. Myrrh, *a perfume*

## N.

s. Nail, *an iron pin*
s. Nard, *an odorous shrub*
a. Neap, *low, scanty*
a. Next, *nearest*
s. Niche, *a place for a statue*
a. Ninth, *before the tenth*
s. Noise, *a great sound*
s. Noon, *mid-day*
s. North, *opposite to the south*
s. Notch, *a dent, a hollow cut in any thing*
a. Numb, *chill, torpid*
s. Nurse, *an attendant on the sick*

## O.

s. Oak, *a tree*
a. Odd, *strange: uneven*
s. Oil, *liquid fat*
s. Ought, *somewhat*
s. Ounce, *a weight*
s. Owl, *a bird*
v. Own, *to acknowledge*

## P

- s. Pack, *a parcel, &c.*
- part. Paid, *satisfied*
- s. Paint, *colours of painting*
- s. Pall, *a funeral cloak*
- s. Palm, *a tree: part of the hand*
- v. Parch, *to dry up*
- s. Paste, *dough*
- s. Patch, *piece sewed on*
- s. Paw, *a beast's foot*
- v. Pawn, *to pledge*
- s. Pea, *a vegetable*
- s. Pearl, *a gem*
- s. Phiz, *the face*
- s. Phlegm, *spittle*
- v. Pierce, *to bore through*
- s. Pint, *half a quart*
- s. Pitch, *a clammy substance*
- s. Plague, *a disease : trouble*
- s Plea, *excuse*
- v. Plea$^z$se, *to satisfy*
- s. Pled$^j$ge, *a pawn*
- s. Plight, *condition*
- s. Plough, *a farming instrument*
- v. Pluck, *to strip feathers, to draw*
- v. Plun$^j$ge, *to dip*
- v. Poach, *to boil slightly*
- s. Point, *a sharp end*
- v. Poi$^z$se, *to balance*
- s. Pool, *standing water*
- a. Poor, *needy, not rich*
- s. Porch, *entrance of a house*
- s. Pounce, *a powder for paper*
- v. Pour, *to flow forth*
- s. Prai$^z$se, *commendation*
- v. Preach, *to deliver a sermon*
- s. Pri$^z$sm, *a solid body*
- s. Prize, *a reward gained, booty*
- s. Pro$^z$se, *language not in metre*
- a Proud, *conceited*
- s. Prude, *a precise woman*
- s. Psalm, *a sacred song*
- v. Pull, *to drag along*
- s. Pulp, *the soft part of fruit*
- s. Purse, *a small money bag*

## Q.

- s. Quack, *a pretender to physic*
- v. Quaff, *to drink luxuriously*
- s. Quail, *a bird of game*
- s. Qualm,* *a faintness*
- s. Quart, *two pints*
- v. Quash, *to overthrow*
- v. Quell, *to subdue*
- v. Quench, *to put out*
- a. Quick, *nimble*
- s. Quill, *a feather*
- s. Quilt, *a bed covering*
- s. Quirk, *a subtilty*
- s. Quoif, *a cap*
- v. Quote, *to cite an author, to adduce the words of another.*

## R.

- s. Raft, *a float of timber*
- s. Rail, *a slight fence*
- s. Rain, *water from the clouds*
- v. Rai$^z$se, *to lift : to levy*
- v. Ran$^j$ge, *to rove about*
- a. Rash, *hasty, precipitate*
- s. Rate, *a parish tax : a price*
- a. Raw, *undressed*
- v. Reach, *to take hold*
- s. Realm, *a kingdom*
- s. Ream, *twenty quires*
- v. Reel, *to stagger*
- s. Rhyme, *verse*
- s. Rice, *a kind of esculent grain*
- s. Rid$^j$ge, *top of a furrow*

* Q always sounds like *k*, is never mute, and is ever followed by *u*.

*v.* Rinse, *to wash*
*s.* Risk, *hazard*
*s.* Ròach, *the name of a fish*
*s.* Roar, *a loud noise*
*s.* Rock, *a mass of stone*
*s.* Rogue, *a knave*
*s.* Roof, *the top of a house*
*s.* Rook, *a bird*
*s.* Room, *space ; an apartment*
*s.* Roost, *a perch for fowls*
*a.* Rough,* *uneven : harsh*
*a.* Round, *circular*
*s.* Rout, *an uproar*
*v.* **Rue,** *to lament*

### S.

*s.* Saint, *a godly person*
*s.* Salt, *a mineral substance*
*s.* Sàlve, *a plaster*
*s.* Sash, *a silk belt : a window that lets up and down by pulleys*
*s.* Sauce, *gravy, pickle*
*v.* Scald, *to burn with hot liquors*
*s.* Scale, *a balance*
*s.* Scalp, *skin of the head*
*a.* Scarce, *rare*
*v.* Scare, *to frighten*
*s.* Scarf, *a loose covering for the shoulders*
*s.* Scate, *a flat fish : an iron to slide with*
*s.* Scheme, *contrivance*
*s.* School, *a place for education*
*v.* Scoff, *to mock, to ridicule*
*s.* Sconce, *a branched candlestick*
*s.* Scope, *drift, aim*
*v.* Scorch, *to burn slightly*
*s.* Scream, *a shrill cry*
*s.* Screech, *a harsh cry*

\* *pr.* Ruff.  †*pr.* Sheer.

*s.* Screen, *shelter against cold or light*
*s.* Screw, *an instrument*
*s.* Scroll, *a roll of parchment*
*v.* Scrub, *to rub hard*
*s.* Scud, *a flying cloud*
*v.* Sculk, *to lurk about*
*s.* Scum, *froth, dross*
*s.* Scurf, *a whitish scale*
*s.* Scythe, *a mowing instrument*
*s.* Sêal, *a stamp*
*v.* Sêar, *to burn*
*v.* Search, *to look for*
*s.* Seat, *a chair or bench*
*s.* Sect, *men united in certain tenets*
*s.* Sedge, *a long grass*
*part.* Seen, *beheld*
*v.* Seize, *to lay hold*
*s.* Sense, *faculty, judgment*
*s.* Serge, *a woollen cloth*
*s.* Sheaf, *a bundle of corn*
*v.* Shear, *to slip*
*s.* Sheath, *a scabbard*
*s.* Sheep, *an animal*
*s.* Sheet, *linen for a bed : paper*
*s.* Shelf, *a board to lay things on*
*s.* Shield, *a buckler*
*s.* Shire,† *a county*
*s.* Shòal, *a sand bank*
*s.* Shoe, *for the foot*
*v.* Shook, *did shake*
*s.* Shoot, *a branch*
*s.* Shore, *the sea coast : a prop*
*s.* Shrew, *a scolding woman*
*v.* Shriek, *to scream*
*a.* Shrill, *loud, sharp, piercing*
*s.* Shrimp, *a shell fish*
*s.* Shroud, *a burial cloth*
*s.* Shrub, *a dwarf tree*
*v.* Shrug, *to shrink up*
*part.* Shrunk, *of the verb to shrink*

s. Sieᶨge, *attack on a town*
s. Sieve, *a sifter or bolter*
s. Sigh, *a deep sob*
v. Sinᶨge, *to scorch*
a. Sixth, *VIth, 6th*
s. Size, *bulk, a glutinous substance*
s. Skein, *a length of thread*
v. Sketch, *to chalk out*
s. Skiff, *a small boat*
s. Skill, *ability, experience*
v. Skim, *to take off the scum*
s. Sky, *the firmament*
part. Slain, *killed*
s. Sledᶨge, *a carriage without wheels*
s. Sleep, *repose*
s. Sleet, *small snow*
s. Sleeve, *of a gown*
s. Sleight, *dexterity*
v. Slew, *did slay*
s. Slice, *a piece*
s. Slight, *neglect*
s. Sloop, *a small ship*
s. Slòth, *indolence*
s. Slough, *a deep muddy place*
s. Sluice, *a vent for water*
s. Slur, *slight disgrace*
s. Smatch, *an ill taste*
v. Smear, *to daub*
s. Smelt, *a small sea-fish*
v. Smirk, *to look pleasantly*
s. Smith, *a worker in metal*
a. Smooth, *even*
s. Snail, *an insect*
v. Snarl, *to growl*
v. Snatch, *to catch suddenly*
s. Snout, *nose of a beast*
s. Snow, *frozen particles of water*
s. Snuff, *a sneezing powder*
v. Sòak, *to steep*

s. Sòap, } *a substance used in washing*
s. Sôpe, }
s. Soil, *land, country*
v. Solve, *to explain*
v. Sooth, *to flatter, to soften*
part. Sought,* *searched out*
a. Sound, *perfect, healthy*
s. Soup, *decoction of flesh*
a. Sour, *acid, austere*
s. Sòurce, *a spring, origin*
v. Souse, *to dip in water*
s. South, *opposite to the north*
s. Spaᶻsm, *a violent contraction*
s. Spaw, *mineral water*
s. Spawn, *the milt of fish*
v. Speak, *to talk*
s. Spear, *a lance*
s. Speech, *language*
s. Speed, *haste, despatch*
s. Sphere,† *a globe*
v. Splash, *to dash water*
s. Spleen, *ill humour, peevishness*
v. Spoil, *to rob, to damage*
s. Spoon, *used for eating liquids*
s. Sprain, *a hurt*
v. Sprawl, *to lie on the ground*
v. Spread, *to cover over*
s. Sprout, *shoot of a plant*
a. Spruce, *neat, clean*
v. Spurn, *to kick at, or reject*
s. Squall, *a gust of wind*
s. Square, *four-sided*
v. Squeak, *to cry shrilly*
v. Squeeze, *to press close*
v. Squint, *to look awry*
v. Squirt, *to spirt out*
s. Staff, *a stick*
s. Staᶨge, *a platform*
s. Stain, *a dye, a spot*
v. Stew, *to boil gently*

\* *pr.* Sawt      † *pr.* Sfere

B

*v.* Stick,* *to cleave to*
*v.* Stitch, *to sew with a needle*
*s.* Stock, *a stem, fund of money*
*part.* Stood, *of the verb to stand*
*s.* Storm, *a tempest*
*a.* Stout, *strong, lusty*
*v.* Stow, *to pack up*
*v.* Strain, *to stretch*
*s.* Straw, *a stalk of corn*
*v.* Streak, *to mark in lines*
*s.* Stream, *a current*
*s.* Street, *road through a town or village*
*s.* Strength, *power*
*s.* Stress, *force*
*v.* Stretch, *to reach out*
*v.* Strew, *to scatter*
*a.* Strict, *severe, rigorous*
*s.* Stud, *a fastening for the wristband of a shirt*
*s.* Stuff, *furniture, &c.*
*s.* Suit, *a set, a petition*
*s.* Surge, *a wave*
*s.* Swab, *a kind of mop*
*s.* Swain, *a shepherd*
*v.* Swam, *did swim*
*s.* Sward, *the rind of bacon*
*s.* Swarm, *a multitude*
*v.* Swathe, *to bind with rollers*
*s.* Sway, *rule, command*
*v.* Swear, *to affirm on oath*
*s.* Sweat, *perspiration*
*v.* Sweep, *to clean*
*v.* Swell, *to enlarge*
*v.* Swerve, *to deviate*

* It is not uncommon to write *music, critic, public, &c.* without the *k*: but words of one syllable invariably retain the *k* final. It may, however, be proper to remark here, that, according to the principles stated in Dr. Johnson's Grammar, *c* never ends an English word.

*a.* Swift, *quick, prompt*
*v.* Swim, *to float on water*
*v.* Swing, *to vibrate*
*s.* Switch, *a light cane*
*s.* Swoon, *a fainting fit*
*s.* Sword, *a weapon of war*
*part.* Swung, *of the verb to swing*

T.

*v.* Taint, *to infect*
*v.* Talk, *to speak*
*part.* Taught, *of the verb to teach*
*s.* Taunt, *a biting jest*
*v.* Teach, *to instruct*
*s.* Teeth, *plural of tooth*
*v.* Tempt, *to allure*
*s.* Thatch, *covering of straw*
*s.* Theft, *a stealing*
*s.* Theme, *a subject*
*a.* Thick, *muddy, not thin*
*s.* Thief, *one who steals*
*v.* Thieve, *to steal*
*s.* Thigh, *a part of the body*
*s.* Thong, *a strap of leather*
*part.* Thought, *of the verb to think*
*v.* Thrash, *to beat out corn*
*s.* Threat, *a menace*
*s.* Throat, *fore part of the neck*
*s.* Throng, *a crowd*
*s.* Thrush, *a bird*
*v.* Thrust, *to push hard*
*v.* Thwart, *to oppose*
*s.* Thyme, *an herb*
*s.* Tierce, *42 gallons*
*a.* Tight, *close, not loose*
*s.* Tinge, *a slight colour*
*s.* Tithe, *a tenth part*
*s.* Toad, *a reptile*
*s.* Toll, *a tribute*
*s.* Tongue,* *the organ of speech*
*s.* Tool, *an instrument*

* *pr.* Tung.

s. Tooth, *of the head*
s. Torch, *a flambeau*
v. Touch, *to handle*
a. Tough,* *stiff, ropy*
s. Tour,† *a journey*
s. Town, *a collection of houses*
s. Track, *a beaten path*
s. Tract, *a discourse*
v. Train, *to bring up*
s. Trait, *outline*
s. Trash, *worthless stuff*
s. Trench, *a deep ditch*
s. Trice, *a moment*
s. Trick, *an artifice*
a. Trite, *common*
s. Troop, *a body of soldiers*
v. Trounce, *to punish*
s. Trout, *a fish*
v. Trudge, *to jog on*
s. Trunk, *body of a tree : a kind of chest*
s. Truss, *a bundle of hay*
s. Truth, *a certainty*
s. Tuft, *of grass, &c.*
s. Twang, *a sharp sound*
a. Twelve, *a number*
s. Twig, *a young shoot*
s. Twine, *twisted thread*
v. Twirl, *to turn round*
v. Twit, *to upbraid*
v. Twitch, *to pinch*
s. Type, *a printing letter*

## V U.

a. Vague, *unmeaning*
s. Valves, *folding-doors*
s. Vase, *a vessel with a foot : an ornament*
a. Vast, *very great*
v. Vaunt, *to boast*

* *pr.* Tuff.     † *pr.* Toor.

v. Veer, *to change*
s. Verge, *brink, edge*
s. Verse, *poetry*
v. Vex, *to tease*
v. Vie, *to contend*
s. View, *prospect*
a. Vile, *base, wicked*
s. Vogue, *fashion*
s. Voice, *human sound*
a. Void, *empty*
v. Vouch, *to witness*
s. Vow, *a solemn promise*
v. Urge, *to press earnestly*
s. Use, *practice, help*

## W

v. Waft, *to carry over*
s. Wag, *a merry fellow*
v. Wage, *to begin*
v. Wait, *to stay*
v. Walk, *to go on foot*
s. Wall, *an enclosure of brick or stone*
s. Wand, *a small stick*
s. Wane, *decrease*
s. War, *hostility*
s. Ware, *merchandize*
a. Warm, *a little heated*
v. Warn, *to caution*
s. Wart, *a fleshy pimple*
s. Wasp, *a stinging insect*
s. Watch, *a time-piece*
s. Wax *a hard substance for sealing : production of bees*
s. Wealth, *riches*
v. Wean, *to deprive of gradually*
v. Weave, *to make cloth*
s. Wedge, *to cleave wood with*
s. Weed, *a wild herb*
v. Weep, *to shed tears*
s. Weight,* *heaviness*

* *pr.* Wate.

s. West, *where the sun sets*
s. Wharf, *a place to land goods at*
s. Wheat, *bread corn*
s. Whelp, *a cub*
s. Whiff, *a puff*
s. Whip, *a scourge*
s. Whirl, *a rapid turning*
a. White, *a colour*
v. Wield, *to sway*
s. Wool, *a sheep's fleece*
s. World, *the earth*
s. Worth, *price, value*
s. Wound, *a hurt*
v. Wrap,* *to roll together*
s. Wrath, *extreme anger*
s. Wreath, *a garland*
s. Wreck, *destruction, ruin*
v. Wrench, *to pull by force*
s. Wretch, *a worthless person*
Wrist, *part of the hand*
a. Wroth, *very angry*
part. Wrought, *manufactured*

\* *W* is always silent before *r*.

part. Wrung, *of the verb to ring*
a. Wry, *crooked*

## Y

s. Yacht,† *a pleasure boat*
s. Yarn, *spun wool*
s. Yawl, *a ship's boat*
s. Year, *twelve months*
v. Yearn, *to grieve with*
s. Yeast, *the froth in the working of new ale or beer*
v. Yelp, *to bark as a hound*
v. Yield, *to produce*
s. Yoke, *mark of servitude*
s. Yolk, *the yellow part of an egg*
ad. Yore, *of old time*
a. Young, *youthful*
s. Youth, *tender age*

## Z.

s. Zeal, *great ardour*
s. Zest, *a relish*
s. Zone, *division of the earth*

† *pr.* Yot.

---

*Words of similar Sound, but different in Spelling and Sense*

Parts of Speech.
s. ACTS, *deeds, exploits*
s. Axe, *an instrument used to chop wood*

v. Ail, *to be ill*
Ale, *malt liquor*

s. Air, *one of the elements*
v. Are, *the plural of* is

a. All, *every one*
s. Awl, *a sharp tool*

Parts of Speech.
s. Ant, *an insect*
s. Aunt, *a father's or mother's sister*

s. Bail, *a surety*
s. Bale, *a bundle of goods*

s. Bait, *a lure*
v. Bate, *to lessen*

a. Bald, *without hair*
v. Bawl'd, *cried out*

## SPELLING ASSISTANT.

*s* Ball, *a round substance*
*v* Bawl, *to cry out*

*a* Bare, *naked*
*s* Bear, *a rough savage animal*

*s* Baize, *a coarse cloth*
*s* Bays, *bay trees, bay horses*

*a* Base, *mean*
*s* Bass, *music*

*v* Be, *to exist*
*s* Bee, *an insect*

*s.* Beach, *the sea shore*
*s.* Beech, *a tree*

*s.* Bean, *a sort of pulse*
*part.* Been, *of the verb to be*

*v.* Beat, *to strike*
*s.* Beet, *a plant*

*s.* Beau, *a fop*
*s.* Bow, *to shoot with*

*s.* Beer, *malt liquor*
*s.* Bier, *a frame for the dead*

*s.* Bell, *a sounding instrument*
*s.* Belle, *a fine lady*

*v.* Blew, *did blow*
*s.* Blue, *a colour*

*s.* Boar, *the male swine*
*v.* Bore, *to make a hole*

*s.* Board, *a thin plank*
*v.* Bor'd, *did bore*

*a.* Bold, *courageous: rude*
*v.* Bowl'd, *did bowl*

*s.* Bole, *a corn measure, &c.*
*s.* Boll, *a round stalk or stem*
*s.* Bowl, *a large basin*

*s.* Bough, *a branch*
*v.* Bow, *to bend*

*s.* Boy, *a young lad*
*s.* Buoy, *an anchor mark* †

*s.* Braid, *hair twisted*
*v.* Bray'd, *did bray*

*s.* Bread, *food made of ground corn*
*part.* Bred, *brought up*

*v.* Brew$^z$s, *he breweth*
*s.* Brui$^z$e, *a hurt*

*s.* Bruit, *a report*
*s.* Brute, *a beast*

*conj.* But, *a particle*
*s.* Butt, *a large cask*

*v.* Buy, *to purchase*
*prep.* By, *near*

*v.* Call, *to name*
*s.* Caul, *net work of a wig, &c*

*v.* Can, *am able*
*s.* Can, *a cup*

*s.* Cart, *for carrying goods*
*s.* Chart,\* *a sea map*

\* *pr.* Kart, or Tshart. Some authors give the latter pronunciation the preference.      † *pr.* Boof.

s. Cell, *a small close room: a cave*
v. Sell, *to dispose of*

s. Chair, *to sit on*
s. Chare, *a job of work*

a. Cinque, *five*
v. Sink, *to go down*

v. Cite, *to summon*
s. Sight, *seeing*
s. Site, *situation*

s. Clau*z*se, *a section*
s. Claw*z*s, *talons*

v. Climb, *to get up*
s. Clime, *climate*

a. Coarse, *not fine*
s. Course, *race*
s. Corse, *a carcass or dead body*

v. Creak, *to make a harsh noise*
s. Creek, *a small inlet in the sea*

a. Dear, *costly*
s. Deer, *a forest animal*

s. Dew, *a thin cold vapour*
a. Due, *owing*

a. Dire, *dreadful*
s. Dyer, *one who dyes cloth*

s. Doe, *a female deer*
s. Dough, *leaven or paste*

part. Done, *acted*
s. Dun, *a troublesome creditor*

s. Draft, *a bill*
s. Draught, *a drink*

s. Ear,* *of the head*
ad. Ere, *before*
ad. E'er, *ever*
s. Heir, *to an estate*

ad. Fain, *willingly*
v. Feign, *to dissemble*

a. Faint, *languid*
s. Feint, *a pretence*

a. Fair, *beautiful*
s. Fare, *diet: hire*
s. Fair, *annual market*

s. Feat, *an exploit*
s. Feet, *of the body*

s. Fir, *a tree*
s. Fur, *soft hair*

s. Flea, *an insect*
v. Flee, *to run from danger*

v. Flew, *did fly*
s. Flue, *of a chimney*

ad. Forth, *onward, forward*
a. Fourth, *in number*

a. Foul, *unclean*
s. Fowl, *a bird*

s. Fray*z*s, *quarrels*
s. Phra*z*se, *mode of speech*

v. Freeze, *to congeal*
s. Frieze, *a coarse cloth*

s. Gait, *manner of walking*
s. Gate, *an entrance*

* Walker pronounces this Eer, and the three following Are.

*part.* Gilt, *with gold*
*s.* Guilt, *sin*

*s.* Glaire, *white of an egg*
*s.* Glare, *a bright light*

*s.* Grate, *fire-place*
*a.* Great, *large*

*s.* Groan, *a deep sigh*
*part.* Grown, *increased*

*s.* Hail, *frozen rain*
*a.* Hale, *strong, robust*

*s.* Hair, *of the head*
*s.* Hare, *an animal*

*s.* Hall, *a large room*
*v.* Haul, *to pull about*

*s.* Hart,* *an animal*
*s.* Heart, *the seat of life*

*v.* Heal, *to cure*
*s.* Heel, *of the foot or shoe*

*v.* Hear, *to hearken*
*ad.* Here, *in this place*

*part.* Heard, *of the verb to hear*
*s.* Herd, *a drove*

*v* Hew, *to cut*
*s* Hue, *shade of colour*
*s* Hugh, *a man's name*

*pro.* Him, *that man*
*s.* Hymn, *a holy song*

 * In English there are but two articles, *a* and *the*. The former uniformly becomes *an* before a vowel.

*s.* Hole, *a cavity*
*a.* Whole, *not impaired*

*s.* Hoop, *for a cask*
*v.* Whoop, *to shout*

*pro.* I, *myself*
*s.* Eye, *the organ of sight*

*s.* Ile, } *of a church*
*s.* Aisle,
*s.* Isle, *an island*

*prep.* In. *within*
*s.* Inn, *a house of entertainment*

*s.* Key, *for a lock*
*s.* Quay, *to land goods on*

*v.* Kill, *to deprive of life*
*s.* Kiln, *for drying corn*

*s.* Knap, *the down on cloth*
*s.* Nap, *short sleep*

*s.* Knave, *a rogue*
*s.* Nave, *of a wheel*

*v.* Knead, *to work dough*
*s.* Need, *poverty*

*v.* Knew, *did know*
*a.* New, *not old*

*s.* Knight, *a title of honour*
*s.* Night, *time of darkness*

*v.* Know, *to understand*
*ad.* No, *not so*

*v.* Knows, *he knoweth*
*s.* Nose, *of the face*

*v.* Lade, *to load*
*v.* Laid, *placed*

*s.* Lead, *a metal*
*v.* Led, *did lead*

*v.* Leak, *to let out*
*s.* Leek, *an herb*

*intj.* Lo, *behold*
*a.* Low, *humble*

*v.* Made, *did make*
*s.* Maid, *a woman servant*

*s.* Mail, *armour*
*s.* Male, *of the he kind*

*a.* Main, *principal, chief*
*s.* Mane, *of a horse*

*a.* Mean, *low-minded*
*s.* Mien, *look, countenance*

*s.* Meat, *flesh, food in general*
*a.* Meet, *fit, proper*
*v.* Mete, *to measure*

*s.* Mite, *an insect*
*s.* Might, *power*

*v* Moan, *to lament*
*part.* Mown, *cut down*

*v.* Mu$^z$se, *to think*
*v* Mew$^z$s, *as a cat*

*a.* Naught, *bad*
*s.* Nought, *nothing*

*ad.* Nay, *no*
*v* Neigh, *as a horse*

*ad.* Not, *not so*
*s.* Knot, *a fastening*

*s.* Oar, *of a boat*
*ad.* O'er, *over*
*s.* Ore, *unwrought metal*

*prep.* Of, *concerning*
*prep.* Off, *from*

*a.* One, *in number*
*part.* Won, *of the verb to win*

*s.* Pail, *a vessel for water*
*a.* Pale, *whitish*

*s.* Pain, *a torment*
*s.* Pane, *of glass*

*a.* Pair, *a couple*
*v.* Pare, *to cut*
*s.* Pear, *a fruit*

*s.* Pau$^z$se, *a stop*
*s.* Paw$^z$s, *beasts' feet*

*s.* Peace, *quietness*
*s.* Piece, *a part*

*s.* Peal, *on the bells*
*s.* Peel, *the rind of fruit*

*s.* Peer, *a nobleman*
*s.* Pier, *the column or support of an arch*

*s.* Place, *situation*
*s.* Plaice, *a flat fish*

*a.* Plain, *clear, evident*
*s.* Plane, *a flat surface*

# SPELLING ASSISTANT.

s. Plait, *a fold*
s. Plate, *wrought silver*

s. Pole, *a long stick*
s. Poll, *the head*

s. Praise, *commendation*
v. Prays, *beseeches*
v. Preys, *seizes, plunders*

v. Pray, *to beseech*
s. Prey, *booty, plunder*

v. Pries, *searches into*
s. Prize, *gain in battle*

s. Rain, *water*
v. Reign, *to rule*
s. Rein, *of a bridle*

v. Raise, *to lift*
s. Rays, *of the sun*
v. Raze, *to demolish*

s. Rap, *a knock*
v. Wrap, *to fold up*

part. Read, *of the verb to read*
a. Red, *a colour*

s. Rear, *the back part* }
a. Rare, *uncommon* } *

s. Rest, *ease*
v. Wrest, *to force*

a. Right, *correct*
s. Rite, *a tenet*
s. Wright, *a workman*
v. Write, *with a pen*

\* The words are incorrectly classed: the first is pronounced Rere, the second Rare.

s. Ring,* *for the finger*
v. Wring, *to twist*

s. Road, *the highway*
v. Rode, *did ride*
v. Row'd, *did row*

s. Roe, *of a fish*
s. Row, *a rank*

s. Rote, *by heart*
v. Wrote, *did write*

a. Rough, *uneven: unpolished*
s. Ruff, *for the neck*

s. Rye, *corn*
a. Wry, *crooked*

s. Sail, *of a ship*
s. Sale, *selling*

s. Scene, *of a stage*
part. Seen, *beheld*

s. Sea, *the ocean*
v. See, *to observe*

s. Seam, *of a garment*
v. Seem, *to appear*

v. Sees, *he beholds*
v. Seize, *to catch hold*

v. Sent, *did send*
s. Scent, *a smell*
s. Cent, *a hundred*

\* *G*, at the end of a word, is always hard.

*v.* Shone, *did shine*
*part.* Shown, *directed*

*s.* Sign, *a token*
*s.* Sine, *a line in geometry*

*s.* Sloe, *a wild fruit*
*a.* Slow, *tardy*

*ad.* So, *thus*
*v.* Sow, *to sow seed*
*v.* Sew, *with a needle*

*s.* Sole, *of a shoe or foot: a fish*
*s.* Soul, *spirit*

*v.* Soar, *to rise high*
*s.* Sore, *a diseased part*

*a.* Some, *a part of*
*s.* Sum, *of money*

*s.* Son, *a male child*
*s.* Sun, *the luminary that makes the day*

*v.* Stare, *to look earnestly*
*s.* Stair, *a step*

*v.* Steal, *to thieve*
*s.* Steel, *refined iron*

*s.* Stile, *steps in a field*
*s.* Style, *language*

*a.* Straight, *not crooked*
*a.* Strait, *narrow*

*s.* Tacks, *small nails*
*s.* Tax, *a rate*

*s.* Tail, *of an animal*
*s.* Tale, *a story*

*s.* Tare, *an allowance in weight*
*v.* Tear, *to rend*

*s.* Team, *of horses*
*v.* Teem, *to produce*

*pro.* Their, *of them*
*ad.* There, *in that place*

*v.* Threw, *did throw*
*prep.* Through, *quite through*

*s.* Throne, *a seat of state*
*part.* Thròwn, *hurl'd*

*s.* Tier, *a row of guns*
*s.* Tear, *from the eyes*

*v.* Tòld, *related*
*v.* Tòll'd, *did toll*

*prep.* To, *unto*
*ad.* Too, *also*
*a.* Two, *in number*

*s.* Toe, *of the foot*
*v.* Tow, *to drag along*

*a.* Vain, *conceited*
*s.* Vein, *a blood-vessel*

*s.* Vale, *a valley*
*s.* Veil, *a covering*

*v.* Wade, *to walk through water*
*v.* Weigh'd, *in a scale*

*s.* Wale, *a rising part*
*s.* Whale, *the largest of all fish*

SPELLING ASSISTANT. 25

*s.* Ware,* *merchandize*
*v.* Wear, *to have on*

*v.* Waste, *to consume*
*s.* Waist, *the middle*

*s.* Way, *a road, passage*
*v.* Weigh, *to poise : to judge*

\* The *e* final in monosyllables, distinguishes the sharp sound of *a* from its flat sound, as in war, ware ; star, stare ; tar, tare ; &c.

*a.* Weak, *feeble : unfortified*
*s.* Week, *seven days*

*s.* Weight, *heaviness*
*v.* Wait, *to stay*

*s.* Wood, *timber*
*v.* Would, *was willing*

*s.* Yew, *a tree*
*pro.* You, *yourself*
*s.* Ewe, *a female sheep*

## WORDS OF TWO SYLLABLES.

Parts of Speech.

### A.

† *Accented on the first.*

*s.* AB-BA, *father*
*s.* Ab-bot, *governor of a monastery*
*s.* Ab-bess, *governess of a nunnery*
*s.* Ab-bey, *a monastery*
*a.* Ab-ject, *mean, contemptible*
*s.* Ac-cent, *strength of pronunciation*
*a.* A-çid, *sour, sharp*

† *Accent* is the laying of a peculiar stress of the voice on a certain letter or syllable in a word, that it may be better heard than the rest, or distinguished from them : as, in the word *abáse*, the stress of the voice must be on the letter *a*, and the second syllable, *báse*, which take the accent.—*Murray.*

Parts of Speech.

*s.* A-cre,‡ *a measure of land*
*a.* Ac-tive, *nimble, quick*
*s.* Ac-tor, *one who performs*
*s.* Ad-age, *a proverb*
*s.* Ad-der, *a poisonous reptile*
*a.* Ad-verse, *contrary, unprosperous*
*s.* A-gent, *a deputy or substitute*
*part. a.* Ail-ing, *unhealthy*
*v.* Am-ble, *to pace to trip*
*s.* Am-bush, *a lying in wait*
*a.* Am-ple, *large, wide*
*s.* An-chor, *a ship's hold fast*
*s.* An-gel, *a celestial being*
*s.* An-gle,§ *the point where two lines meet*
*s.* An-guish, *excessive pain.*
*s.* An-nals, *yearly chronicles*
*s.* An-them, *a divine hymn*

‡ *pr.* A-kur.   § *pr.* Ang-gl.

s. An-tick, *a buffoon*
s. An-vil, *a smith's iron*
s. Ar-bour, *a shady place*
s. Ar-chive²s, *records*
a. Arc-tic, *northern*
a. Ar-dent, *fervent*
a. Art-ful, *cunning, sly*
s. Ar-tist, *a professor of any art*
s. As-pect, *look, countenance*
s. At-las, *a book of maps*
v. Au-dit, *to examine accounts*
a. A-zure,* *light blue*

*Accented on the last.*

v. A-base, *to humble*
v. A-bate, *to diminish*
v. A-bet, *to aid, to incite*
v. Abide, *to continue*
v. A-bound, *to be over and above*
s. A-bode, *a dwelling place*
ad. A-breast, *side by side*
v. A-bridge, *to shorten*
a. Ab-rupt, *sudden, unexpected*
v. Ab-scond, *to hide one's self*
v. Ab-²solve, *to pardon*
v. Ab-sorb, *to swallow up*
v. Ab-stain, *to keep from*
a. Ab-struse, *obscure, difficult*
a. Ab-surd, *unreasonable*
v. A-bu²se, *to affront rudely*
v. Ac-cede, *to comply with*
s. Ac-cess, *admittance*
v. Ac-cord, *to agree with*
v. Ac-cost, *to address*
v. Ac-crue, *to arise from*
v. Ac-cu²se, *to impeach*
v. A-chieve, *to perform*
v. A-cute, *quick of apprehension*
v. Ac-quit, *to discharge*
v. Ad-apt, *to suit, to make fit*

* pr. A-zhure.

v. Ad-dict, *to be prone to*
s. Ad-dress, *politeness: direction*
s. Ad-ept, *a proficient*
v. Ad-duce, *to allege*
v. Ad-here, *to stick close*
v. Ad-journ, *to put off*
v. Ad-judge, *to pass sentence*
v. Ad-just, *to put in order*
v. A-dopt, *to make one's own*
v. A-dorn, *to embellish*
v. Ad-vert, *to take notice*
s. A-dult, *grown up*
v. Af-firm, *to assure*
v. Af-fix, *to fasten to*
a. A-ghast, or } *astonished*
a. A-gast,
a. A-lert, *brisk, lively*
v. Al-ledge, *to affirm*
v. Al-lude, *to refer to*
v. Al-lure, *to entice*
s. Al-ly, *a confederate*
v. An-nex, *to join to*
v. An-nounce, *to give notice*
v. An-noy, *to injure*
v. An-nul, *to abolish*
v. Ap-pal,† *to terrify*
v. Ap-pea²se, *to pacify*
v. Ap-plaud, *to commend*
s. Ap-plau²se, *public praise*
v. Ap-ply, *to have recourse to: to suit: to put or lay on*
v. Ap-point, *to ordain*
v. Ap-prize, *to inform*
v. Ap-proach, *to draw near*
v. Ap-prove, *to like*
v. Ar-raign, *to indict*
v. Ar-range, *to set in order*
v. Ar-rest, *to sieze on*
v. As-cribe, *to impute to*
v. As-sail, *to assault*
v. As-pire, *to aim at*

* pr. Ap-pawl.

v. As-sault, *to attack*
s. As-sent, *consent*
v. As-sert, *to affirm*
v. As-sign, *to appoint*
s. As-size, *the sitting of judges*
v. As-suage, *to ease*
v. As-sume, *to claim*
prep. A-thwart, *across*
v. A-tone, *to make amends*
v. At-test, *to certify*
s. At-tire, *apparel, clothes*
v. At-tract, *to allure*
v. A-vail, *to benefit*
v. A-venge, *to vindicate*
v. A-ver, *to declare positively*
v. A-vert, *to keep off*
a. A-verse, *not favourable to*
v. A-void, *to shun*
v. A-vow, *to justify*
v. Aug-ment, *to increase*
v. A-wait, *to attend*
a. A-ware, *vigilant, cautious*

## B.

*Accented on the first.*

s. Bái-liff, *a land steward: an officer of justice*
v. Bal-ançe, *to settle*
v. Baf-fle, *to elude*
v. Bal-lot, *to elect*
a. Bane-ful, *hurtful*
s. Bank-er, *a trader in money*
s. Bank-rupt, *an insolvent person*
v. Ban-ish, *to expel the country*
part. Bar-bed, *bearded, furnished with armour*
a. Bar-ren, *unfruitful*
s. Ba-sis, *foundation*
s. Bea-con, *a signal of alarm*
s. Bi-as, *bent, inclination*

s. Bil-low. *a wave*
s. Blem-ish, *an imperfection*
v. Bor-row, *to take on credit*
s. Boun-ty, *generosity*
s. Brack-et, *a piece of metal or wood for support*
v. Bran-dish, *to flourish*
a. Bra-zen, *made of brass: impudent*
s. Bride-groom, *a new-married man*
a. Brit-tle, *apt to break*
s. Bro-ker, *one who does business for others*
a. Bru-mal, *winter-like*
s. Brush-wood, *small wood*
s. Buck-ler, *a shield*
s. Buck-ram, *stiff cloth*
s. Bud-get, *a bag*
a. Bul-bous, *round, knotty*
s. Bûl-wark, *a strong defence*
s. Bung-ler, *a clumsy person*
s. Bur-then, or Bur-den, *a load*
s. Bur-gess, *a member of a corporation*
v. Burn-ish, *to make bright*
s. But-ler, *head servant*
s. But-tress, *a prop*

*Accented on the last.*

v. Be-guile, *to deceive*
v. Be-môan, *to lament*
a. Be-nign, *kind, liberal*
v. Be-queath, *to give by will*
v. Be-reave, *to deprive of*
v. Be-witch, *to fascinate*
s. Block-ade, *blocking up a town*
v. Bom-bard, *to attack with bombs*
s. Bom-bast, *rant*

*s.* Brig-ade, *a division of soldiers*
*s.* Bu-reau,* *drawers with a flap to write on*
*v.* Bur-lesque,† *to ridicule*

## C.

*Accented on the first.*

*s.* Cà-ble, *a rope to hold a ship at anchor*
*s.* Ca-dençe,‡ *fall of the voice*
*a.* Cal-id, *hot, burning*
*a.* Cal-lous, *gristly insensible*
*a.* Cal-low, *unfeathered*
*s.* Cam-phire, *a drug*
*v.* Can-çel, *to blot out*
*s.* Can-çer, *a virulent sore*
*a.* Can-did, *ingenuous*
*s.* Can-dour, *sincerity*
*s.* Can-vass, *a soliciting: a sort of cloth*
*s.* Cap-tive, *a prisoner*
*s.* Car-bine, *a horse musket*
*s.* Car-cass, *a dead body*
*s.* Car-go, *a ship's lading*
*s.* Car-nage, *slaughter, havoc*
*s.* Car-tridge, *a charge of powder*
*s.* Car-ving, *sculpture*
*s.* Cas-tle, *a fortified place*
*s.* Cau-dle, *a mixed gruel*
*s.* Cav-ern, *a den*
*s.* Cauʷse-way, *a raised passage*
*s.* Caus-tic, *a burning application*
*s.* Ce-rate, *a kind of salve*
*s.* Ceil-ing, *the roof of a room*

*s.* Chair-man, *a president*
*s.* Chal-içe, *a communication*
*v.* Chal-lenge, *to bid defiance*
*s.* Chan-cel, *the east end of a church*
*s.* Chan-nel, *a narrow sea or river*
*s.* Cha-os, *a confused mass*
*s.* Chap-el, *a place of worship*
*s.* Chap-let, *a wreath*
*s.* Char-ter, *a privilege*
*s.* Chat-tels, *household goods*
*a.* Cheer-ful, *full of life*
*a.* Cheer-less, *sad, comfortles*
*v.* Cher-ish, *to support, to nourish*
*s.* Chief-tain, *a leader*
*s.* Chiʷs-el, *a carpenter's tool*
*s.* Cho-rus, *a concert in which all unite*
*v.* Chris-ten, *to baptize*
*a.* Chur-lish, *surly, ill-bred*
*s.* Chem-ist, *one who separates bodies by fire*
*s.* Ci-pher, *an arithmetical character (0)*
*s.* Çir-cle, *an orb or round figure*
*s.* Çir-cuit, *a going about*
*s.* Çis-tern, *a vessel to hold water*
*s.* Çit-ron, *a foreign fruit*
*v.* Çiv-il, *polite, obliging*
*s.* Claim-ant, *one who demands*
*s.* Clam-our, *noise, outcry*
*s.* Clas-sic, *an author of the first rank*
*s.* Clea-ver, *a chopping knife*
*a.* Clem-ent, *mild, merciful*
*s.* Cli-mate, *temperature of the air, &c.*
*s.* Cli-ent, *one who acts by a lawyer*
*s.* Clus-ter, *a bunch*
*s.* Cof-fer, *a money chest*

\* *pr.* Bu-ro.   † *pr.* Bur-lesk.
‡ C has two sounds. Before *e, i,* and *y,* it has the sound of *s*; and that of *k* in all other cases. It is also hard when it ends a syllable; as in *victim, flaccid, sick, city,* &c.

a. Co-gent, *forcible*
s. Coin-age, *making of money*
s. Col-league, *an associate*
s. Col-lege, *a public place of learning*
s. Col-umn, *a round pillar*
s. *Com-bat, *a battle*
s. Com-et, *a blazing star*
s. Com-ment, *explanation*
s. Com-merce, *trade*
s. Com-pact, *an agreement*
v. *Com-pass, *to surround*
a. Com-plex, *of many parts*
s. *Com-rade, *a companion*
a. Con-cave, *hollow in the inside*
s. Con-cord, *harmony*
s. Con-course, *a crowd*
s. Con-flict, *contest, struggle*
s. Con-flux, *a flowing together*
s. Con-gress, *an assembly*
s. Con-quest, *victory*
s. Con-serve, *a sweetmeat*
s. Con-sort, *a wife or husband*
s. Con-strue, *to interpret*
s. Con-tact, *close union*
a. Con-trite, *truly penitent*
s. Con-vent, *a nunnery*
a. Con-vex, *round, like the surface of a spherical body*
s. Cor-net, *an ensign or standard bearer*
s. Cor-nice, *projection under the ceiling of a room, &c.*
s. Cor-sair, *a pirate, a plunderer on the sea*
a Cos-tive, *bound in the body*
s. †Cov-ert, *a retreat*
v. †Cov-et, *to desire*
s. Cour-age, *bravery*
s. Coun-tess, *an earl's wife*
s. Coun-try, *a kingdom*

\* *pr.* Cum.  † *pr.* Cuv.

s. Coun-ty, *a shire*
s. Cred-it, *reputation: trust*
a. Crim-son, *deep red*
s. Cri-sis, *a critical time*
s. Crit-ic, *one skilled in criticism*
s. Crys-tal, *a lucid mineral*
s. Cul-ture, *improvement*
s. Cu-rate, *a parish priest*
s. Cur-rent, *a running stream*
s. Cus-tom, *fashion: king's duties*
s. Cut-ler, *a knife maker*
s. Cyn-ic, *a snarler: a follower of Diogenes*
s. Cy-press, *a tree*

*Accented on the last.*

s. Ca-bàl, *a factious gang*
v. Ca-jole, *to flatter*
s. Ca-lash, *an open chariot*
v. Cal-cine, *to burn to a calx*
s. Cam-paign, *action of armi in the field*
s. Ca-nal, *an artificial river*
s. Ca-noe *an Indian boat*
s. Ca-price,† *whim, fancy*
v. Ca-reen, *to caulk or stop leaks*
s. Ca-reer, *swift motion*
v. Ca-ress, *to fondle*
v. Ca-rouse, *to drink hard*
s. Car-tel, *an exchange of prisoners*
s. Cas-cade, *a waterfal*
s. Cash-ier, *cash keeper*
s. Cha-grin,‡ *ill humour, vexation*
v. Chas-tise, *to punish*
v. Co-here, *to stick to*
v. Com-bine, *to join together*
v. Com-mand, *to order*
v. Com-mence, *to begin*
v. Com-mend, *to praise*

† *pr.* Ka-preese.  ‡ *pr.* Sha-green.

## THE SCHOLAR'S

*v.* Com-mit, *to imprison: to in-* [*trust*
*v.* Com-mune, *to converse*
*v.* Com-pare, *to estimate*
*v.* Com-pel, *to force*
*v.* Com-pile, *to collect*
*v.* Com-plain, *to murmur*
*a.* Com-plete, *perfect*
*v.* Com-ply, *to yield to*
*v.* Com-pòrt, *to behave*
*v.* Com-po$^z$se, *to put together: to appease or quiet*
*v.* Com-pri$^z$se, *to contain*
*v.* Com-pute, *to calculate*
*v.* Con-çeal, *to keep secret*
*v.* Con-çede, *to grant*
*s.* Con-çeit, *fancy: pride*
*v.* Con-çeive, *to comprehend*
*a.* Con-çise, *brief, short*
*v.* Con-clude, *to finish*
*v.* Con-cur, *to agree with*
*v.* Con-demn, *to find guilty: to censure*
*v.* Con-dense, *to make thick*
*v.* Con-dole, *to sympathise with*
*v.* Con-duçe, *to contribute to*
*v.* Con-fer, *to bestow*
*v.* Con-fess, *to acknowledge*
*v.* Con-fide, *to rely on*
*v.* Con-firm, *to establish*
*v.* Con-form, *to comply with*
*v.* Con-found, *to perplex, to stupify*
*v.* Con-front, *to face or oppose*
*v.* Con-fu$^z$se, *to perplex*
*v.* Con-fute, *to convict of error*
*v.* Con-geal, *to freeze*
*v.* Con-join, *to put together*
*v.* Con-nect, *to fasten together*
*v.* Con-nive, *to wink at a fault*
*v.* Con-sign, *to make over*
*v.* Con-sist, *to be composed of*
*v.* Con-sole, *to comfort*

*v.* Con-spire, *to plot together*
*v.* Con-struct, *to build, to form*
*v.* Con-strain, *to force*
*v.* Con-sult, *to advise with*
*v.* Con-sume, *to destroy or waste*
*v.* Con-tain, *to comprehend*
*v.* Con-temn, *to despise*
*s.* Con-tempt, *disdain*
*v.* Con-tend, *to strive with*
*a.* Con-tent, *satisfied with*
*v.* Con-trive, *to invent*
*s.* Con-tròl, *restraint*
*v.* Con-vene, *to assemble* [*point*
*v.* Con-verge, *to tend to one*
*v.* Con-vey, *to make over*
*v.* Con-voke, *to call together*
*v.* Cor-rect, *to punish: to set right*
*v.* Cor-rode, *to eat away*
*v.* Cor-rupt, *to infect: to bribe*

### D.

*Accented on the first.*

*v.* Dàb-ble, *to splash*
*a.* Dain-ty, *nice in diet*
*v.* Dam-age, *to injure*
*s.* Dam-ask, *flowered silk*
*s.* Dan-ger, *risk, hazard*
*s.* Dar-nel, *a weed*
*s.* Das-tard, *a coward*
*s.* Dea-con, *a minister*
*s.* Debt-or, *one who owes money*
*a.* De-çent, *modest, becoming*
*s* De-ist, *one who denies revelation*
*s.* Del-uge, *a flood*
*s.* Des-pot, *an absolute prince*
*v.* Dic-tate, *to point out*
*s.* Di-et, *food: an assembly*

s. Dig-it, *a figure, any number under ten*
s. Dis-cord, *strife*
a. Dis-mal, *dreary*
s. Dis-tich, *two lines in verse*
s. Dis-trict, *a province*
a. Dole-ful, *mournful*
s. Do-lour, *grief, lamentation*
s. Dol-phin, *a beautiful sea-fish*
s. Do-nor, *a benefactor*
a. Dor-mant, *sleeping, concealed*
s. Do-tage, *silly fondness*
s. Doz-en, *twelve things*
s. Dra-ma, *the action of a play*
s. Dra-per, *a seller of cloth*
a. Drea-ry, *dismal*
v. Driz-zle, *to fall in slow drops*
s. Drop-sy, *a watery disease*
s. Dro-ver, *a driver of cattle*
a. Drow-sy, *sleepy, stupid*
s. Drug-gist, *a seller of drugs*
s. Drug-get, *woollen stuff*
a. Duc-tile, *flexible*
s. Du-el, *a single fight*
s. Duke-dom, *title of a duke*

### Accented on the last.

v. De-bár, *to keep from*
v. De-base, *to humble*
v. De-bate, *to dispute*
v. De-cant, *to pour off*
v. De-cay, *to wither*
s. De-cease, *death*
s. De-ceit, *fraud*
v. De-cide, *to determine*
v. De-claim, *to harangue*
s. De-cline, *decay*
v. De-coy, *to insnare*
s. De-cree, *an edict*
v. De-cry, *to speak ill of*
v. De-duce, *to infer from*

v. De-duct, *to subtract*
v. De-face, *to spoil*
v. De-fame, *to discredit*
s. De-fault, *a failure*
v. De-feat, *to overthrow*
s. De-fect, *blemish, failing*
s. De-fence, *resistance*
v. De-fend, *to protect*
v. De-fer, *to delay*
v. De-fine, *to explain*
v. De-form, *to disfigure*
v. De-fraud, *to cheat*
v. De-fray, *to bear expenses*
v. De-fy, *to challenge*
v. De-grade, *to disgrace*
s. De-gree, *quality, station*
v. De-ject, *to cast down*
v. De-lay, *to put off*
s. De-light, *pleasure, joy*
v. De-lude, *to deceive*
s. De-mand, *a claim*
v. De-mean, *to behave*
v. De-mise, *to bequeath*
v. De-mur, *to object*
a. De-mure, *grave, affected*
v. De-note, *to signify*
v. De-nounce, *to proclaim*
v. De-part, *to go away*
v. De-pend, *to rely on*
v. De-pict, *to portray, to describe*
v. De-plore, *to lament*
v. De-plume, *to unfeather*
v. De-pose, *to give evidence : to dethrone*
v. De-prave, *to corrupt*
v. De-press, *to cast down*
v. De-prive, *to bereave*
v. De-pute, *to appoint*
v. De-ride, *to mock*
v. De-rive, *to draw from*
v. De-scend, *to come down*
v. De-scribe, *to delineate*

*v.* De-scry', *to discern*
*s.* De-²sert, *merit, worth*
*v.* De-sign, *to project*
*v.* De-sist, *to leave off*
*v.* De-spair, *to be without hope*
*v.* De-spatch, *to hasten, to send off*
*v.* De-spoil, *to rob, to deprive*
*v.* De-spond, *to despair*
*s.* De-spite, *malice*
*s.* De²s-²sert, *the last course at a feast*
*v.* De-tach, *to separate*
*s.* De-tail, *the particulars*
*v.* De-tain, *to keep*
*v.* De-ter, *to frighten*
*v.* De-tect, *to discover*
*v.* De-test, *to abhor*
*v.* De-tract, *to lessen, to slander*
*s.* De-vice, *a contrivance*
*v.* De-vi²se, *to invent*
*a.* De-void, *empty, vacant*
*v.* De-volve, *to fall by succession*
*v.* De-vote, *to dedicate*
*a.* De-vout, *pious, sincere*
*a.* Dif-fuse, *copious*
*v.* Di''-gest, *to dissolve, to range in order*
*v* Di''-gress, *to go from*
*v.* Di''-late, *to widen*
*v.* Di²s-arm, *to deprive of arms*
*v.* Di²s-band, *to discharge soldiers*
*v.* Di²s-burse, *to lay out money*
*v.* Dis-card, *to dismiss from service*
*v.* Di²s-cern, *to perceive*
*v.* Dis-claim, *to disown*
*v.* Dis-clo²se, *to reveal*
*s.* Dis-côurse, *conversation, a treatise*
*a.* Dis-creet, *wise, prudent*
*v.* Dis-cuss, *to debate, to examine*

*s.* Di²s-dain, *scorn, contempt*
*s.* Di²s-ea²se, *a distemper*
*v.* Di²s-gui²se, *to conceal*
*s.* Di²s-gust, *dislike*
*a.* Di²s-junct, *disjoined*
*v.* Di²s-may, *to terrify*
*v.* Di²s-mount, *to alight from a horse*
*v.* Di²s-own, *to deny*
*v.* Dis-pel, *to drive away*
*v.* Dis-pense, *to distribute, to excuse*
*v.* Dis-play, *to exhibit* [late
*v.* Dis-po²se, *to incline, to regu-*
*v.* Di²s-robe, *to undress*
*v.* Dis-sect, *to anatomise*
*v.* Dis-sent, *to differ*
*v.* Di²s-²solve, *to melt*
*v.* Dis-suade, *to advise against*
*v.* Dis-tend, *to stretch out*
*a.* Dis-til, *clear, separate*
*v.* Dis-tinct, *to drop*
*v.* Dis-tort, *to wrest, or twist*
*v.* Dis-u²se, *to discontinue*
*v.* Di''-vert, *to entertain*
*v.* Di''-vest, *to strip off*
*a.* Di''-vine, *heavenly*
*v.* Di''-vorce, *to put away*
*v.* Di''-vulge, *to make known*
*s.* Dra-goon, *a horse soldier*

## E.

*Accented on the first.*

*a.* Ea-ger, *earnest*
*s.* Ea-gle, *a large bird: the Roman standard*
*s.* Ear-nest, *steadfast*
*a.* Earth-en, *made of earth*
*ad.* East-ward, *towards the east*
*v.* Ech-o, *to resound*

*s.* E-dict, *a proclamation*
*s.* Ef-fort, *exertion*
*s.* E-gress, *a going forth*
*s.* Em-blem, *a moral device*
*s.* Em-pire, *a kingdom*
*s.* En-dive, *a salad herb*
*s.* En-gine, *a machine*
*s.* En-trails, *the bowels*
*s.* En-vy, *spite, malice*
*a.* Ep-ic, *heroic*
*a.* E-qual, *even*
*s.* E-ra, or } *particular date*
   Æ-ra,
*s.* Er-ror, *mistake*
*s.* Es-sençe, *the substance of a thing*
*s. pl.* Eth-ics, *moral philosophy*
*s.* Europe, *a quarter of the world*
*s.* Ex-ile, *banishment*
*s.* Ex-it, *departure*
*a.* Ex-tant *that is in being*

*Accented on the last.*

*s.* E-clát,* *show, lustre*
*v.* E-clipse, *to darken*
*v.* Ef-façe, *to destroy*
*s.* Ef-fect, *issue*
*s.* Ef-fects, *goods*
*v.* E-ject, *to throw out*
*v.* E-lapse, *to glide or pass away*
*v.* E-lect, *to choose*
*v.* E-lope, *to run away*
*v.* E-lude, *to shift off*
*v.* Em-balm, *to preserve dead bodies*
*v.* Em-bark, *to go on shipboard*
*v.* Em-braçe, *to fold in one's arm*
*v.* Em-broil, *to disturb, confuse*
*v.* E-merge, *to rise out of*

*\* pr. E-klaw.*

*v.* E-mit, *to send forth*
*v.* En-act, *to decree*
*v.* En-çhant, *to bewitch*
*v.* En-clo²se, *to fence in*
*v.* En-crôaçh, *to invade*
*v.* En-dear, *to make beloved*
*v.* En-dorse, *to write on the back*
*v.* En-dow, *to bestow upon*
*v.* En-dure, *to suffer*
*v.* En-forçe, *to put in force*
*v.* En-gage, *to undertake: to fight*
*v.* En-grôss, *to write plain: also monopolize*
*v.* En-hançe, *to increase in value*
*v.* En-large, *to make large*
*a.* E-nough,† *sufficient in quantity*
*a.* E-now, (*pl.* of E-nough,) *sufficient in number* (obsolete)
*v.* En-rage, *to provoke*
*v.* En-riçh, *to make rich*
*v.* En-rôl, *to register*
*v.* En-sue, *to follow*
*v.* En-sure,‡ *to make sure*
*s.* En-tail, *a settlement in law*
*v.* En-tiçe, *to allure*
*a.* En-tire, *complete*
*v.* En-treat, *to beg earnestly*
*v.* E-quip, *to furnish, to dress*
*v.* E-rase, *to rub out*
*v.* E-rect, *to build, to raise*
*v.* Es-çape, *to get away*
*v.* E-vade, *to elude*
*s.* Event, *issue, consequence*
*v.* E-vinçe, *to prove*
*a.* Ex-act, *accurate*
*v.* Ex-alt,§ *to lift up*

† *pr.* E-nuf.
‡ *pr.* En-shure.
§ Ex. *pr.* egs.

*v.* Ex-cel, *to surpass*
*s.* Ex-cess, *superfluity*
*v.* Ex-cite, *to stir up*
*v.* Ex-clude, *to shut out*
*a.* \*Ex-empt, *free from*
*v.* \*Ex-ert, *to endeavour strong*
*v.* \*Ex-hale, *to breathe out,*
*v.* \*Ex-haust, *to empty*
*v.* \*Ex-hort, *to encourage*
*v.* \*Ex-ist, *to have a being*
*v.* Ex-pand, *to open*
*s.* Ex-panse, *the firmament*
*v.* Ex-pel, *to drive out*
*v.* Ex-pend, *to lay out.*
*s.* Ex-pense, *cost, charges*
*a.* Ex-pert, *dexterous*
*v.* Ex-pire, *to die.*
*v.* Ex-plain, *to illustrate*
*v.* Ex-plode, *to decry*
*s.* Ex-ploit, *a great action*
*v.* Ex-plore, *to search into*
*v.* Ex-port, *to send abroad,*
*v.* Ex-punge, *to blot out*
*v.* Ex-tend, *to stretch out*
*s.* Ex-tent, *the utmost*
*a.* Ex-tinct, *at an end*
*v.* Ex-tol, *to praise*
*v.* Ex-tort, *to wrest from*
*a.* Ex-treme, *the utmost*
*v.* Ex-trude, *to thrust out*
*v.* \*Ex-ult, *to rejoice, to triumph*

### F.
*Accented on the first.*

*s.* Fab-ric, *a building*
*s.* Fac-tor, *an agent*
*a.* Faith-ful, *sincere, trusty*
*v.* Fam-ish, *to starve*
*a.* Fa-mous, *celebrated*
*s.* Fan-cy, *thought, taste*

\* Ex. pr. egs.

*s.* Fath-om, *six feet*
*s.* Fa-vour, *kindness*
*a.* Fee-ble, *weak, infirm*
*s.* Fel-on, *a criminal*
*a.* Fer-tile, *fruitful*
*s.* Fer-vour, *zeal, warmth*
*a.* Fi-bres,\* *the threads of veins, plants, &c.*
*a.* Fic-kle, *changeable*
*s.* Fig-ure, *shape, image*
*a.* Fi-nal, *last*
*s.* Fi-nis, *the end*
*a.* Fi-nite, *limited, bounded*
*a.* Fla-grant, *notorious*
*v.* Flat-ter, *to praise falsely*
*s* Fla-vour, *relish*
*part.* Fled-ged, *feathered*
*s.* Fleet-ness, *swiftness*
*s.* Flex-ure, *a bending*
*a.* Flor-id, *red, blooming*
*s.* Flor-ist, *one skilled in flowers*
*s.* Flu-id, *water, &c.*
*a.* Flu-ent, *ready in speech*
*v.* Flus-ter, *to confuse*
*s.* Fod-der, *food for cattle*
*s.* Foi-ble, *a failing*
*s.* For-age, *provisions*
*a.* Fo-reign, *of another country*
*s.* For-feit, *a fine*
*s.* For-ger, *a counterfeiter*
*a.* For-mal, *affected, precise*
*s.* For-tress, *a strong hold*
*v.* Fos-ter, *to cherish*
*s.* Foun-tain, *a spring of water*
*v.* Foun-der, *to sink*
*v.* Frac-ture, *to break*
*a* Fra-grant, *odorous, smelling sweet.*
*s.* Frag-ment, *a broken piece*
*s.* Frail-ty, *weakness*

\* *pr.* Fi-burs.

## SPELLING ASSISTANT. 35

- a. Frantic, *mad, crazy*
- s. Fren-zy, *distraction of mind*
- a. Fri″-)gid, *cold, impotent*
- s. Frol-ic, *jocund, merry*
- s. Fron-tier, *the borders of a country*
- a. Fru-gal, *economical*
- a. Fruit-less, *ineffectual*
- v. Frus-trate, *to disappoint*
- v. Fur-bish, *to brighten*
- s. Fur-nace, *an enclosed fire place*
- s. Fur-row, *a trench*
- a. Fu-tile, *silly, trifling*
- a. Fu-ture, *time to come*

*Accented on the last.*

- s. Fa-tigue,* *weariness*
- s. Fin-ançe, *revenue*
- v. Fo-ment, *to bathe, to incite*
- v. For-bear, *to let alone*
- v. Fore-bode, *to foretell*
- v. Fore-go, *to give up*
- a. For-lorn, *hopeless, wretched*
- v. For-swear, *to swear falsely*

### G.

*Accented on the first.*

- s. Gam-ut, *a scale of music*
- v. Gar-gle, *to wash the throat*
- s. Gar-ment, *wearing apparel*
- v. Gar-nish, *to adorn*
- a. Gau-dy, *superfluously showy*
- s. Gan-grene, *a mortification*
- s. Gaug-ing, *measuring of casks*
- a. Gen-tle, *mild, meek*
- Ges-ture, *posture*
- a. Ghast-ly, *pale, wan*

*pr.* Fa-teeg.

- s. Gher-kin, *a small cucumber*
- s. Gid-dy, *thoughtless*
- v. Glit-ter, *to shine, to sparkle*
- s. Glut-ton, *a great eater*
- s. Gos-pel, *the New Testament*
- a. Goth-ic, *antiquated*
- v. Gov-ern, *to rule, to manage*
- s. Gram-mar, *the science of speaking or writing a language correctly: the book which teaches it*
- s. Gran-deur, *magnificence*
- v. Grap-ple, *to struggle with*
- a. Grate-ful, *thankful*
- ad. Grat-is, *for nothing*
- s. Gra-ver, *a graving tool*
- s. Griev-ance, *uneasiness*
- s. Gross-ness, *coarseness*
- v. Grov-el, *to be mean*
- a. Ground-less, *void of truth*
- s. Gui-dance, *direction*
- a. Guil-ty, *not innocent*

*Accented on the last.*

- s. Ga-zette, *a newspaper*
- a. Gen-teel, *polite, graceful*

### H.

*Accented on the first.*

- s. Hab-it, *custom, dress*
- v. Ham-per, *to entangle*
- v. Hand-cuff, *to fetter*
- a. Hand-some, *beautiful*
- s. Har-row, *a farming implement*
- s. Har-vest, *time of reaping corn*
- s. Hatch-et, *a small axe*
- s. Ha-ven, *a harbour for ships*
- a. Haugh-ty, *proud, lofty*
- s. Ha-voc, *slaughter, destruction*

s Haw-ker, *a pedlar*
s. Haz-ard, *chance, dange*
a. Head-y, *rash, self-willed*
a. Heart-felt, *felt at heart*
a. Hea-then, *a pagan*
a. Hec-tic, *consumptive*
v. Hec-tor, *to boast*
a. Heed-less, *careless*
a. Hein-ous,\* *enormous*
s. Heif-er, *a young cow*
s. Hel-met, *a head piece*
s. Hem-lock, *a poisonous plant*
s. Her-bal, *a book of plants*
s. Her-mit, *a solitary person*
s. He-ro, *a person of valour*
s. Hig-ler, *a travelling poulterer*
s. Hire-ling, *one who serves for wages*
ad. Hith-er, *to this place*
a. Hoa-ry, *gray-headed*
s. Hom-aʲge, *respect, submission*
a. Hon-est,† *just, sincere*
s. Hon-our, *esteem, reputation*
s. Hor-ror, *dread*
s. Hos-taʲge, *a public pledge*
a. Hos-tile, *enemy like*
v. Hov-er,‡ *to keep near*
a. Hum-ble, *modest, submissive*
a. Hu-mid, *damp, moist*
s. Hu-mour, *whim, fancy*
s. Hyˢ-ᶻsop, *the name of a purgative plant*

\* *pr.* Hay-nus.
† There are several words in which *h* is not sounded; as, *hour, heir, honour, honest, hospital, hostler, humour, humble,* &c. In expressing these words we say, *an hour, an heir,* &c. because *a* always becomes *an* before a silent *h*. But if the *h* be sounded, the *a* only is to be used: as *a house, a hand, a heart.*
‡ *pr.* Huv-ver

*Accented on the last.*

s. Ha-rângue, *an oration or speech*
s. Har-poon, *a dart to strike whales with*
a. Hu-mane, *tender, compassionate, kind*

## I. J.

*Accented on the first.*

a. I-dle, *slothful*
s. Im-aʲge, *a picture or statue*
s. Im-post, *a tax*
s. Im-pulse, *persuasion*
s In-come, *rent, revenue*
s In-dex, *a table of reference*
s. In-gress, } *entrance*
   In-let, }
v. In-jure, *to wrong*
s. In-mate, *a lodger*
s. In-quest, *judicial inquiry*
s. In-road, *invasion*
s. In-sect, *any small living creature*
s. In-sight, *inspection, knowledge*
s. In-stance, *example, proof*
s. In-stinct, *a natural impulse*
a. Irk-some, *troublesome, tedious*
s. Is-land,§ *land surrounded by water*
s. Is-sue, *event, end*
ad. I-tem, *also*
v. Jan-gle, *to wrangle*
s. Jal-ap, *a medicine*
s. Join-ture, *a maintenance*
s. Junc-ture, *a critical period*
s. Jun-to, *a cabal, a faction*

§ *pr.* I-land.

*Accented on the last.*

v. Il·lúde, *to mock, to deceive*
v. Im-bibe, *to suck in*
v. Im-brue, *to soak or steep*
a. Im-mense, *very great*
v. Im-merse, *to dip or plunge*
v. Im-mure, *to confine*
v. Im-pair, *to make worse*
v. Im-part, *to communicate*
v. Im-peach, *to accuse*
v. Im-pede, *to obstruct*
v. Im-pel, *to urge, to force*
v. Im-pend, *to hang over*
v. Im-plant, *to ingraft*
v. Im-plore, *to beseech*
v. Im-ply, *to mean*
v. Im-po²se, *to lay upon*
v. Im-press, *to stamp*
v. Im-print, *to fix on the mind*
a. Im-pure, *unclean*
v. Im-pute, *to ascribe to*
v. In-case, *to cover*
v. In-cense, *to provoke*
v. In-cite, *to spur on*
v. In-clude, *to contain*
v. In-cur, *to fall under*
v. In-dent, *to notch*
v. In-dict,* *to charge with some crime, to write, &c.*
a. In-ert, *sluggish*
v. In-fect, *to corrupt*
v. In-fer, *to conclude from*
v. In-fest, *to annoy or trouble*
a. In-firm, *feeble, weak*
v. In-flict, *to impose a punishment*
v. In-form, *to tell or acquaint*
v. In-fringe, *to violate*
v. In-fu²se, *to pour in*
v. In-spect, *to look into*

\* *pr* In-dite.

v. In-spire, *to endue with*
v. In-stil, *to infuse*
a. In-tense, *excessive*
s. In-tent, *design, purpose*
v. In-ter, *to bury under ground*
s. In-trigue,† *a plot, cabal*
v. In-trude, *to enter uninvited*
v. In-veigh,‡ *to rail against*
v. In-vert, *to turn upside down*
v. In-vest, *to clothe with*
v. In-volve, *to fold in*
v. In-ure, *to accustom*
v. Jap-an, *to varnish*
a. Je-june, *empty in style*
a. Jo-cose, *merry, facetious*
s. Jon-quille,§ *a flower*

### K.

*Accented on the first.*

s. Kén-nel, *a water course*
s. Ker-²sey, *a coarse cloth*
s. Kid-der, *an engrosser of corn*
s. King-dom, *a country*
a. Kna-vish, *dishonest*
s. Knight-hood, *the dignity of a knight*
s. Knuc-kle, *a joint*

### L.

*Accented on the first.*

s. Lá-bel, *a direction*
s. La-bour, *toil, work*
s. Lan-cet, *a surgeon's instrument*
a. Lan-guid, *faint, weak*

† *pr.* In-treeg.   ‡ *pr.* In-vay.
§ *pr.* Jon-kille.

*v.* Lan-guish, *to pine away*
*a.* La-tent, *lying hid*
*s.* Lat-tice, *a window formed of grate work*
*v.* Lav-ish, *to scatter with profusion*
*s.* Law-yer, *a counsellor or pleader*
*a.* Le-gal, *lawful*
*s.* Leg-ate, *a pope's ambassador*
*s.* Le-gend, *a fabulous tale*
*s.* Lei-ᶻsure,* *freedom from business*
*a.* Lev-el, *even, flat*
*s.* Li-bel, *defamatory writing*
*s.* Li-çense, *permission*
*s.* Lim-ner, *a painter*
*a.* Lim-pid, *clear, transparent*
*s.* Lin-guist, *one skilled in language*
*s.* Liq-uor, *drink, water, &c.*
*a.* Liv-id, *bluish*
*a.* Lo-cal, *belonging to a place*
*s.* Lo-gic,† *the art of reasoning*
*a.* Loy-al, *faithful*
*a.* Lu-cid, *bright, shining*
*s.* Lu-cre,‡ *gain, profit*
*s.* Lug-gage, *weight or burden*
*s.* Lus-tre,§ *brightness*
*a.* Lyr-ic, *belonging to the harp*

### M.

*Accented on the first.*

*s.* Mág-net, *a loadstone*
*part.* Maim-ed, *hurt or wounded*
*s.* Mal-içe, *spite, ill will*
*s.* Mam-mon, *the god of wealth*

\* *pr.* Lee-zhure.    † *pr.* Lod-jik.
‡ *pr.* Lu-kur.    § *pr.* Lus-tur.

*v.* Man-age, *to rule or govern*
*s.* Man-date, *a judicial command*
*v.* Man-gle, *to cut or wound*
*s.* Man-or, *a jurisdiction*
*s.* Man-tle, *a cloak*
*s.* Mar-ble, *a fine stone*
*s.* Mar-gin, *the brim or edge*
*s.* Mar-shal, *an officer of superior rank in the army*
*s.* Mar-tyr, *one who dies for the truth*
*v.* Mar-vel, *to wonder*
*a.* Mas-sy, *solid, weighty*
*a.* Match-less, *not to be equalled*
*s.* Mat-trass, *a quilted bed to lie under another*
*ad.* Mau-gre,‖ *in spite of*
*s.* Max-im, *a principle*
*s.* May-or, *a chief magistrate*
*s.* Mead-ow, *pasture, land*
*a.* Mea-gre, *lean, thin*
*s.* Med-al, *an ancient coin*
*s.* Mem-brane, *a fibrous substance*
*v.* Men-ace, *to threaten*
*a.* Men-tal, *intellectual*
*s.* Mer-çer, *a dealer in silk*
*s.* Mer-it, *worth*
*s.* Mes-sage, *an errand*
*s.* Me-ter, *a measurer*
*s.* Me-tre, *poetic measure*
*s.* Mid-night, *twelve at night*
*a.* Migh-ty, *powerful*
*v.* Min-gle, *to mix together*
*a.* Mi-nor, *less: one under age*
*s.* Mir-ror, *a looking-glass*
*s.* Mis-chief, *hurt, damage*
*s.* Mi-tre, *an episcopal crown*
*s.* Mod-el, *frame, fashion*
*a.* Mod-ern, *new, recent*
*a.* Mod-est, *discreet in behaviour*

‖ *pr.* Maw-gur.

a. Mo-dish, *fashionable*
s. Mo-ment, *an instant: also importance*
s. Mon-arch, *king, sovereign*
a. Mon-strous, *prodigious*
a. Mo-ral, *belonging to manners*
s. Mortar, *a vessel to pound in: a cement for building: a bomb cannon*
v. Mort-gage, *to pledge lands, &c.*
s. Mo-tive, *incitement*
a. Mot-ley, *mixed*
s. Mot-to, *a short sentence*
a. Mòurn-ful, *sorrowful*
a. Mun-dane, *worldly*
v. Mur-mur, *to grumble*
s. Mus-çle, *fleshy fibre, shell fish*
s. Myr-tle, *a kind of shrub*

*Accented on the last.*

v. Main-táin, *to support*
v. Mal-treat, *to treat ill*
v. Ma-nure, *to dung the ground*
s. Ma-rine,* *belonging to the sea*
a. Ma-ture, *ripe, perfect*
s. Mar-quee,† *an officer's field tent*
s. Mis-deed, *a crime*
s. Mis-trust, *suspicion*
v. Mo-lest, *to disturb*
a. Mo-rose, *cross, surly*

### N.

*Accented on the first.*

s. Nátive, *one born in the land*
s. Na-ture, *disposition*
s. Na-vy, *a fleet of ships of war*
a. Nee-dy, *poor, distressed by want*

\* *pr.* Mareen.   † *pr.* Markee.

a. Ner-vous, *vigorous*
a. Neth-er, *lower*
a. Neu-ter, *of neither party*
s. Nig-gard, *a covetous person*
s. Ni-tre, *saltpetre*
a. No-cent, *hurtful*
a. Noi-some, *loathsome*
s. Non-age, *under age*
v. Non-plus, *to puzzle*
ad. North-ward, *towards the north*
s. Nos-trum, *a quack medicine*
a. Nov-el, *new, unusual*
s. Nov-içe, *an inexperienced person*
v. Nou-rish, *to keep or maintain*
s. Nui-sançe, *an offensive thing*
s. Nur-ture, *support, education*

### O.

*Accented on the first.*

s. Ob'-long, *four-sided, right-angled figure, longer than broad*
s. O-çean,‡ *the sea*
s. O-dour, *scent or smell*
s. Of-fal, *refuse, waste meat*
s. Off-spring, *progeny*
s. O-men, *a prognostic or sign*
a. Op-tic, *belonging to the sight*
a. O-ral, *by the mouth or voice*
s. Ord-nançe, *heavy cannon*
s. Or-dure,§ *dung, filth*
s. Or-phan, *a fatherless and motherless child*
s. Os-trich, *a very large African fowl*
a. O-val, *egg-like*
a. O-vert, *open, manifest*
a. Out-rage, *a violent assault*
s. Oys-ter, *a shell-fish*

‡ *pr.* O-shun.   § *pr.* Or-jure.

*Accented on the last.*

v. O-béy, *to submit*
a. O-blique,* *crooked, not direct*
a. Ob-scene, *filthy, lewd*
a. Ob-scure, *dark*
v. Ob-struct, *to hinder*
v. Ob-trude, *to thrust in upon*
a. Ob-tuse *blunt*
a. Oc-cult, *secret*
v. Oc-cur, *to offer itself*
v. O-mit, *to leave out*
v. Op-po$^z$se, *to thwart*
v. Op-press, *to overburden*
v. Or-dain, *to appoint*

## P.

*Accented on the first.*

s. Pác-ket, *a parcel*
s. Pa-gan, *a heathen*
s. Pal-açe, *a splendid mansion*
a. Pal-try, *pitiful, mean*
v. Pam-per, *to indulge*
s. Pam-phlet, *a stitched book*
s. Pan-ic, *sudden fear*
a. Pa-pal, *belonging to the pope*
s. Pa-pist, *a popish religionist*
v. Par-boil, *to boil in part*
s. Parçh-ment, *skins of sheep*
s. Par-ley, *a conference*
s. Par-lour, *a lower room*
a. Pas-sive, *apt to bear or suffer*
s. Pas-tor, *a church minister*
s. Pas-ture, *grass, land*
s. Pat-ent, *an exclusive grant*
s. Pa-thos, *warmth, passion*
s. Pa-tron, *a protector*
s. Pau-per, *a poor person*
s. Pea$^z$s-ant, *a countryman*

* *pr.* by Walker ob-like, by many *pr.* ob-leek.

s. Ped-ant, *a pretended scholarship*
s. Ped-ler, *one who sells small ware*
a. Pee-vish, *fretful, hard to please*
a. Pe-nal, *exacting punishment*
s. Pen-ançe, *mortification*
a. Pen-sive, *sad, sorrowful*
s. Per-il, *danger, hazard*
v. Per-ish, *to die, to decay*
v. Pes-ter, *to harass, to disturb*
s. Pes-tle, *a tool to beat in a mortar*
s. Phan-tom,† *a fancied vision*
s. Phœ-nix, *an extraordinary bird*
s. Phi-al, *a small bottle*
s. Phy$^z$s-ic, *medicines*
v. Pil-fer, *to steal*
s. Pil-grim, *a holy traveller*
v. Pil-laǰge, *to plunder*
s. Pi-lot, *one who directs a ship' course*
s. Pin-naçe, *a small sea vessel*
a. Pi-ous, *religious*
s. Pi-rate, *a sea-robber*
a. Plaç-id, *gentle, mild*
a. Plain-tiff,‡ *a complainant*
s. Plat-form, *a model*
s. Plough-share, *the iron of a plough*
s. Plu-maǰge, *feathers*
v. Plun-der, *to rob*
a. Plu-ral, *many*

† *ph* at the beginning of words or syllables always sounds like *f;* except in the words *phthisis, ph-thisick, ph-thisical, apophthegm,* where it has no sound at all.

‡ Many persons pronounce this word *Plan-tiff;* but it is more correct to restore the dipthong, and speak it as if written *Plane-tiff.*

*a.* Poign-ant,* *sharp, satirical*
*v.* Pol-ish, *to brighten, to civilize*
*s.* Pom-mel, *a knob on a sword or saddle*
*a.* Pom-pous, *splendid, showy*
*v.* Pon-der, *to consider*
*s.* Pon-tiff, *a high priest*
*a.* Pòrt-ly, *comely*
*s.* Pòr-trait, *a picture drawn from life*
*s.* Pòst-a<sup>j</sup>ge, *carriage of letters*
*s.* Pos-ture, *position*
*a.* Po-tent, *powerful*
*s.* Prac-tiçe, *custom, &c.*
*s.* Preb-end, *a church dignity*
*s.* Pre-çept, *a command*
*s.* Pre-çinct, *a jurisdiction*
*s.* Prel″-ate, *a bishop* [*tory*
*s.* Pre-lude, *something introduc-*
*s.* Pres-sure, *force, impression*
*s.* Pri-mate, *the chief archbishop*
*a.* Pri-or, *before*
*a.* Pris-tine, *ancient*
*a.* Priv-y, *in the secret*
*s.* Prob-lem, *a proposition*
*s.* Pro-cess, *a proceeding*
*s.* Proc-tor, *an advocate*
*s.* Prod-uct, *the thing produced*
*s.* Prof-it, *advantage, gain*
*v.* Prof-fer, *to offer*
*s.* Prog-ress, *advancement*
*s.* Proj-ect, *design*
*s.* Pro-logue, *preface*
*s.* Pro-noun, *a personal noun*
*s.* Proph-et, *an inspired person*
*s.* Pros-pect, *a view*
*v.* Pros-trate, *stretched on the ground*
*s.* Prov-erb, *a common saying*
*s.* Prov-ince, *division of a kingdom*

* *pr.* Poe-nant

*a.* Pru-dent, *discreet*
*s.* Prow-ess, *bravery*
*s.* Prox-y, *a deputy*
*s.* Psal-mist, *a writer of psalms*
*s.* Psal-ter, *a book of psalms*
*a.* Pur-blind, *short sighted*
*s.* Pur-port, *meaning*
*s.* Pus-tule, *a pimple*
*a.* Pu-trid, *rotten, offensive*

*Accented on the last.*

*s.* Par-áde, *great show*
*s.* Par-ole, *word of honor*
*v.* Par-take, *to take part with*
*s.* Par-terre,† *a flower garden*
*s.* Pa-trol, *a night-watch*
*v.* Per-form, *to do*
*v.* Per-mit, *to allow*
*v.* Per-plex, *to trouble*
*v.* Per-sist, *to continue steadfas*
*v.* Per-spire, *to sweat*
*v.* Per-suade, *to advise*
*v.* Per-tain, *to belong to*
*v.* Per-vade, *to go through*
*a.* Per-verse, *froward*
*v.* Per-vert, *to turn from the right*
*v.* Pe-ru<sup>z</sup>se, *to read over*
*a.* Po-lite, *elegant of manners*
*v.* Por-tend, *to forbode*
*v.* Pòst-pone, *to delay*
*v.* Pre-çede, *to go before*
*a.* Pre-çise, *formal, exact*
*v.* Pre-clude, *to hinde*
*v.* Pre-dict, *to foretell*
*v.* Pre-fer, *to regard more*
*v.* Pre-fix, *to put before*
*v.* Pre-mi<sup>z</sup>se, *to speak of before*
*a.* Pre-pense, *a fore-thought*
*v.* Pre-sa<sup>j</sup>ge, *to foretoken*

* *pr.* Par-táre.

42     THE SCHOLAR'S

*v.* Pre-scribe, *to appoint*
*v.* Pre-side, *to rule over*
*v.* Pre-²sume, *to conjecture*
*s.* Pre-tençe, *excuse*
*v.* Pre-tend, *to allure falsely*
*s.* Pre-text, *a colourable excuse*
*v.* Pre-vail, *to overcome*
*v.* Pre-vent, *to obstruct*
*v.* Pro-cure, *to get*
*a.* Pro-fane, *impious*
*s.* Pro-file,* *the side face*
*v.* Pro-fess, *to declare*
*a.* Pro-found, *deep learned*
*a.* Pro-lix, *long, tedious*
*v.* Pro-long, *to delay*
*v.* Pro-mote, *to advance*
*v.* Pro-mulge, *to publish*
*v.* Pro-nounçe, *to utter*
*v.* Pro-po²se, *to offer*
*v.* Pro-pound, *to propose*
*v.* Pro-rogue, *to put off*
*v.* Pro-tect, *to defend*
*v.* Pro-test, *to declare positively*
*v.* Pro-tract, *to keep back*
*v.* Pro-trude, *to push forward*
*v.* Pro-vide, *to take care of*
*v.* Pro-voke, *to anger*
*v.* Pur-loin, *to filch, to steal*
*s.* Pur-suit, *a running after*

## Q.

*Accented on the first.*

*s.* Quá-drant, *the fourth part of a circle*
*s.* Quag-mire, *a bog*
*s.* Quar-to, *four leaves to a sheet*
*s.* Que-rist, *an inquirer*
*v.* Quib-ble, *to equivocate*

*pr.* **Pro-feel.**

*s.* Quin-²sy, *a disease in the throat*
*s.* Quiv-er, *a case for arrows*
*s.* Quo-rum, *a bench of justices*
*s.* Quo-ta, *a share*

## R.

*Accented on the first.*

*s.* Ráb-ble, *an assemblage of low people*
*s.* Rai-ment, *garment*
*v.* Ral-ly, *to jest : to recover order*
*a.* Ram-pant, *wanton*
*s.* Ran-cour, *inveterate malignity*
*a.* Ran-dom, *without aim*
*v.* Ran-sack, *to rifle*
*v.* Ran-som, *to redeem*
*a.* Rap-id, *swift*
*s.* Rap-ine, *pillage*
*s.* Rap-ture, *transport*
*s.* Rash-ness, *hastiness*
*v.* Rav-age, *to lay waste*
*s.* Rea-²son, *clearness of faculties*
*a.* Re-çent, *new, late*
*s.* Rec-tor, *a parson*
*s.* Re-flux, *a flowing back*
*s.* Ref-uge, *a place of safety*
*a.* Re-gal, *royal, kingly*
*s.* Re-gent, *a ruler for another*
*s.* Rel-ict, *a widow*
*a.* Rel-ish, *to like or approve*
*s.* Rem-nant, *a fragment*
*v.* Ren-der, *to give back*
*s.* Rep-tile, *a creeping thing*
*v.* Res-pite, *to put off*
*v.* Rev-el, *to riot licentiously*
*s.* R*h*u-barb,* *a medical root*
*a.* Ri-gid,† *very strict*

* *H* is always silent after *r*.
† *pr.* **Rid-jid.**

*s.* Riot, *tumult, sedition*
*s.* Ri-val, *a competitor*
*a.* Ro-guish, *knavish*
*s.* Ro<sup>z</sup>s-in, *an inflammable gum*
*s.* Ros-trum, *a kind of pulpit*
*a.* Roy-al, *kingly*
*s.* Ru-bric, *a book of church laws*
*a.* Rug-ged, *uneven, harsh*
*r.* Rum-ble, *to make a hollow noise*
*v.* Rum-mage, *to search places*
*s.* Ru-mour, *report, hearsay*
*a.* Rup-ture, *a breaking*
*a.* Ru-ral, *belonging to the country*
*a.* Rus-tic, *clownish*

*Accented on the last.*

*v.* Re-bóund, *to leap back*
*v.* Re-buke, *to reprove*
*v.* Re-call, *to call back*
*v.* Re-cant, *to retract*
*v.* Re-çede, *to depart from*
*s.* Re-çeipt, *an acquittance*
*s.* Re-çess, *a withdrawing*
*v.* Re-çite, *to relate or rehearse*
*v.* Re-claim, *to amend in life*
*v.* Re-cline, *to lean backwards*
*a.* Re-cluse, *shut up*
*v.* Re-coil, *to fly back*
*v.* Re-count, *to relate*
*s.* Re-còurse, *application*
*v.* Re-crùit, *to supply*
*v.* Re-cur, *to have recourse to*
*v.* Re-deem, *to recover*
*v.* Re-dound, *to conduce*
*v.* Re-dress, *to remedy*
*v.* Re-duçe, *to make less : to sub-due*
*v.* Re-fer, *to direct to*
*v.* Re-fine, *to purify*
*v.* Re-fit, *to fit again*

*v.* Re-flect, *to throw back : to think*
*v.* Re-form, *to grow better*
*v.* Re-frain, *to keep from*
*v.* Re-fresh, *to revive*
*v.* Re-fund, *to pay back*
*v.* Re-fute, *to disprove*
*v.* Re-gain, *to get again*
*v.* Re-gale, *to entertain*
*v* Re-gard, *to respect*
*v.* Re-gret, *to lament*
*v.* Re-hearse, *to relate*
*v.* Re-ject, *to cast off*
*s.* Re-lapse, *a falling back*
*v.* Re-late, *to tell*
*v.* Re-lax, *to loosen*
*v.* Re-lease, *to set at liberty*
*v.* Re-lent, *to feel compassion*
*s.* Re-lief, *assistance, comfort*
*s.* Re-mark, *observation*
*v.* Re-mind, *to put in mind*
*a.* Re-miss, *careless*
*v.* Re-mit, *to send back*
*s.* Re-morse, *check of conscience*
*a.* Re-mote, *far distant*
*v.* Re-new, *to begin afresh*
*s.* Re-nown, *fame*
*v.* Re-pair, *to mend : to go to*
*s.* Re-past, *a meal*
*v.* Re-peal, *to revoke*
*v.* Re-peat, *to say or do again*
*v.* Re-pel, *to drive back*
*v.* Re-pent, *to be sorry for*
*v.* Re-pine, *to murmur*
*a.* Re-plete, *abounding*
*s.* Re-po<sup>z</sup>se, *sleep, peace*
*v.* Re-press, *to crush, restrain*
*s.* Re-prieve, *a pardon*
*v.* Re-pròaçh, *to upbraid*
*v.* Re-prove, *to blame*
*v.* Re-pulse, *to drive off*
*s.* Repute, *credit, esteem*

v. Re-quest, *to solicit*
v. Re-quite, *to reward*
v. Re-sent, *to return an injury*
v. Re-serve, *to keep in store*
v. Re-side, *to live in a place*
v. Re-sign, *to give up*
v. Re-sist, *to oppose*
v. Re-sort, *to repair to*
v. Re-sound, *to echo*
s. Re-source, *a fund of support*
v. Re-spect, *to regard*
v. Re-spire, *to breathe*
v. Re-strain, *to keep in*
s. Re-sult, *issue, conclusion*
v. Re-sume, *to begin again*
v. Re-tail, *to sell by parcels*
v. Re-tain, *to keep*
v. Re-tard, *to delay*
v. Re-tire, *to go away*
v. Re-tort, *to throw back*
v. Re-tract, *to unsay*
s. Re-treat, *a retiring*
v. Re-trench, *to cut off*
v. Re-trieve, *to recover*
v. Re-veal, *to discover*
s. Re-venge, *return of an injury*
v. Re-vere, *to venerate, to love*
s. Re-verse, *contrary*
v. Re-vert, *to return*
v. Re-view, *to examine*
v. Re-vile, *to reproach*
v. Re-vise, *to review*
v. Re-vive, *to recover*
v. Re-voke, *to make void*
v. Re-volt, *to rebel*
v. Re-volve, *to turn in mind*
a. Ro-bust, *strong, sinewy*
s. Ro-mance, *a feigned story*

## S

*Accented on the first*

s. Sá-ble, *a dark fur; black*
s. Sa-bre, *a Turkish sword*
a. Sa-cred, *holy, consecrated*
s. Sal-vage, *recompense to a ship for recovery, or rescue*
s. Sam-ple, *a specimen*
a. San-guine, *confident, full of hope*
s. Sap-phire,* *a precious stone*
s. Sar-casm, *a satirical jest*
v. Saun-ter, *to idle, to drone*
s. Scab-bard, *a sheath for a sword*
s. Scan-dal, *defamation*
s. Scep-tic, or Skep-tic, } *one who doubts*
s. Scep-tre,† *a royal staff*
s. Sched-ule, *a small scroll*
s. Scho-lar, *a pupil; a learned man*
s. Sci-ence, *knowledge, skill*
s. Sci-on, *a young shoot*
v. Scrib-ble, *to write badly*
s. Scrip-ture, *the sacred writings*
v. Scru-ple, *to doubt, to hesitate*
s. Sculp-tor, *a carver or engraver*
s. Sculp-ture, *carved work*
a. Se-cret, *private*
s. Sei-zure, *a seizing*
a. Self-ish, *interested*
s. Sen-ate, *a council*
s. Sen-tence, *a decree*
s. Se-quel, *the conclusion*
s. Ser-mon, *a pious, instructive discourse*
a. Ser-vile, *mean, base*

* pr. Saf-fyr.   † pr. Sep-tur.

v. Sev-er, *to part asunder*
s. Sew-er, *a drain or passage for water*
s. Sex-ton, *a church officer*
a. Shal-low, *not deep*
s. Sham-bles, *butchers' stalls*
a. Shame-ful, *disgraceful*
a. Shame-less, *void of shame*
s. Shar-per, *a sly cheat*
v. Shat-ter, *to break to pieces*
s. Shel-ter, *protection, security*
s. Sher-iff, *a crown officer*
s. Ship-wreck, *destruction of a ship by rocks, &c.*
ad. Shrewd-ly, *acutely*
v. Shriv-el, *to wrinkle*
v. Shud-der, *to tremble*
v. Shuf-fle, *to mingle together*
s. Sic-kle, *a reaping hook*
s. Sig-nal, *a sign given*
s. Sig-net, *a seal*
a. Sil-van, *woody*
s. Sin-ew, *a tendon or muscle*
s. Sir-up,* *a vegetable juice boiled with sugar*
a. Skil-ful, *experienced*
a. Skil-led, *well versed in*
s. Skir-mish, *a slight encounter*
s. Slaugh-ter, *destruction with the sword*
a. Slen-der, *thin, small*
a. Sloth-ful, *lazy, idle*
s. Slov-en, *a nasty person*
v. Slum-ber, *to doze*
v. Smoth-er, *to suffocate*
s. Smug-gler, *one who cheats the revenue*
v. So-journ, *to tarry, to stay*
s. Sol-ace, *comfort, consolation*
a. So-lar, *belonging to the sun*
a. Sol-emn, *awful*
     * *pr.* Sur-rup.

a. Sol-id, *firm compact*
a. Sol-vent *able to pay*
s. Son-net, *a poem of 14 lines*
s. Soph-ist,† *a captious disputant*
a. Sor-did, *mean, covetous*
s. Sor-rel, *an herb*
s. Sor-row, *grief, anxiety*
ad. South-ward, *towards the south*
v. Spar-kle, *to glitter*
v. Spat-ter, *to sprinkle with dirt*
a. Spee-dy, *very quick*
s. Spend-thrift, *a prodigal*
s. Spike-nard, *a foreign plant*
a. Spi-ral, *of a screw-like form*
a. Spite-ful, *full of malice*
a. Splen-did, *noble, magnificent*
s. Splen-dour, *glory, brightness*
s. Spokes-man, *one who speaks for others*
s. Spon-sor, *surety*
a. Spot-less, *without blemish*
a. Spright-ly, *lively, agreeable*
v. Sprin-kle, *to wet with drops*
s. Squad-ron, *part of an army or fleet*
a. Squal-id, *foul, nasty*
a. Squal-ly, *windy, stormy*
v. Squan-der, *to lavish*
a. Squeam-ish, *weak-stomached*
a. Sta-ble, *sure, lasting*
a. Stag-nant, *motionless*
v. Stam-mer, *to falter in speaking*
s. Stand-ard, *a fixed weight*
s. Stand-ish, *an inkstand*
a. State-ly, *pompous, majestic*
s. Stat-ue, *an image of metal, stone, &c.*
s. Stat-ure, *height of any animal*
s. Stat-ute, *an act of parliament, a law.*
     † *pr.* Sof-fist.

a. Stead-y, firm, constant
s. Steer-age, steering
a. Ster-ile, barren
a. Ster-ling, genuine
ad. Stern-ly, severely
s. Stew-ard, a manager
s. Stick-ler, a warm advocate
s. Stig-ma, a mark of infamy
s. Sti-pend, salary, wages
s. Stom-ach, a part of the body
s. Store-house, a warehouse
s. Sto-ry, a tale; a floor
s. Stow-age, warehouse room
v. Strag-gle, to wander
v. Stran-gle, to choke or stifle
s. Stream-er, a small flag
s. Strict-ness, severity, exactness
s. Strip-ling, a youth
s. Struc-ture, a building; form
v. Strug-gle, to strive or contend
a. Stub-born, obstinate
s. Stu-dent, a scholar
s. Stub-ble, short straw
s. Stum-ble, a trip in walking
a. Stu-pid, dull, senseless
s. Stu-por, insensibility
a. Stur-dy, strong, hardy
s. Sub-stance, essence
a. Sub-tile, thin, fine
a. Sub-tle,* crafty, cunning
s. Sub-urb's, the out parts of a city
s. Suc-cour, help, relief
a. Sud-den, unexpected
s. Suf-frage, a vote
a. Sui-tor, a petitioner
a. Sul-len, gloomy, forbidding
v. Sul-ly, to soil, to tarnish
s. Sul-tan, the Turkish emperor
a. Sul-try, hot and close
    * pr. Sut-tle.

s. Sum-mit, the highest part
v. Sum-mon, to cite
s. Sum-mon's, a call of authority
a. Sun-dry, several
a. Sup-ple, pliant
s. Sur-face, the outside
v. Sur-feit, to make sick with eating, &c.
s. Sure-ty, bail, security
s. Sur-name, a family name
s. Sur-plice, a priest's white garb
s. Sur-plus, remainder
v. Swad-dle, to wrap up
a. Swar-thy, blackish
s. Swiv-el, a thing for another to turn upon
s. Sym-bol, a badge
s. Symp-tom, an indication
s. Syn-od, an ecclesiastical meeting
s. Syn-tax, construction of words
s. Syr-inge, a squirting instrument
s. Sys-tem, a method

*Accented on the last.*

v. Se-cede, to withdraw from
v. Se-clude, to shut out
v. Se-crete, to hide
a. Se-cure, perfectly safe
a. Se-date, quiet, serene
v. Se-duce, to mislead
v. Se-lect, to choose
a. Se-rene, calm, quiet
a. Se-vere, harsh, unfeeling
a. Sin-cere, honest, true
s. Spin-et, a musical instrument
v. Sub-due, to conquer
v. Sub-join, to add
a. Sub-lime, grand, lofty

## SPELLING ASSISTANT.

v. Sub-mit, *to yield*
v. Sub-orn, *to procure false witness*
v. Sub-scribe, *to sign*
v. Sub-side, *to sink gradually*
v. Sub-sist, *to live*
v. Sub-vert, *to overthrow*
v. Suc-ceed, *to follow, to prosper*
s. Suc-cess, *prosperity*
a. Suc-cinct, *brief, short*
v. Suf-fice,* *to be enough*
v. Sug-gest,† *to hint*
a. Su-perb, *elegant*
a. Su-pine, *negligent*
v. Sup-plant, *to displace*
v. Sup-ply, *to furnish*
v. Sup-port, *to endure*
v. Sup-po$^z$se, *to imagine*
v. Sup-press, *to put a stop to*
a. Su-preme, *the highest*
v. Sur-char$^j$ge, *to overload*
s. Sur-mi$^z$se, *suspicion*
v. Sur-mount, *to overcome*
v. Sur-pass, *to excel*
s. Sur-pri$^z$se, *amazement*
v. Sur-round, *to enclose*
v. Sur-vey, *to overlook: to measure*
v. Sur-vive, *to outlive*
v. Sus-pect, *to fear or mistrust*
v. Sus-pend, *to delay*
s. Sus-pense, *uncertainty*

* Or *pr.* Suf-fize.
† *pr.* Sud-jest. When two *g*gs come together, they are both hard, (except in the words *suggest, exaggerate*,) though *e, i,* or *y* follow; as *dagger, stagger, begging, craggy, foggy,* &c.

T.

*Accented on the first.*

s. Tá-bor, *a small drum*
a. Tac-it, *silent*
s. Tal-ent, *capacity, genius*
v. Tal-ly, *to score, to agree*
s. Tal-on, *claw of a bird*
v. Tam-per, *to meddle with*
s. Tan-kard, *a pot with a lid*
s. Ta-per, *a wax candle*
s. Tap-ster, *a drawer of beer*
a. Tar-dy, *slow*
s. Tar-get, *a shield*
v. Tar-nish, *to sully or soil*
v. Tar-ry, *to loiter or lag*
s. Tart-ness, *sharpness, sourness*
s. Tas-sel, *a bunch of fringe*
a. Taunt-ing, *insulting*
a. Taw-dry, *ridiculously gay*
s. Tem-per, *natural disposition*
s. Tem-pest, *a violent storm*
s. Tem-ple, *a place of worship*
s. Ten-ant, *that rents of another*
a. Ten-der, *soft, kind*
s. Ten-don, *a sinew*
s. Ten-et, *a doctrine or opinion*
s. Ten-or, *intent, meaning*
s. Ten-ter, *a hook*
s. Ten-ure, *term of holding land*
s. Ter-race, *a bank of earth*
s. Ter-ror, *great fear*
s. Tes-ter, *the cover of a bed*
a. Tes-ty, *peevish*
s. Tex-ture, *composure*
s. The-sis, *a composition*
s. Thick-et, *a close wood*
a. Thirs-ty, *dry*
s. This-tle, *a weed*
ad. Thith-er, *to that place*
s. Thral-dom, *slavery*

s. Tick-et, *a note*
s. Til-lage, *the ploughing of land*
s. Tim-brel, *a musical instru-* [ment
a. Tim-id, *fearful*
s. Tinc-ture, *a colouring*
v. Tin-kle, *to clink*
s. Ti-tle, *an inscription*
s. Tit-tle, *a small particle*
a. Toil-some, *laborious*
s. To-ken, *a sign or mark*
s. Ton-nage,* *a duty on goods*
s. Top-ic, *head of a discourse*
s. Tor-ment, *misery anguish*
a. Tor-pid, *benumbed*
s. Tor-rent, *a rapid stream*
a. Tor-rid, *burning hot*
s. Tor-toiˢse, *an animal*
s. Tor-ture, *exquisite pain*
a. To-tal, *the whole*
a. To-ward, *docile, compliant*
s. Tow-er, *a citadel*
s. Traf-fic, *trade, commerce*
a. Tra-gic, *disastrous, mournful*
s. Trai-tor, *an enemy to his country*
v. Tram-ple, *to tread on*
a. Tran-quil, *quiet, still*
s. Tran-script, *a copy*
s. Tran-sit, *a passing over*
s. Trans-port, *ecstasy, rapture*
s. Trav-el, *a journey*
v. Trav-erse, *to cross, to survey*
s. Trea-cle, *the spume of sugar*
s. Trea-ˢson, *disloyalty*
s. Trea-tiˢse, *a discourse*
s. Tre-mour, *a shaking or trembling*
a. Trep-id, *fearful*
s. Tres-pass, *offence, injury*
s. Tri-al, *test: examination*
s. Trib-ute, *a tax*

    * pr. Tun-nage.

s. Tri-fle, *of small importance*
a. Trip-le, *threefold*
s. Tri-umph, *exultation*
s. Troop-er, *a horse soldier*
s. Tro-phy, *a token of victory*
s. Trow-el, *a mason's tool*
s. Tru-ant, *an absentee*
a. Trus-ty, *faithful*
a. Tu-mid, *swelled*
s. Tu-mour, *a morbid swelling*
s. Tu-mult, *riot, uproar*
a. Tur-bid, *thick, muddy*
a. Tur-gid, *puffed up*
s. Tur-ret, *a little tower*
s. Tu-tor, *a teacher*
s. Twi-light, *the faint light before sunrise and after sunset*
v. Twin-kle, *to sparkle*
v. Twit-ter, *to make a noise like swallows*
s. Ty-rant, *a despotic governor*
s. Ty-ro, *a beginner*

   *Accented on the last.*

v. Tra-dúce, *to slander*
v. Trans-act, *to carry on*
v. Tran-scend, *to surpass*
v. Tran-scribe, *to copy out*
v. Trans-fer, *to make over*
v. Trans-fix, *to pierce through*
v. Trans-form, *to change*
v. Trans-fuˢse, *to pour through*
v. Trans-gress, *to violate*
v. Trans-late, *to remove, to interpret*
v. Trans-mit, *to convey*
v. Trans-mute, *to change*
v. Trans-pierçe, *to run through*
v. Tran-spire, *to escape from secrecy*
v. Trans-plant, *to remove*
v. Trans-pòrt, *to convey*

*v.* Trans-pose, *to change places*
*a.* Trans-verse, *across*
*v.* Tre-pan, *to insnare*
*s.* Trus-tee, *a guardian*

## V U

*Accented on the first.*

*a.* Vá-cant, *empty*
*s.* Va-grant, *a stroller*
*s.* Val-ançe, *short bed curtains*
*a.* Val-id, *binding, good in law*
*s.* Val-ley, *a bottom between two hills*
*s.* Val-our, *courage, bravery*
*s.* Val-ue, *price, worth*
*v.* Van-ish, *to disappear*
*v.* Van-quish, *to overcome*
*a.* Vap-id, *dead, flat*
*s.* Va-pour, *a water exhalation*
*v.* Var-nish, *to gloss*
*v.* Va-ry, *to alter*
*s.* Vas-sal, *a slave*
*a.* Vault-ed, *arched*
*s.* Vel-lum, *a kind of parchment made of calf skin*
*a.* Ve-nal, *mercenary, base*
*s.* Ven-om, *poison*
*v.* Ven-ture, *to hazard*
*a* Ver-bal, *by word of mouth*
*a.* Ver-dant, *green*
*s.* Ver-dict, *the report of juries*
*s.* Ver-dure, *greenness*
*a.* Ver-nal, *belonging to the spring*
*s.* Ver-sion, *translation*
*s.* Ver-tex, *the highest part*
*s.* Ves-per, *the evening*
*s.* Ves-sel, *a ship, &c.*
*s.* Ves-tige, *footstep, trace*

*s.* Ves-try, *a parish meeting*
*s.* Ves-ture, *a garment*
*s.* Vi-and, *meat, food*
*v.* Vi-brate, *to move* **to and fro**
*s.* Vic-ar, *a parson*
*s.* Vice-roy, *a deputy king*
*s.* Vic-tim, *a sacrifice*
*s.* Vic-tor, *a conqueror*
*s.* Vig-il, *a holiday eve*
*s.* Vig-our, *strength, energy*
*s.* Vil-lage, *a small country* **town**
*s.* Vi-ol, *a fiddle*
*s.* Vir-tue, *moral conduct*
*s.* Vis-age, *the face*
*s.* Vis-count, *a nobleman*
*a.* Vis-cous, *clammy*
*v.* Vis-it, *to go to see*
*s.* Vis-or, or Viz-ard, } *a mask*
*s.* Vis-ta. *a prospect*
*a.* Vi-tal, *living*
*a.* Viv-id, *lively, vigorous*
*a.* Vo-cal, *belonging to the* **voice**
*a.* Vo-lant, *flying*
*s.* Vol-ley, *a discharge of shot*
*s.* Vol-ume, *a single book*
*s* Vor-tex, *a whirlpool*
*s* Vouch-er, *a witness*
*s.* Voy-age, *travel by sea*
*a.* Vul-gar, *low, mean*
*s.* Um-ber, *a colour*
*s.* Um-brage, *offence*
*s.* Um-pire, *an arbitrator*
*s.* Un-cle, *a father's or* **mother's** *brother*
*s.* U-nit, *the number* 1
*a.* Up-right, *standing, just*
*s.* Up-roar, *a great noise*
*s.* Up-shot, *issue, end*
*a.* Ur-gent, *pressing, earnest*
*s.* U-sage, *treatment,* **custom**
*v.* Ut-ter, *to speak*

## THE SCHOLAR'S

*Accented on the last.*

*a.* Ver-bose, *tedious*
*v.* Vouch-safe, *to condescend*
*a.* Un-couth,* *strange, unusual*
*v.* Un-fold, *to spread*
*v.* U-nite, *to join*
*v.* Un-moor, *to loose a ship*
*v.* Un-nerve, *to weaken*
*v.* Up-hold, *to support*
*v.* U-surp, *to seize illegally*

## W

*Accented on the first.*

*s.* Wá-ger, *a bet*
*s.* Wain-scot, *a lining the rooms*
*s.* Wal-let, *a travelling bag*
*v.* Wal-low, *to roll in the mire*
*v.* Wan-der, *to ramble*
*v.* War-ble, *to sing*
*s.* War-den, *a guardian or keeper*
*s.* Ward-robe, *a place for apparel*
*s.* War-fare, *military service*
*s.* War-rant, *a writ of authority*
*s.* War-ren, *a place for rabbits*
*a.* Way-ward, *perverse, peevish*
*a.* Wealth-y, *very rich*
*s.* Weath-er, *state of the air*
*a.* Wear-i-some, *heavy, tiresome*
*s.* Wel-fare, *happiness*

\* *pr. Unkooth.*

*v.* West-ward, *towards the west*
*s.* Whar-fage, *duty for wharfing*
*s.* Wher-ry, *a light river boat*
*a.* Whole-some, *good, healthful*
*s.* Wick-et, *a small gate*
*s.* Wid-ow, *a woman whose hus-band is dead*
*a.* Wil-ful, *full of one*
*v.* Win-now, *to sift*
*v.* Wran-gle, *to quarrel*
*s.* Wrap-per, *a cloth or paper to wrap, &c*
*v.* Wres-tle, *to grapple with*
*v.* Wrin-kle, *to crease or fold*

## Y.

*Accented on the first.*

*s.* Yeo-man, *a gentleman, a farmer, &c.*
*s.* Young-ster, *a young person*
*a.* Youth-ful, *young*

## Z.

*Accented on the first.*

*s.* Ze-bra, *a wild ass*
*a.* Zea-lous, *with passionate ar-dour*
*s.* Ze-nith, *the point over the* **head**

SPELLING ASSISTANT.   61

## WORDS OF THREE SYLLABLES.

Parts of
Speech.

### A.

*Accented on the first.*

v. AB′-DI-CATE, *to resign*
v. Ab-ro-gate, *to abolish*
a. Ab-so-lute, *peremptory*
s. Ab-sti-nence, *temperance*
s. Ac-ci-dent, *chance*
a. Ac-cu-rate, *exact*
a. Ac-tu-al, *real, certain*
v. Ac-tu-ate, *to prompt*
a. Ad-e-quate, *equal to*
s. Ad-jec-tive, *a word added to a noun, to denote its quality, as good, bad, &c.*
s. Ad-ju-tant, *a military officer*
s. Ad-mi-ral, *a naval commander*
s. Ad-vo-cate, *a pleader*
a. Af-fa-ble, *civil, courteous*
s. Af-flu-ence, *riches, abundance*
v. Ag-gran-dize, *to make great*
v. Ag-gra-vate, *to provoke*
s. Ag-gre-gate, *the total*
v. Ag-i-tate, *to put in motion*
s. Ag-o-ny, *violent pain*
s. Al-der-man, *a city magistrate*
s. A-li-en, *a foreigner*
s. Al-i-ment, *food, nourishment*
s. Al-ma-nac, *a yearly calendar*
s. Al-pha-bet, *the letters of a language*
s Al-ti-tude, *height of a place*
a. Am-bi-ent, *encircling*
s. Am-nes-ty, *a general pardon*
v. Am-pli-fy, *to enlarge*

Parts of
Speech.

v. Am-pu-tate, *to cut off* [ment
s. An-ar-chy, *want of govern-*
s. An-ces-tor$^z$s, *forefathers*
s. An-cho-ret, or ⎱ *a hermit*
   An-cho-rite, ⎰
a. And-i-ron, *an iron utensil, used to support the wood or coal in fire places*
s. An-ec-dote, *secret history*
s. An-i-mal, *any thing which has life*
v. An-i-mate, *to encourage, to give life to*
a. An-nu-al, *yearly*
v. An-te-date, *to date before*
s. An-ti-dote, *a counter poison*
s. An-ti-pope, *a false pope*
a. Anx-i-ous,* *solicitous*
s. Ap-a-thy, *want of feeling*
s. Aph-o-ri$^z$sm,† *a general rule*
s. Ap-o-logue, *a moral tale*
a. Ap-po-$^z$site, *fit, suitable*
s. Ap-ti-tude, *fitness, tendency*
s. A″-que-duct, *a conduit or pipe*
a. A-que-ous, *watery*
a. A″-qui-line, *hooked*
s. Ar-bi-ter, *an umpire*
v. Ar-bi-trate, *to decide*
s. Ar-chi-tect,‡ *a master builder*
a. Ar-du-ous,§ *hard to perform*
s. Ar-gu-ment, *reasoning*
s. Ar-ma-ment, *a naval force*
a. Ar-ro-gant, *proud, overbearing*
v. Ar-ro-gate, *to assume*

\* *pr.* Ank-shus.    † *pr.* Af-o-rizm.
‡ *pr.* Ar-ke-tekt.    § *pr.* Ar-ju-us.

s. Ar-ti-cle, *a term, a part of speech*
s. Ar-ti-fiçe, *trick, fraud*
s A-the-ist, *one who denies a God*
v. As-pi-rate, *to pronounce strong*
s. At-ti-tude, *posture*
a. Au-di-ble, *easy to be heard*
s. Au-di-ençe, *a hearing*
s. Av-a-riçe, *covetousness*
s. Av-e-nue, *a passage or entrance*
s. Av-er-age, *a mean proportion*
s. Ax-i-om,* *a self-evident principle*

*Accented on the second.*

v. A″-bán-don, *to forsake*
s. A″-base-ment, *an humbling*
s. A″-bate-ment, *a lessening*
s A-bet-tor, *an encourager*
s. Ab-hor-rençe, *aversion*
v. A-bol-ish, *to destroy, make void*
a. A-bor-tive, *untimely*
s. A-brid'g-ment, *a shortening*
part. Ab-stract-ed, *separated*
a. A-bun-dant. *plentiful*
a. A-bu-sive. *apt to abuse*
s. Ac-çep-tançe, *a receiving*
s. Ac-com-pliçe, *a partner in a crime*
v. Ac-com-plish, *to perform*
s. Ac-compt-ant, or } *one skilled*
   Ac-count-ant,   } *in accounts*
a. Ac-cor-dant, *agreeing with*
v. Ac-cou-tre,† *to equip, to dress*
v. Ac-cus-tom, *to use one's self to*
s. A″-chieve-ment, *a deed, an escutcheon*

* pr. Ak-shum.   † pr. Ak-koo-tur.

a. Ad-he-rent, *sticking to*
a. Ad-ja-çent. *lying near to*
s. Ad-journ-ment, *putting off to another day*
v. Ad-mon-ish, *to warn, to advise*
s. Ad-van-tage, *benefit*
s. Ad-ven-ture. *an occurrence*
s. Af-fi-ançe, *hope, trust*
a. Af-fron-tive, *abusive*
s. Ag-gres-sor, *the beginner of a quarrel*
s. Al-li-ançe, *connexion*
s. Al-lot-ment. *the part given to any one*
a. Al-ter-nate. *by turns*
s. A-pos-tate. *one who renounces his religion*
s. Ap-par-el, *clothing*
a. Ap-pa-rent. *clear, certain*
s. Ap-pen-dage. *something added*
s. Ap-pen-dix, *a supplement*
s. Ar-ca-num, *a mystery*
s. Arch-án-gel, *a chief angel*
s. Arch-bish-op, *a chief bishop*
s. Ar-ma-da. *a great fleet*
s. As-sail-ant. *one who attacks*
s. As-sas-sin, *a private murderer*
s. As-sem-blage. *a collection*
s. As-ses-sor. *one who settles*
a. As-trin-gent, *binding*
v. As-ton-ish, *to amaze*
ad. A″-sun-der, *in two parts*
s. A″-sy-lum, *a place of refuge*
s. At-tach-ment. *regard*
s. At-ten-dançe. *waiting, service*
v. At-trib-ute, *to impute to*
a. Au-then-tic, *of good authority*
a. Au-tum-nal, *belonging to autumn*
a. Ath-let-ic. *strong, sinewy*

*Accented on the last.*

s. Ab-sen-tée, *one who absents himself*
v. Ac-qui-esce, *to comply with*
v. Ad-ver-ti$^z$se, *to give public notice*
s. Am-bus-cade, *a lying in wait*
v. Ap-per-tain, *to belong to*
v. Ap-pre-hend, *to seize on: to understand*
v. As-çer-tain, *to make certain*

B.

*Accented on the first.*

s. Bách-e-lor, *an unmarried man*
a. Bar-ba-rous, *cruel, uncivilized*
s. Bar-o-net, *a title of honour*
s. Bar-ris-ter, *a lawyer*
s. Bat-te-ry, *a platform of cannon*
s. Ben-e-fiçe, *an ecclesiastical living*
s. Ben-e-fit, *kindness, profit*
s. Bev-er-a$^j$ge, *drink*
s. Big-ot-ry, *superstition*
s. Blas-phe-my, *impious language*
a. Bois-ter-ous, *stormy*
a. Boun-ti-ful, *liberal, generous*
s. Bra-ve-ry, *true courage*
s. Brev-i-ty, *shortness*
s. Broi-de-ry, *embroidery, flower-work*
s. Bur-gla-ry, *house-breaking*

*Accented on the second.*

s. Bal-có-ny, *a small gallery of wood or stone on the outside of a house*

a. Bal-sam-ic, *healing*
part. Bé-numb-ed, *deprived of feeling*
v. Be-to-ken, *to foreshow*
v. Be-wil-der, *to mislead, to puzzle*
s. Bi-tu-men, *a pitchy substance*
s. Bra″-va-do, *a boasting*

*Accented on the last.*

s. Ba″-ga-télle, *a trifle*
s. Ber-ga-mot, *a perfume*
s. Brig-a-dier, *a military officer*
s. Buc-a-nier,* *an American pirate*

C.

*Accented on the first.*

s. Cáb-i-net, *a little chest*
v. Cal-cu-late, *to reckon*
s. Cal-um-ny, *slander*
s. Can-di-date, *one who solicits*
s. Can-o-py, *a covering over the head*
s. Cap-tious-ly, *peevishly*
v. Cap-ti-vate, *to charm*
a. Car-di-nal, *chief or principal*
s. Car-ri-a$^j$ge, *conveyance, also behaviour*
s. Car-ri-er, *one who carries*
s. Car-ti-la$^j$ge, *a gristle*
a. Ca$^z$s-u-al, *accidental*
s. Ca$^z$s-u-ist, *a subtile disputer*
s. Cat-a-logue, *a list*
s. Cat-a-ract, *a cascade*
s. Cat-e-chi$^z$sm, *instruction by question and answer*

* *pr.* Buk-ka-neer.

*a.* Cath-o-lic, *universal*
*s.* Cav-al-ry, *horse troops*
*s.* Ca-ve-at, *a caution*
*s.* Cav-i-ty, *hollowness*
*v.* Çel-e-brate, *to praise*
*s* Çen-tu-ry, *one hundred years*
*v.* Çer-ti-fy, *to give notice*
Çham-pi-on, *a combatant*
*s.* Chan-çel-lor, *an officer of state*
*s.* Char-ac-ter, *description*
*s.* Char-i-ty, *benevolence*
*s.* Chas-tise-ment, *punishment*
*s.* Chas-ti-ty, **purity**
*a.* Chol-er-ic, *passionate*
*s.* Chor-is-ter,* *a singer in ca-
   the-dral*
*a.* Çir-cu-lar, **round**
*v.* Çir-cu-late, *to move round*
*a.* Çir-cum-spect, *cautious, pru-
   dent*
*s.* Çir-cum-stançe, *incident, event*
*s.* Çit-a-del, *a fortress*
*v.* Çiv-il-ize, *to polish manners*
*a.* Clam-o-rous, *noisy, loud*
*v.* Clar-i-fy, *to make clean*
*s.* Clem-en-çy, *mildness*  [gy
*a.* Cler-i-cal, *relating to the cler-*
*s.* Cog-ni-zançe, *knowledge*
*s.* Col-lo-quy, *a conference*
*s* Col-o-nel,† *the commander of a
   regiment*
*s.* Col-o-ny, *a plantation*
*s.* †Com-ba-tant, *a fighter*
*s.* Com-e-dy, *a play*
*a.* Com-i-cal, *facetious, droll*
*a.* Com-pe-tent, *fit, qualified*
*v.* Com-pro-mise, *to settle*
*s.* Con-fer-ençe, *a discourse*
*a.* Con-fi-dent, **positive**, *bold*

*s.* Con-flu-ençe, *a flowing together*
*a.* Con-gru-ous, *suitable*
*a.* Con-ju-gal, *belonging to marriage*
*s.* Con-scien.çe,† *the testimony
   of one's own mind*
*a.* Con-scious, *inwardly per-
   suaded*
*v.* Con-se-crate, *to make sacred*
*s.* Con-se-quençe, **an** *effect, importance*
*a.* Con-so-nant, *agreeable, fit*
*s.* Con-sta-ble,‡ *a common peace
   officer*
*s.* Con-stan-çy, *firmness*
*a.* Con-sti-tute, *to make, to appoint*
*s.* Con-ti-nent, *land not disjoined by the sea from other lands*
*a.* Con-tra-band, **unlawful**
*v.* Con-tro-vert, *to dispute*
*a.* Con-ver-sant, *acquainted with*
*a.* Co-pi-ous, *abundant, full, &c.*
*a.* Cor-di-al, *sincere, reviving*
*s.* Cor-o-net, *a nobleman's crown*
*a.* Cor-pu-lent, *bulky, stout*
*s.* *Cov-e-nant, *an agreement*
*v.* Coun-te-nançe, *to favour*
*a.* Coun-ter-feit, *forged, fictitious*
*s.* Coun-ter-part, *a correspondent
   part*
*s.* Cour-te-sy,* *civility*
*a.* *Cov-e-tous, *greedy of gain*
*s.* †Coz-en-age, *fraud, deceit*
*a.* Cred-i-ble, *worthy of credit*
*s.* Cre-di-tor, *one who gives credit*

§ *pr.* Kon-shense.  ‡ *pr.* Cun-sta-b'l
   *pr.* Cuv.
* This word, when it is used to signify an act of reverence, is pronounced
+ *pr.* Kor-is-ter.      + *pr.* Kur-nel, in two syllables; as, *pr.* Kurtsee.
‡ *pr.* Cum.                + *pr.* Cuz.

*a.* Cred-u-lous, *apt to believe*
*a.* Crim-i-nal, *faulty*
*a.* Crit-i-cal, *judicious, accurate*
*s* Crit-i-ci*z*sm, *the art of judging*
*s.* Cru-ci-fix, *a representation of our Saviour on the cross*
*s.* Cru-di-ty, *indigestion*
*a.* Crys-tal-line, *clear, bright*
*a.* Cul-pa-ble, *blame-worthy*
*v.* Cul-ti-vate, *to improve, to manure*
*a.* Cum-ber-some, *troublesome*
*a.* Cu-ra-ble, *easy of cure*
*s.* Cur-ren-çy, *circulation*
*a.* Cur-so-ry, *hasty, careless*
*s.* Cus-to-dy, *imprisonment, care, security*
*s.* Cus-tom-er, *one who buys any thing*
*a.* Cyn-i-cal, *churlish*

*Accented on the second.*

*s.* Ca-thé-dral, *an episcopal church*
*s.* Chi-me-ra,\* *an idle conceit*
*a* Clan-des-tine, *secret, sly*
*a.* Co-e-qual, *equal with*
*a.* Co-er-çive, *restraining*
*s.* Col-lec-tor, *a tax-gatherer*
*a.* Col-lu-sive, *fraudulent*
*s.* Com-mençe-ment, *beginning*
*s.* Com-mit-tee, *a select society*
*v.* Com-pen-sate, *to make amends*
*a.* Com-pla-çent, *civil, kind*
*s.* Com-pli-ançe, *submission*
*s.* Com-po-*z*sure, *tranquillity*
*a.* Com-pul-sive, *forcible*
*part.* Con-çeit-ed, *opinionated*
*v.* Con-cen-trate, *to unite in a point*
*a* Con-çen-tric, *having the same centre*

• *pr.* Ky-me-ra, *or* Ke-me-ra

*s.* Con-çern-ment, *affair, business*
*a.* Con-clu-sive, *decisive, convincing*
*a.* Con-cord-ant, *agreeing with*
*s.* Con-cur-rençe, *agreement, assent, union*
*s.* Con-do-lençe, *grief for another's loss*
*a.* Con-du-çive, *promoting*
*v.* Con-fis-cate, *to forfeit to the public*
*s.* Con-form-ist, *one who conforms*
*s.* Con-jec-ture, *a guess, idea*
*s.* Con-junc-ture, *a peculiar time*
*s.* Con-ni-vançe, *pretended ignorance*
*a.* Con-sis-tent, *conformable*
*a.* Con-sum-mate, *complete, perfect*
*v.* Con-tem-plate, *to meditate*
*s.* Con-tex-ture, *a knitting together*
*a.* Con-tin-gent, *accidental*
*s.* Con-trac-tor, *a bargainer*
*v.* Con-trib-ute, *to bear a part*
*s.* Con-vey-ançe, *act of removing any thing*
*v.* Cor-ro-sive, *of a gnawing quality*

*Accented on the last.*

*v.* Can-non-áde, *to batter with cannon*
*v.* Cav-al-cade, *a show of horsemen*
*s.* Cav-a-lier,† *a knight*
*v.* Çir-cum-vent, *to over-reach*
*v.* Çir-cum-vest, *to clothe around*
*v.* Co-a-lêsce, *to unite together*
*v.* Co-in-çide, *to concur*

† *vr.* Ka-va-leer.

a. Com-plai-²sant, *very obliging*
v. Com-pre-hend, *to include, to conceive*
v. Con-de-scend, *to yield to*
s. Con-nòis-seur,* *a nice judge*
v. Con-tra-dict, *to deny*
v. Cor-res-pond, *to suit, to agree: to keep up a commerce with another by letters*
v. Coun-ter-act, *to thwart*
v. Coun-ter-mand, *to contradict an order*

### D.

*Accented on the first.*

Déc-a-logue,† *the ten commandments*
s De-çen-çy, *modesty*
v. Dec-o-rate, *to adorn*
v. Ded-i-cate, *to devote to*
s. Def-er-ençe, *respect, submission*
s. De-i-ty, *the Almighty Father*
a. Def-i-nite, *limited*
s. Del-e-gate, *a commissioner*
a. Del-i-cate, *dainty, nice*
s. Dem-a-gogue, *a factious ringleader*
s. Den-si-ty, *thickness*
v. Dep-re-cate, *to pray against*
s. Dep-u-ty, *one who acts for another*
v. Der-o-gate, *to disparage*

* *pr.* Kon-nes-sarc.
† *pr.* Dek-a-log.—In this word the diphthong *ue* is entirely sunk, as well as in the words *dialogue, synagogue,* &c; but in the words *prorogue, disembogue,* &c, it is not entirely sunk, for it has the evident effect of lengthening the final syllable.

a. Des-o-late, *uninhabited: laid waste*
a. Des-pe-rate, *violent, furious*
s. Des-po-ti²sm, *absolute power*
s. Des-ti-ny, *fate, doom*
a. Des-ti-tute, *left forsaken*
s. Det-ri-ment, *hurt, damage*
v. De-vi-ate, *to go from*
a. De-vi-ous, *swerving from*
a. Dex-te-rous, *expert*
s. Di-a-dem, *a royal crown*
s. Di-a-gram, *a mathematical scheme*
s. Di-a-lect, *manner of expression*
s. Di-a-logue, *alternate discourse*
s. Di-a-ry, *a day-book*
a. Dif-fi-dent, *dubious, bashful*
v. Dig-ni-fy, *to exalt, to honour*
s. Dig-ni-ty, *rank, honour*
s. Dis-ci-pline, *regular order*
v. Dis-lo-cate, *to disjoint*
s. Dis-pu-tant, *a disputer*
v. Dis-si-pate, *to disperse: to spend lavishly*
a. Dis-so-lute, *loose, wanton*
a. Dis-so-nant, *untuneful*
s. Div-i-dend, *a share*
a. Doç-i-ble, *teachable*
s. Doc-u-ment, *a precept, instruction*
v. Dog-ma-tize, *to assert positively*
a. Dol-o-rous, *grievous, sad*
s. Don-a-tive, *a gift or present*
a. Drop-si-cal, *subject to or diseased with the dropsy*
a. Du-bi-ous, *doubtful*
v. Dul-ci-fy, *to sweeten*
s. Du-pli-cate, *an exact copy*
a. Du-ra-ble, *lasting, firm*
a. Du-ti-ful, *obedient, respectful*

## SPELLING ASSISTANT.        57

*Accented on the second.*

s. De-báse-ment, *a degrading*
s. De-ben-ture, *a writ, or written instrument, by which a debt is claimed*
s. De-can-ter, *a flint glass bottle*
v. De-çi-pher, *to explain, to unravel*
v. De-çi-sive, *conclusive*
s. De-co-rum, *decency, order*
a. De-crep-it, *worn out with age*
a. De-fec-tive, *faulty, imperfect*
s. De-fend-ant, *the person prosecuted*
a. De-fen-sive, *state of defence*
s. De-fi-ançe, *a challenge*
s. De-lin-quent, *an offender*
a. De-lu-sive, *apt to deceive*
s. De-mean-our, *behaviour*
s. De-mer-it, *ill-deserving*
v. De-mol-ish, *to raze, to destroy utterly*
v. De-mon-strate, *to prove by argument*
s. De-mur-ra$^j$ge, *charge for delaying ships*
s. De-pô-nent, *a witness on oath*
s. De-pòrt-ment, *conduct*
v. De-pos-it, *to stake or lay down*
a. De-scrip-tive, *describing*
a. De-$^z$si-rous, *wishing for*
a. De-spot-ic, *arbitrary, absolute*
v. De-ter-mine, *to fix, to settle*
v. De-vel-ope, *to unfold*
s. Dic-ta-tor, *a ruler*
a. Di-dac-tic, *preceptive*
a. Dif-fu-sive, *spreading widely*
s. Di-lem-ma, *a vexatious alternative*
v. Di''-min-ish, *to make less*
s. Di''-rec-tor, *a superintendent*

v. Di$^z$s-a-ble, *to render incapable*
s. Di$^z$s-as-ter, *great misfortune*
a. Di$^z$s-as-trous, *unfortunate*
s. Di$^z$s-burse-ment, *a laying out*
s. Di$^z$s-cern-ment, *judgment*
s. Dis-çi-ple, *a scholar, a follower*
v. Dis-com*-fit, *to overthrow*
a. Dis-cor-dant, *disagreeing*
v. Dis-cov†-er, *to find out*
v. Dis-cour-a$^j$ge, *to dishearten*
s. Dis-cred-it, *ignominy, reproach*
v. Dis-fig-ure, *to deface*
a. Di$^z$s-graçe-ful, *shameful*
a. Di$^z$s-gust-ful, *causing strong dislike*
a. Di$^z$s-hon-est, *void of probity*
s. Di$^z$s-hon-our, *infamy, disgrace, censure*
v. Di$^z$s-man-tle, *to strip*
v. Dis-par-a$^j$ge, *to undervalue*
v. Dis-peo-ple, *to depopulate*
v. Dis-pir-it, *to discourage*
s. Dis-plea$^z$s-ure, *anger*
s. Dis-po-$^z$sal, *a regulation*
v. Dis-qui-et, *to trouble, to vex*
v. Dis-sem-ble, *to play the hypocrite*
s. Dis-sen-ter, *a non-conformist that is, one who dissents from or does not conform to the ceremonies of the established church*
s. Dis-ser-viçe, *injury, mischief*
s. Dis-tem-per, *sickness, disease*
v. Dis-tin-guish, *to discern between*
a. Dis-tract-ed, *deranged in mind*
v. Dis-trib-ute, *to deal out*
a. Dis-trust-ful, *doubtful of*
s. Dis-tur-bançe, *confusion, tumult*

* pr. Cum.         pr. Cuv

*a.* Diur–nal, *daily*
*a.* Do-mes-tic, *belonging to the house*
*a.* Dra-mat-ic, *theatrical*

Accented on the last.

*a.* Deb-on-áir, *gay, sprightly*
*s.* Dev-o-tee, *a bigot*
*v.* Dis-al-low, *not to allow*
*v.* Dis-ap-prove, *to dislike*
*s.* Dis-be-lief, *want of faith*
*v.* Dis-com-po$^z$se, *to unsettle*
*v.* Dis-em-bark, *to leave shipboard*
*v.* Dis-em-bôgue, *to discharge into the sea*
*v.* Dis-en-ga$^j$ge, *to set free*
*s.* Dis-hab-ille, *an undress*
*v.* Dis-po$^z$s-$^z$sess, *to deprive of*
*s.* Dis-regard, *neglect*
*s.* Dis-re-pute, *dishonour*
*v.* Dis-u-nite, *to separate*
*v.* Dom-i-neer, *to hector, to behave with insolence*

E.

Accented on the first.

*s.* E'c-sta-çy, *excessive joy*
*a* Ed-i-ble, *eatable*
*s.* Ed-i-fiçe, *a building*
*v.* Ed-i-fy, *to improve by instruction*
*s.* Ed-i-tor, *one who prepares a manuscript for the press*
*v.* Ed-u-cate, *to instruct*
*s.* Ef-fi-gy, *representation in painting, &c.*
*s.* E-go-ti$^z$sm, *self-commendation*
*a.* El-e-gant, *handsome, grand*
*s.* El-e-gy, *a funeral song*

*s.* El-e-ment, *the first principle*
*v.* El-e-vate, *to raise, to exalt*
*s.* El-o-quençe, *the power of oratory*
*a.* El-o-quent, *endowed with oratory*
*s.* Em-bas-sy, *a public message*
*s.* Em-bry-o, *imperfect state*
*s.* Em-e-rald, *a green, precious stone*
*s.* Em-i-grant, *one who deserts his country*
*s.* Em-i-nençe, *excellency, height loftiness*
*a.* Em-i nent, *high, dignified*
*s.* Em-pe-ror, *a sovereign prince*
*s.* Em-pha-sis, *strong pronunciation*
*s.* Em-pi-ric, *a pretended doctor, a quack*
*v.* Em-u-late, *to rival*
*a.* Em-u-lous, *desirous to excel*
*s.* En-e-my,* *a foe, opponent*
*s.* En-er-gy, *force, efficacy*
*s.* En-mi-ty, *hatred, variance*
*s.* En-ter-pri$^z$se, *a hazardous undertaking*
*s.* En-ti-ty, *a being*
*a.* En-vi-ous, *full of enmity*
*s.* Ep-i-cure, *a glutton*
*s.* Ep-i-gram, *a pointed poem*
*s.* Ep-i-logue, *an address after a play*
*s.* Ep-i-taph, *a monumental inscription*

* It is not uncommon to hear boys, and, in fact, grown persons, pronounce this and many other words, beginning with a vowel, as if *h* preceded it: thus, out, they term *hout*; enemy, *henemy*; &c. And it is no less faulty to sink or render mute the letter *h*, when it ought to be sounded

s. Ep-i-thet, *a quality*
a. E-qua-ble, *even, uniform*
ad. E-qual-ly, *in like manner*
s. E″-qui-pa͡ge, *attendance, retinue*
s. E-qui-poiᶻse, *equality of weight*
s. E″-qui-ty, *justice, candour*
a. Es-cu-lent, *eatable: good for food*
v. Es-ti-mate, *to set a value on*
s. Eu-cha-rist,* *the sacrament of the Lord's supper*
s. Eu-lo-͡gy, *a panegyric*
s. Ev-i-dençe, *a witness*
a. Ev-i-dent, *clear, plain*
s. Ex-çel-lençe, *dignity, high rank*
a. Ex-çel-lent, *of great worth*
v. Ex-e-crate, *to abominate*
v. Ex-e-cute, *to perform*
s. Ex-er-çiᶻse, *employment: a task*
s. Ex-i-gençe, *necessity*
s. Ex-or-çiᶻsm, *conjuration*
v. Ex-pe-dite, *to hasten*
v. Ex-pi-ate, *to atone for*
s. Ex-ple-tive, *a filling up*
v. Ex-pli-cate, *to explain*
a. Ex-qui-ᶻsite, *excellent, choice*
v. Ex-tri-cate, *to disentangle*

*Accented on the second.*

a. Ec-çén-tric, *irregular*
s. E-clip-tic, *a circle in the heavens made by the sun's apparent annual motion*
a. Ef-fec-tive, *operative*
s. Ef-ful-͡gençe, *a shining forth*
a. Ef-ful-͡gent, *highly splendid*
s. E-ject-ment, *an expelling*

* *Eu* is always sounded like long *u:*
pr. Yu-ka-rist.

a. E-las-tic, *springy*
s. E-lope-ment, *a running away*
s. Em-bar-go, *an arrest of ships*
v. Em-bar-rass, *to perplex*
v. Em-bel-lish, *to beautify*
v. Em-bez-zle, *to secrete goods*
a. E-mer-͡gent, *pressing*
v. Em-pan-nel, *to swear a jury*
a. Em-phat-ic, *forcible*
v. Em-pow-er, *to authorize*
v. En-am-el, *to paint with mineral colours*
v. En-çir-cle, *to surround*
s. En-clo-ᶻsure, *a place enclosed*
v. En-coun-ter, *to meet with: to fight, to attack*
v. En-cour-a͡ge, *to animate*
v. En-cum-ber, *to clog, to embarrass*
s. En-deav-our, *attempt, effort*
s. En-dorse-ment, *the writing one's name on a bill of exchange, &c.*
s. En-dow-ment, *a gift natural or acquired*
v. En-er-vate, *to weaken*
v. En-fee-ble, *to make weak*
v. En-fran-chiᶻse, *to make free*
s. En-ga͡ge-ment, *a sea fight, &c.*
v. En-͡gen-der, *to beget, produce*
s. E-nig-ma, *a riddle or obscure question*
s. En-lar͡ge-ment, *a setting at liberty*
v. En-light-en, *to illuminate*
v. En-li-ven, *to make lively*
v. En-no-ble, *to dignify*
a. E-nor-mous, *very large: wicked in a high degree*
v. En-tan-gle, *to perplex*
s. En-tiçe-ment, *an allurement*
v. En-vel-ope, *to cover*

v. En-ven-om, *to poison*
. En-vi-ron, *to surround*
s. En-vi-ron²s, *places adjacent*
s. E-pis-tle, *a letter*
s. E-qua-tor, *the equinoctial line*
s. pl. Er-ra-ta, *errors in printing*
a. Er-rat-ic, *wandering*
v. Es-tab-lish, *to make firm*
a. E-ter-nal, *everlasting*
a. E-va-sive, *crafty, shuffling*
a. E-vent-ful, *full of incidents*
s. *Ex-ac-tor, *an extortioner*
v. *Ex-am-ine, *to inquire into*
s. *Ex-am-ple, *a pattern or model*
a. Ex-ces-sive, *beyond due bounds*
s. Ex-che″-quer, *the king's treasury*
s. Ex-ci²se-man, *a revenue officer*
a. Ex-clu-sive, *leaving out*
v. Ex-cul-pate, *to clear from*
s. *Ex-em-plar, *a pattern*
v. *Ex-hib-it, *to produce or show*
s. *Ex-ist-ence, *a state of being*
a. *Ex-ot-ic, *foreign*
a. Ex-pec-tant, *waiting in expectation*
a. Ex-pen-sive, *costly*
a. Ex-plic-it, *clear, plain*
s. Ex-po-²sure, *a making public*
a. Ex-pres-sive, *full of expression*
a. Ex-ten-sive, *wide, large*
a. Ex-ter-nal, *outward*
v. Ex-tin-guish, *to put out*
v. Ex-tir-pate, *to root out*
a. Ex-trin-sic, *the outside*
a. *Ex-uc-cous, *without moisture, dry*

Accented on the last.
s. En-¹gi″-neer, *one skilled in fortification*

\* pr egs.

v. En-ter-tain, *to treat, to please*
s. Es-ca-lade, *the scaling of walls*
s. Es-cru-toire, *a kind of desk upon drawers*

F

Accented on the first.

v. Fáb-ri-cate, *to build, to invent*
a. Fab-u-lous, *feigned*
ad. Fac-tious-ly, *in a turbulent or disorderly manner*
s. Fac-to-ry, *a residence of traders abroad*
s. Fac-ul-ty, *ability, power*
s. Fal-la-cy, *deceit, craft*
a. Fal-li-ble, *liable to error*
s. Fal-si-ty, *an untruth*
a. Fan-ci-ful, *full of whim*
v. Fas-ci-nate, *to bewitch*
a. Fath-om-less, *bottomless*
s. Fa-vour-ite, *a person or thing beloved*
s. Fe-al-ty, *homage, duty*
a. Fea-²si-ble, *that may be done*
a. Fec-u-lent, *full of dregs*
a. Fed-er-al, *relating to a contract*
s. Fel-low-ship, *partnership*
s. Fel-o-ny, *a capital crime*
v. Fer-til-ize, *to make fruitful*
s: Fer-ven-cy, *ardour, devotional zeal*
v. Fes-ti-val, *a day of civil or religious joy*
a. Fig-u-rate, *of a certain and determinate form*
s. Fil-a-ment, *a fibre, a thread*
a, Fi-na-ble, *that admits a fine*
v. Fi-ne-ry, *fine attire*
a. Fin-ic-al, *affected, foppish*

*s.* Fir-ma-ment, *the sky, the heavens*
*s.* Fish-e-ry, *the place where fish abound*
*s.* Fis-tu-la, *an ulcer*
*s.* Fla<sup>j</sup>g-e-let,* *a musical pipe*
*s.* Flat-te-ry, *false praise*
*a.* Flat-u-lent, *windy*
*a.* Flex-i-ble, *easily bent*
*a.* Flow-er-ed, *wrought with flowers*
*v.* Fluc-tu-ate, *to waver*
*s.* Flu-en-çy, *readiness of speech*
*s.* Fo-li-a<sup>j</sup>ge, *the leaves*
*s.* Fo-li-o, *a book of the largest size*
*s.* Fop-pe-ry, *fantasticalness, foolery, folly*
*a.* Fôr-çi-ble, *strong, impetuous*
*s.* Fórd-a-ble, *that may be waded over*
*s.* For-fei-ture, *act of forfeiting*
*s.* Fôr-<sup>j</sup>ge-ry, *counterfeiting*
*s.* For-mal-ist, *a precise person*
*v.* For-ti-fy, *to strengthen*
*s.* For-ti-tude, *magnanimity of mind*
*a.* For-tu-nate, *successful*
*a.* Frac-tion-al, *belonging to a broken number*
*a.* Fran-<sup>j</sup>gi-ble, *easily broken*
*a.* Frat-ri-çide,† *the murderer of a brother*
*a.* Frau-du-lent, *deceitful*
*ad.* Fri<sup>j</sup>g-id-ly, *coldly, dully*
*a.* Friv-o-lous, *silly, trifling*
*a.* Frol-ick-some, *merry, flighty*
*v.* Fruc-ti-fy, *to make fruitful*
*s.* Fu-<sup>j</sup>gi-tive, *a deserter*
*v.* Ful-mi-nate, *to thunder*
*v.* Fu-mi-gate, *to perfume*

*pr.* Fladje-e-let.   † *pr.* Frat-tre-side.

*ad.* Fu-ming-ly, *angrily, in a rage*
*s.* Fu-ner-al, *a burial*
*a.* Fu-ri-ous, *headstrong*
*s.* Fur-ni-ture, *household goods*
*s.* Fur-ri-er, *a dealer in furs*
*a.* Fu-si-ble, *capable of being melted*

Accented on the second.

*s.* Fa-nát-ic, *an enthusiast*
*a.* Fan-tas-tic, *capricious*
*a.* Fo-ren-sic, *belonging to court, of judicature*
*s.* Fore-stal-ler, *a monopolizer*
*a.* Fra-ter-nal, *brotherly*
*a.* Fre-net-ic, *mad, distracted*

G.

Accented on the first.

*s.* Gál-ax-y, *the milky way*
*s.* Gal-lan-try, *bravery, polite address*
*s.* Gar-ri-son, *a fortified place*
*a.* Gar-ru-lous, *talkative*
*a.* Gen-er-al, *common*
*a.* Gen-er-ous, *liberal, munificent*
*a.* Ge-ni-al, *nourishing*
*s.* Ge-ni-us, *nature, disposition*
*a.* Gen-u-ine, *natural, true*
*v.* Ger-min-ate, *to put forth buds*
*s.* Gib-ber-ish, *nonsensical talk*
*v.* Gla-ci-ate, *to turn into ice*
*s.* Glim-mer-ing, *a faint light*
*a.* Glob-u-lar, *round, spherical*
*v.* Glo-ri-fy, *to praise, to worship*
*a.* Glo-ri-ous, *illustrious, excellent, noble*
*s.* Glos-sa-ry, *a dictionary of old words*
*a.* Glu-ti-nous, *clammy*

s. Glut-to-ny, *excess of eating*
a. Gor-ge-ous, *splendid, pompous*
v. Gor-man-dize, *to eat greedily*
s. Gov-ern-ment, *supreme power, manageableness*
s. Gov-er-nor, *a ruler or commander*
s. Gov-er-ness, *a female teacher*
ad. Grace-ful-ly, *elegantly, with pleasing dignity*
a. Grad-u-al, *done by degrees*
s. Gran-a-ry, *a storehouse for threshed corn*
v. Grat-i-fy, *to indulge*
s. Grat-i-tude, *thankfulness*
v. Grav-i-tate, *to tend to the centre*
s. Grav-i-ty, *seriousness, weight*
s. Guar-di-an, *one who has the care of an orphan: a superintendent*

*Accented on the second and third.*

a. Gi-gan-tic, *of huge stature*
a. Gym-nas-tic, *athletic*
s. Gas-co-nade, *a brag, a boast*
s. Ga-zet-teer, *name of a newspaper, a writer of gazettes, &c.*
s. Gren-a-dier, *a tall foot soldier*

## H.

*Accented on the first.*

s. Háb-i-tude, *habit, custom*
a. Hal-cy-on, *peaceable, calm*
a. Hal-low-ed, *made holy*
s. Hand-i-craft, *a working trade*
ad. Hap-pi-ly, *fortunately*
s. Har-bin-ger, *a forerunner*
s. Har-mo-ny, *melody, concord*

s. Harp-si-chord, *a musical instrument with keys*
a. Haz-ard-ous, *dangerous*
s. Hec-a-tomb, *a sacrifice of one hundred oxen*
s. Hem-i-sphere, *half of a globe*
s. Hep-ta-gon, *a figure of seven sides*
s. Her-bal-ist, *one skilled in herbs*
s. Her-e-tic, *one who propagates heretical opinions in opposition to the Christian religion*
s. Her-o-ine, *a female hero*
v. Hes-i-tate, *to doubt, to pause*
s. Hex-a-gon, *a figure of six sides*
a. Hid-e-ous, *horrible*
s. Hin-der-ance, *an impediment*
s. His-to-ry, *a narration of facts*
ad. Hith-er-to, *to this time*
s. Hom-i-cide, *man-slaughter*
s. Hon-es-ty, *sincerity*
a. Hor-ri-ble, *frightful*
s. Hos-pi-tal, *a house for the sick and poor*
v. Hu-ma-nize, *to civilize*
s. Hu-mor-ist, *a whimsical person*
a. Hu-mor-ous, *comical, jocular*
s. Hur-ri-cane, *a tempest*
s. Hus-ban-dry, *tillage, frugality*
s. Hy-a-cinth, *a flower*
s. Hyp-o-crite, *a dissembler in religion, &c.*

*Accented on the second.*

a. He-ró-ic, *brave, noble*
s. Ho-ri-zon, *the circle which bounds our view*
a. Hor-rif-ic, *causing horror*
s. Hy-e-na, *a fierce animal*
s. Hys-ter-ics, *fits peculiar to women*

## I. J.

*Accented on the first.*

s. Id-i-om, *a peculiar manner of speaking*
s. Id-i-ot, *a fool*
s. I-dle-ness, *laziness, sloth*
v. I-dol-ize, *to dote on*
s. Ig-no-rançe, *want of knowl-* [ledge
v. Im-i-tate, *to copy from*
a. Im-mi-nent, *impending, threatening*
t. Im-pi-ous, *ungodly*
s. Im-ple-ment, *a tool*
v. Im-pli-cate, *to involve*
t. Im-po-tent, *unable, feeble*
v. Im-pre-cate, *to curse*
s. Im-pu-dence, *immodesty*
a. Im-pu-dent, *bold, saucy*
s. In-çi-dent, *an event*
v. In-di-cate, *to show*
a. In-di-gent, *needy, poor*
s. In-di-go, *a drug for dying*
a. In-do-lent, *lazy, careless*
s. In-dus-try, *diligence*
a. In-fa-mous, *notoriously bad*
s. In-fa-my, *disgrace*
s. In-fan-çy, *childhood*
s. In-fan-try, *the foot soldiers of an army*
s. In-fer-ençe, *conclusion*
s. In-fi-del, *a heathen, an unbeliever*
a. In-fi-nite, *boundless*
v. In-flu-ençe, *to sway, to bias*
s. In-ju-ry, *wrong, offence*
s. In-no-çençe, *harmlessness*
a. In-no-çent, *without guilt*
v. In-no-vate, *to change*
v. In-so-lençe, *haughtiness, pride*
a. **In-so-lent,** *overbearing*

v. In-sti-gate, *to excite to ill*
v. In-sti-tute, *to establish*
s. In-stru-ment, *a tool, a deed of contract*
a. In-su-lar, *belonging to an island*
s. In-te-ger, *a whole number*
a. In-te-gral, *whole, complete*
s. In-tel-lect, *understanding*
s. In-ter-côurse, *mutual correspondence*
s. In-ter-est, *use-money, advantage, influence*
s. In-ter-im, *the mean time*
s. In-ter-lude, *a short prelude*
s. In-ter-val, *a space between*
s. In-ter-view, *a joint meeting*
v. In-ti-mate, *to hint, to suggest*
a. In-tri-cate, *perplexed*
v. In-vo-cate, *to call upon*
s. I-ro-ny, *a manner of speaking quite contrary to what we mean*
v. Ir-ri-tate, *to provoke to anger*
s. Jav-e-lin, *a spear, or half pike*
s. Jeal-ou-sy, *suspicion*
a. Joc-u-lar, *jocose, waggish*
a. Jo-vi-al, *gay, merry*
s. Ju-bi-lee, *a celebration*
s. Ju-gu-lar, *belonging to the throat*
v. Jus-ti-fy, *to vindicate*
a. Ju-ve-nile, *youthful, young*

*Accented on the second.*

a. I-dé-al, *imaginary*
a. Ig-no-ble, *mean of birth*
a. Il-le-gal, *contrary to law*
a. Il-li"-çit, *unlawful*
a. Il-lu-sive, *deceitful*
v. Il-lus-trate, *to make clear*
v. I-mag-ine, *to conceive*
v. Im-bit-ter, *to make unhappy*
a. Im-mod-est, *wanting delico*

*a.* Im-mor-al, *depraved in morals*
*a.* Im-mor-tal, *everlasting*
*a.* Im-per-fect, *incomplete*
*a.* Im-pliç-it, *entirely obedient*
*s.* Im-por-tançe, *concernment*
*a.* Im-por-tant, *of great consequence*
*s.* Im-pos-tor, *a false pretender*
*v.* Im-pri$^z$s-on, *to put in prison*
*a.* Im-prop-er, *unfit, not just*
*s.* Im-prove-ment, *act of improving*
*a.* Im-pru-dent, *unwise*
*a.* In-ac-tive, *sluggish, idle*
*part.* In-car-nate, *made flesh*
*s.* In-çen-tive, *a motive*
*a.* In-çes-sant, *unceasing*
*s.* In-ci$^z$s-ure, *a cut or gash*
*a.* In-clem-ent, *severe*
*a.* In-clu-sive, *comprehending*
*a.* In-con-stant, *not steady*
*v.* In-cul-cate, *to impress on the mind*
*a.* In-cum-bent, *one in office*
*v.* In-cur-vate, *to bend*
*part.* In-debt-ed, *in debt for favours or money received*
*a.* In-de-çent, *unbecoming*
*s.* In-den-ture, *a deed indented*
*a.* In-dig-nant, *angry*
*a.* In-do″-cile, *unteachable*
*s.* In-duçe-ment, *motive for doing a thing*
* In-dul-gence, *fondness*
*a.* In-dul-gent, *kind, tender*
*a.* In-fer-tile, *unfruitful*
*s.* In-for-mer, *one who gives intelligence*
*v.* In-hab-it, *to dwell in*
*a* In-he-rent, *innate, inborn*
*v.* In-her-it, *to possess by birthright*

*v.* In-hib-it, *to forbid*
*a.* In-hu-man, *cruel*
*s.* In-jus-tiçe, *unfairness*
*s.* In-qui-ry, *search* [*lish*
*a.* In-sip-id, *without taste or re-*
*a.* In-sol-vent, *unable to pay*
*a.* In-struc-tive, *conveying knowledge*
*s.* In-su-rançe, *security*
*s.* In-ten-dant, *a governor*
*s.* In-ter-ment, *a burial*
*a.* In-ter-nal, *inward*
*v.* In-ter-pret, *to explain*
*s.* In-ter-stiçe, *space between*
*a.* In-tes-tate, *dying without a will*
*a.* In-tes-tine, *internal* [*fence*
*s.* In-trençh-ment, *a line of de-*
*a.* In-trep-id, *courageous*
*a.* In-trin-sic, *secret, also real*
*s.* In-tru-der, *one who intrudes*
*s.* In-va-der, *one who invades*
*a.* In-val-id, *of no force*
*s.* In-vec-tive, *satire, abuse*
*a.* In-ven-tive, *ready at expedients*
*s.* In-ven-tor, *a finder out*

Accented on the last.

*a.* Im-ma-túre, *not ripe*
*a.* Im-po-lite, *ungenteel*
*v.* Im-por-tune, *to press earnestly*
*v.* In-com-mode, *to trouble*
*a.* In-com-pact, *not well joined*
*a.* In-cor-rect, *faulty*
*a.* In-cor-rupt, *pure, honest*
*a.* In-di-rect, *unfair, underhand*
*a.* In-dis-creet, *unwise*
*a.* In-se-cure, *unsafe*
*a.* In-sin-çere, *unfaithful*
*v.* In-ter-çede, *to entreat for*
*v.* In-ter-çept, *to stop, to seize*
*v.* In-ter-fere, *to intermeddle*

v. In-ter-lard, *to put between*
v. In-ter-leave, *to insert blank leaves*
v. In-ter-line, *to write between*
v. In-ter-mix, *to mix among*
v. In-ter-po²se, *to place between*
v. In-ter-rupt, *to hinder*
v. In-ter-sect, *to cross each other*
v. In-ter-sperse, *to scatter between*
v. In-ter-vene, *to come between*
v. In-tro-duçe, *to bring in*
s. In-va-lid,* *one disabled by sickness or by wounds*

### K.

*Accented on the first.*

s. Kíl-der-kin, *a beer measure of 18 gallons*
s. Kna-ve-ry, *deceitful dealing*
s. Knead-ing-trough,† *a trough in which dough is worked together*

### L.

*Accented on the first.*

s. Láb-y-rinth, *a maze full of windings*
v. Laç-er-ate, *to tear in pieces*
s. La-i-ty, *the people distinguished from the clergy*
s. Lar-çe-ny, *petty theft*
a. Lat-er-al, *growing out on the side, &c.*
s. Lat-i-tude, *breadth*
s. Lat-in-ist, *one skilled in Latin*
a. Lau-da-ble, *praiseworthy*
s. Lau-da-num, *the tincture of opium*

* pr. In-va-leed.   † pr. Need-in-trof.

a. Lax-a-tive, *loosening or opening*
a. La-zi-ness, *idleness*
s. Lec-tu-rer, *one who gives lectures*
s. Leg-a-çy, *a bequeathed gift*
v. Le-gal-ize, *to make lawful*
s. Le-ᴊgi-ble, *easily read*
a. Le-ni-ent, *softening*
a. Len-i-tive, *of a softening quality*
s. Len-i-ty, *mildness, mercy*
v. Lev-i-gate, *to smooth, to polish, to grind*
s. Lev-i-ty, *careless behaviour*
a. Li-a-ble, *subject to*
s. Li-bel-ler, *a defamatory writer*
a. Li-bel-lous, *slanderous*
a. Lib-er-al, *bountiful*
v. Lib-er-ate, *to set free*
s. Lib-er-tine, *a dissolute liver*
s. Lib-er-ty, *freedom, leave*
s. Li-bra-ry, *a large collection of books*
a. Lim-it-ed, *bounded*
s. Li-ne-aᴊge, *race, progeny*
a. Lin-e-al, *in a right line*
s. Lit-a-ny, *a general prayer*
a. Lit-er-al, *according to the letter*
v. Lit-i-gate, *to contest in law*
s. Lit-ur-gy, *a form of prayer*
s. Live-li-hood, *living*
s. Log-a-rithm²s, *artificial numbers*
a. Loᴊg-i-cal, *pertaining to logic*
s. Lon-ᴊgi-tude, *length, &c.*
s. Loy-al-ty, *fidelity, adherence*
a. Lu-bri-cous, *slippery*
a. Lu-cra-tive, *gainful*
a. Lu-di-crous, *laughable*
a. Lu-mi-nous, *shining*
s. Lu-na-çy, *madness*
s. Lu-na-tic, *a madman*

*s.* Lux-u-ry, *voluptuousness*

Accented on the second.
*a.* La-cón-ic, *concise, short*
*s* Lieu-ten-ant,* *a second in rank*

# M.

Accented on the first.
*v.* Máç-er-ate, *to make lean*
*s.* Mag-is-trate, *one in the commission of the peace*
*s.* Mag-ne-ti$^z$sm, *the power of the loadstone*
*v.* Mag-ni-fy, *to praise highly, to increase in size*
*s.* Mag-ni-tude, *greatness*
*s.* Ma-jes-ty, *high dignity*
*s.* Main-te-nance, *support*
*r.* Mal-a-dy, *a disease, sickness*
*s.* Male-con-tent, *a discontented person*
*s.* Man-a-cles, *fetters for the hands*
*a.* Man-i-fest, *clear, evident*
*a.* Man-i-fold, *a great many*
*s.* Man-i-ple, *a handful*
*a.* Man-u-al, *performed by the hand*
*s.* Man-u-script, *a written book not printed*
*a.* Mar-gi-nal, *written on the edge*
*s.* Mar-i-ner, *a seaman* [*sea*
*a.* Mar-i-time, *belonging to the*
*s.* Mar-shal-ler, *one that arranges*
*s.* Mar-tyr-dom, *death of a martyr*
*a.* Mar-vel-lous, *wonderful*
*a.* Mas-cu-line, *manlike*
*s.* Mas-sa-cre,* *slaughter*
*a.* Mas-ter-ly, *skilful*

* *pr.* Lev-ten-nant.    *pr.* Mas-sa-kur.

*s.* Mas-ter-piece, *capital performance*
*s.* Mas-te-ry, *superiority*
*s.* Ma-tri-çide, *a mother-killer*
*s.* Mech-an-i$^z$sm, *the construction of an engine*
*v.* Me-di-ate, *to interpose*
*a.* Med-i-cal, *physical*
*v.* Med-i-cate, *to heal or cure*
*s.* Med-i-cine, *a physical remedy*
*v.* Med-i-tate, *to think on*
*s.* Me-di-um, *a middle state*
*s.* Mel-o-dy, *harmony of sound*
*s.* Mem-o-ry, *the rational faculty*
*s.* Men-di-cant, *a beggar*
*s.* Me-ni-al, *a domestic*
*v.* Men-su-rate, *to measure*
*a.* Mer-can-tile, *commercial*
*s.* Mer-chan-di$^z$se, *trade, goods*
*s.* Mer-cu-ry, *quicksilver*
*s.* Mer-ri-ment, *mirth*
*s.* Mes-sen-ger, *one who carries an errand*
*a.* Met-al-line,‡ *impregnated with metal*
*s.* Met-a-phor, *a rhetorical figure of speech*
*s.* Me-te-or, *a fiery vapour in the sky*
*v.* Meth-o-dize, *to dispose in order*
*s.* Mi-cro-co$^z$sm, *the little world*
*s.* Mi-cro-scope, *a magnifying glass for viewing diminutive objects*   [*fire*
*a.* Mil-i-tant, *engaged in war-*
*v.* Mil-i-tate, *to oppose*
*s.* Mi-li-tia, *the train bands*
*a.* Mim-i-cal, *apish*

‡ Sheridan and Johnson have placed the accent on the *second* syllable.

Min-er-al, *a fossil*
s. Min-i-on, *a favourite, a dar-* [ling
s. Min-is-try, *agency of the state*
s. Mir-a-cle, *something above human power*
s. Mis-an-thrope, *a hater of mankind*
a. Mis-chie-vous, *harmful*
s. Mis-cre-ant, *a vile wretch*
s. Mis-si-on, *a sending*
v. Mit-i-gate, *to ease*
s. Mit-ti-mus, *a warrant of commitment*
s. Moc-ke-ry, *ridicule, scorn*
v. Mod-er-ate, *temperate, sober*
s. Mod-es-ty, *decency, purity of manners*
v. Mod-i-fy, *to shape*
v. Mod-u-late, *to tune*
v. Mol-li-fy, *to assuage*
s. Mon-ar-chy, *a kingly government*
s. Mon-i-tor, *one who warns of faults*
s. Mon-o-dy, *a serious poem*
s. Mon-u-ment, *a tomb, statue, &c.*
s. Mor-al-ist, *a moral writer*
ad. Mor-tal-ly, *deadly*
s. Mort-ga-ger, *one who gives a mortgage*
v. Mor-ti-fy, *to grow dead: to vex, to humble*
s. Mo-ti-on, *a moving, a proposal*
a. Moun-tain-ous, *full of mountains, hilly*
a. Mul-ti-form, *of many shapes*
v. Mul-ti-ply, *to increase in number*
s. Mul-ti-tude, *many*
a. Mus-cu-lar, *full of muscles*
s. Mu-si-cal, *harmonious*

a. Mu-ta-ble, *changeable*
v. Mu-ti-late, *to mangle*
a. Mu-ti-nous, *seditious*
s. Mu-ti-ny, *sedition*
a. Mu-tu-al, *reciprocal*
s. Myr-i-ad, *ten thousand*
s. Mys-te-ry, *a secret*
a. Mys-ti-cal, *obscure*

*Accented on the second.*

a. Mag-nét-ic, *attractive*
a. Ma-jes-tic, *august, stately*
a. Ma-lig-nant, *malicious*
s. Man-da-mus, *a writ in the King's Bench*
s. Ma-nœu-vre, *skilful management*
a. Ma-ter-nal, *motherly* [ing
s. Me-an-der, *a serpentine wind-*
s. Me-chan-ic, *a tradesman*
s. Me-men-to, *a remembrance*
v. Mis-con-strue, *to interpret wrong*
s. Mis-for-tune, *ill success*
a. Mis-trust-ful, *suspicious*
a. Mo-men-tous, *important*
a. Mo-nas-tic, *monkish*
s. Mu-se-um, *a repository of curiosities*

*Accented on the last.*

s. Mag-a-zine,* *a storehouse for provisions, &c. a miscellaneous pamphlet*
s. Mas-que-rade, *a masked ball*
v. Mis-ap-ply, *to apply amiss*
v. Mis-in-form, *to tell falsely*
s. Moun-tain-eer, *a dweller in mountains*

* *pr.* Mag-ga-zeen.

## N.

*Accented on the first.*

s. Nár-ra-tive, *a relation*
s. Na-ti-on, *a people distinct from others*
a. Nat-u-ral, *according to nature*
v. Nav-i-gate, *to sail on the sea*
v. Nau-se-ate,* *to loathe or abhor*
a. Nau-se-ous,† *loathsome*
a. Nau-ti-cal, *pertaining to sea affairs*
a. Neb-u-lous, *cloudy*
a. Neg-a-tive, *denying*
a. Neg-li-gent, *careless*
a. Neigh-bour-ly,‡ *friendly, sociable*
s. Ni-ce-ty, *accuracy*
a. Nig-gard-ly, *avaricious, mean*
a. Nom-i-nal, *in name only*
v. Nom-i-nate, *to appoint*
a. Not-a-ble, *careful, bustling*
s. No-ta-ry, *a scrivener*
v. No-ti-fy, *to make known*
s. No-ti-on, *an idea, thought*
s. Nov-el-ty, *newness*
a. Nox-i-ous,§ *hurtful*
a. Nu-me-ral, *relating to numbers*
v. Nu-mer-ate, *to count*
a. Nu-mer-ous, *containing many*
s. Nun-ne-ry, *a house of nuns*
a. Nup-ti-al, *pertaining to marriage*
s. Nu-tri-ment, *food, aliment*
a. Nu-tri-tive, *nourishing*

*Accented on the second.*

s. Nar-cis-sus, *the daffodil flower*

\* pr. Naw-she-ate.  † pr. Naw-shus.
‡ pr. Nay-bur-ly.  § pr. Nok-shus.

s. Nar-ra-tor, *a relator*
a. Noc-tur-nal, *nightly*

## O.

*Accented on the first.*

s. O'b-lo-quy, *odium, slander*
s. Ob-se-quies, *funeral rites*
a. Ob-so-lete, *out of use*
s. Ob-sta-cle, *hinderance*
a. Ob-sti-nate, *stubborn*
v. Ob-vi-ate, *to prevent*
a. Ob-vi-ous, *plain, apparent*
s. Oc-ci-dent, *the west*
v. Oc-cu-py, *to possess*
s. Oc-ta-gon, *a figure of eight sides*
a. Oc-u-lar, *known by the eye*
a. Oc-u-list, *one skilled in the eyes*
a. O-di-ous, *abominable*
s. O-di-um, *hatred, disgrace*
a. O-dor-ous, *sweet of smell*
a. Of-fi-cer, *one in office*
a. Om-in-ous, *ill boding*
v. On-er-ate, *to load*
v. Op-er-ate, *to act*
s. O-pen-ness, *fair dealing*
s. O-pi-ate, *a drug*
s. O-pi-um, *a medicine that causes sleep*
a. Op-po-site, *in front*
s. Op-u-lence, *riches*
a. Op-u-lent, *wealthy*
s. Or-ches-tre,‖ *a musical gallery*
s. Or-a-cle, *an answer from God*
s. Or-a-tor, *a man of eloquence*
s. Or-di-nance, *an injunction*
s. Or-gan-ist, *a player on the organ*

‖ pr. Or-kes-tur.

*s.* O-ri-ent, *the east*
*s.* Or-i-fiçe, *an opening*
*s.* Or-i-ʲgin, *beginning* [*tion*
*s.* Or-na-ment, *beauty, decora-*
*a.* Or-tho-dox, *sound in belief*
*s.* O-ver-ture, *proposal*
*s.* Out-law-ry, *out of the protection of the law*
*s.* O-ver-sight, *a mistake*
*s.* Over-throw, *a defeat*

Accented on the second.

*a.* Ob-dú-rate, *obstinate inflexible*
*s.* O-bei-sançe,* *request*
*s.* Ob-ᶻser-vançe, *respect, attention*
*s.* Oc-cur-rençe, *what happens*
*s.* Oc-ta-vo, *8 leaves to the sheet*
*a.* Of-fen-sive, *displeasing*
*s.* Op-po-nent, *an adversary*
*a.* Op-pres-sive, *cruel, overwhelming*
*s.* Op-pres-sor, *one who oppresses*

Accented on the last.

*a.* Op-por-túne, *convenient*
*a.* O-ver-cast, *clouded*
*v.* O-ver-come, *to subdue*
*v.* O-ver-flow, *to run over*
*v.* O-ver-look, *to superintend*
*s.* O-ver-seer, *a superintendent: a parish officer*
*v.* O-ver-ween, *to think too highly*
*v.* O-ver-whelm, *to crush*

P.

Accented on the first.

*v.* Páç-i-fy, *to appease*
*v.* Pal-li-ate, *to lessen a fault*

\* *Or pr.* O-ba-zanse.

*a.* Pal-pa-ble, *plain, that may be felt*
*v.* Pal-pi-tate, *to beat at the heart*
*s.* Par-a-ble, *a similitude*
*s.* Par-a-dox, *a seeming contradiction*
*s.* Par-a-graph, *a distict part of a discourse*
*a.* Par-al-lel, *equal*
*s.* Par-a-pet, *a wall breast high*
*s.* Par-a-phraᶻse, *a loose interpretation* [*men*
*s.* Par-a-site, *a flatterer of rich*
*s.* Paʺ-ren-taʲge, *kindred*
*s.* Par-i-ty, *likeness, equality*
*s.* Par-ri-çide, *one who murders his father*
*s.* Par-ox-ysm,* *the return of a fit with increased malignity*
*a.* Par-ta-ble, *divisible*
*s.* Par-ti-cle, *a small portion of a great substance*
*s.* Par-vi-ty, *smallness*
*a.* Pas-sa-ble, *possible to be passed: tolerable*
*a.* Pas-sion-ate, *soon angry*
*a.* Pas-to-ral, *rural, rustic*
*ad.* Pa-tient-ly, *quietly* [*mily*
*s.* Pa-tri-arch, *the head of a fa-*
*s.* Pa-tri-ot, *a lover of his country*
*s.* Pat-ron-aʲge, *support, protection* [*fend*
*v.* Pat-ron-ise, *to protect or de-*
*s.* Pau-çi-ty, *fewness*
*v.* Pay-a-ble, *due, that ought to be paid* [*breast*
*a.* Pec-to-ral, *belonging to the*
*s.* Ped-an-try, *affectation of great learning*

\* *pr.* Par-rok-sizm.

s. Ped-es-tal, *the basis of a pillar*
s. Ped-i-gree, *descent from ancestors*
s. Pen-al-ty, *a fine or punishment*
s. Pen-du-lum, *a hanging weight which vibrates*
v. Pen-e-trate, *to dive into*
a. Pen-i-tent, *contrite for sin*
s. Pen-ta-gon, *a figure of five sides*
s. Pen-u-ry, *extreme want*
s. Per-fi-dy, *treachery*
v. Per-fo-rate, *to pierce through*
a. Per-il-ous, *hazardous*
s. Pe-ri-od, *circuit: length of duration*
s. Per-ju-ry, *false oath*
a. Per-ma-nent, *lasting*
s. Per-qui-ᶻsite, *something over settled wages*
s. Per-son-aᴊge, *a person of distinction* [person
a. Per-son-al, *belonging to a*
v. Per-son-ate, *to represent another*
a. Per-ti-nent, *fit, well adapted*
a. Per-vi-ous, *seen through*
s. Pes-ti-lence, *the plague*
v. Pet-ri-fy, *to change into stone*
a. Pet-u-lent, *saucy, perverse*
a. Phyᶻs-i-cal, *medicinal*
s. Pi-e-ty, *duty to the Almighty*
s. Pin-na-cle, *the summit of a spire*
a. Pit-e-ous, *sorrowful*
a. Plau-ᶻsi-ble, *seemingly fair*
s. Pleaᶻs-an-try, *merriment, gayety*
a. Plen-a-ry, *full, entire*
s. Plen-i-tude, *fulness*

a. Plen-te-ous, *abundance*
s. Pleu-ri-sy, *a disease*
a. Pli-a-ble, *easy to bend*
s. Po-e-try, *verse*
s. Poign-an-cy, *high relish*
s. Pol-i-cy, *prudence*
s. Po-li-ty, *civil government*
s. Pol-y-gon, *a figure of many angles*
a. Pon-der-ous, *heavy*
s. Pop-u-lace, *the vulgar*
a. Pop-u-lar, *pleasing to the people*
v. Pop-u-late, *to people*
a. Pop-u-lous, *well inhabited*
s. Por-phy-ry, *a fine spotted marble*
a. Pòrt-a-ble, *that may be carried*
s. Pòr-trai-ture, *a painted resemblance*
a. Poᶻs-i-tive, *sure, certain*
a. Post-hu-mous, *published after one's death*
a. Po-ta-ble, *fit to drink.*
s. Pov-er-ty, *necessity, want*
a. Pow-er-ful, *mighty* [tice
a. Prac-ti-cal, *belonging to prac-*
s. Pre-am-ble, *introduction*
s. Pre̦c-e-dent, *example*
s. Pre″-ci-pice, *steep place*
s. Pref-er-ence, *the choice*
s. Pre-ju-dice, *judgment beforehand*
s. Prem-i-seᶻs, *houses, land*
s. Pre-mi-um, *a reward* [church
s. Preᶻs-by-ter, *an elder of the*
s. Pre-sci-ence,* *foreknowledge*

*\* pr.* Pre-she-ense. The two concluding syllables of the words *prescience* and *omniscience* are generally pronoun-

s. Pre²s-i-dent, *a ruler*
a. Prev-a-lent, *prevailing*
a. Pre-vi-ous, *going before*
a. Pri-ma-ry, *first in order*
a. Prim-i-tive, *ancient*
a. Prin-çi-pal, *chief*
s. Prin-çi-ple, *first cause, motive*
s. Priv-i-le-¹ge, *peculiar advantage*
s. Priv-i-ty, *private knowledge*
a. Prob-a-ble, *likely*
ad. Prob-a-bly, *in all likelihood*
s. Prob-i-ty, *honesty*
a. Prod-i-gal, *profuse, lavish*
s. Prod-i-¹gy, *a preternatural thing*
a. Prof-li-gate, *wicked*
s. Proj-ge-ny, *offspring*
a. Prom-i-nent, *jutting out*
s. Promp-ti-tude, *readiness*
v. Prop-a-gate, *to spread abroad*
s. Prop-er-ty, *individual right*
v. Proph-e-sy, *to foretell*
v. Pros-e-cute, *to continue: to pursue by law*
s. Pros-e-lyte, *a convert*
a. Pros-pe-rous, *successful*
s. Prov-en-der, *food for cattle*
s. Prov-i-dençe, *divine protection*
s. Prov-i-dent, *cautious, prudent*
s. Psal-mo-dy, *a singing of psalms*
a. Pu-e-rile, *childish*
v. Pul-ver-ize, *to reduce to dust*
a. Punc-tu-al, *exact*
s. Pun-ish-ment, *chastisement*
a. Pur-ga-tive, *cleansing*
s. Pur-çha-ser, *one who buys*
v. Pu-ri-fy, *to make clean*

ced with a much more marked distinction than in the word *conscience*, which common usage has turned into a dissyllable.

s. Pu-ri-ty, *unspotted virtue*
s. Pu-ri-tan, *a sectary*
v. Pu-tre-fy, *to rot*
s. Py-ra-mid, *a pillar terminating in a point, whose sides are triangles*

*Accented on the second*

a. Pa-cif-ic, *peaceful*
a. Pa-ren-tal, *pertaining to parents*
s. Par-ta-ker, *a sharer*
a. Pa-ter-nal, *fatherly*  [*sions*
a. Pa-thet-ic, *moving the passions*
a. Pe-dan-tic, *vain, conceited*
a. Pel-lu-çid, *clear, bright*
s. Per-spec-tive, *a distant view*
a. Per-sua-sive, *able to persuade*
s. Pe-ru-²sal, *a reading over*
s. Pome-gran-ate, *a kind of fruit*
s. Pòrt-man-teau,* *a travelling chest*
s. Pre-çe-dençe, *priority of place*
a. Prc-çe-dent, *going before*
a. Pre-çep-tive, *instructive*
s. Pre-çep-tor, *a teacher*
ad. Pre-çise-ly, *exact*  [*ment*
s. Pre-con-tract, *a prior engagement*
s. Pre-cur-sor, *a forerunner*
s. Pre-fer-ment, *higher advançement*
a. Pre-²sump-tive, *presumed: arrogant, confident*
s. Pre-ven-tive, *which prevents*
a. Pri-me-val, *original*  [*duct*
s. Pro-çe-dure, *manner of conduct*
a. Pro-duc-tive, *producing, fertile*
s. Pro-fes-sor, *a public teacher*
s. Prog-nos-tic, *a prediction*
a. Pro-gres-sive, *going forward*

* *pr.* Port-man-to

v. Pro-hib-it, *to forbid*
a. Pro-lif-ic, *fruitful*
v. Pro-mul-gate, *to spread abroad*
s. Pro-po-ᶻsal, *an offer*
s. Pro-vi-ᶻso, *a stipulation*
s. Pur-su-ançe, *in consequence*
v. Pur-su-ant, *according to order*
s. Pur-vey-or, *one who provides victuals*

*Accented on the last.*

s. Pal-i-sáde, *slight paling*
v. Per-se-vere, *to persist*
v. Pre-ex-ist, *to exist before*
a. Pre-ma-ture, *too soon said, or done too early*

## Q.

*Accented on the first.*

s. Quád-ran-gle, *a figure of four sides*
s. Quad-ru-ped, *a four-footed animal*
a. Quad-ru-ple, *fourfold*
v. Qual-i-fy, *to make fit*
s. Qual-i-ty, *kind, sort*
s. Quan-ti-ty, *weight, portion*
a. Quar-rel-some, *inclined to quarrel*
s. Quar-ter-age, *quarterly allowance*
a. Quer-u-lous, *complaining*
s Ques-ti-on, *an inquiry*
s. Qui-e-tude, *silence*
a. Quin-tu-ple, *five-fold*
s. Quo-ti-ent, *the number produced by division*

*Accented on the second.*

a. Quad-rát-ic, *belonging to a square*
s. Quan-da-ry, *a doubt*
a. Qui-es-çent, *resting*

*Accented on the last.*

s. Quar-an-tine,* *the space of 40 days*

## R.

*Accented on the first.*

a. Rá-di-ant, *bright, shining*
a. Rad-i-cal, *inbred*
s. Ra-di-us, *the semidiameter*
v. Rar-e-fy, *to make thin*
s. Ra-ri-ty, *any thing uncommon*
v. Rat-i-fy, *to confirm*
s. Ra-ti-o,† *reason or proportion*
a. Rav-en-ous, *greedy*
v. Re-al-ize, *to make real*   [*tion*
s. Re″-çi-pe, *a medical prescrip-*
s. Re-com-pense, *reward*
v. Rec-re-ate, *to divert*
s. Rec-tan-gle, *a right angle*
v. Rec-ti-fy, *to make right*
s. Rec-ti-tude, *moral honesty*
s. Rec-to-ry, *a church living*
s. Ref-er-ençe, *allusion*
s. Re-ᴊgen-çy, *government by proxy*
s. Reᴊg-i-çide, *a king-killer*
s. Reg-i-men, *diet*
s. Re-ᴊgi-on, *a country*
s. Reᴊg-is-ter, *a record*
a. Re-gu-lar, *orderly*

* pr. Kwor-ran-teen
† pr. Ra-she-

SPELLING ASSISTANT.

v. Reg-u-late, *to put in order*
a. Relative, *having relation to*
s. Rem-e-dy, *medicine, cure*
v. Rem-i-grate, *to remove back again*
s. Ren-e-gade, *an apostate*
v. Re-no-vate, *to renew*
s. Rep-ro-bate, *lost to virtue*
a. Re-qui-$^z$site, *necessary*
s. Res-i-dençe, *dwelling place*
s. Re$^z$s-i-due, *remainder*
a. Re$^z$s-o-lute, *determined*
a. Ret-ro-grade, *going backwards*
s. Ret-ro-spect, *a review or consideration of things past*
s. Rev-e-nue,* *public taxes*
s. Rev-er-ence, *honour, respect*
a. Rev-er-end, *worthy of respect*
s. Rhap-so-dy, *loose thoughts*
s. Rhet-o-ric, *the art of oratory*
s. Rheu-ma-ti$^z$-sm, *a painful disease*
s. Rib-ald-ry, *obscene language*
s. Rid-i-cule,† *mockery*
s. Rig-id-ness, *severity*
a. Rig-or-ous, *over-harsh*
a. Ri-ot-ous, *disorderly*
a. Ri$^z$s-i-ble, *exciting laughter*
s. Rit-u-al, *a book of rights or ceremonies*
s. Ri-val-ry, *competition*
s. Riv-u-let, *a little river*
s. Rob-be-ry, *theft*
s. Roy-al-ty, *kingly dignity*
s. Ru-di-ments, *first principles*
a. Ru-in-ous, *fallen to ruin*
a. Ru-mi-nate, *to reflect on*
a. Rus-ti-cal, *boisterous*

* Or pr. Re-ven-ue.
† pr. R**i**d-e-kule. not R**e**d-e-kule

*Accented on the second.*

s. Re-çi-tal, *rehearsal*
s. Re-cor-der, *a law officer*
a. Re-cum-bent, *lying down*
v. Re-dou-ble, *to double again*
a. Re-dun-dant, *overflowing*
s. Re-fine-ment, *an improvement*
s. Re-fresh-ment, *relief, rest*
a. Re-ful-gent, *shining, splendid*
a. Re-gard-less, *inattentive*
s. Re-hear-sal, *a repeating*
v. Re-lin-quish, *to part with*
s. Re-luc-tance, *unwillingness*
a. Re-luc-tant, *unwilling*
s. Re-main-der, *what is left*
s. Re-mit-tançe, *a return of money*
s. Re-mon-strançe, *representation*
v. Re-mon-strate, *to reason with*
s. Ren-coun-ter, *an unexpected adventure*
s. Re-pen-tançe, *sorrow,*
v. Re-plen-ish, *to fill again*
s. Re-plev-in, or  
s. Re-plev-y,  } *a law writ*
s. Re-pri-$^z$sal, *a seizure in recompense*
s. Re-pub-lic, *a commonwealth*
a. Re-pug-nant, *contrary to*
s. Re-qui-tal, *a recompense*
s. Re-$^z$sem-blançe, *likeness*
v. Re-$^z$sem-ble, *to be like*
s. Re-$^z$sent-ment, *a sense of injury*
s. Re-$^z$sist-ançe, *opposition*
a. Re-spect-ful, *submissive*
a. Re-splen-dent, *shining*
s. Re-spon-dent, *he who answers*
a. Re-ten-tive, *apt to remember*
s. Re-tire-ment, *a private abode*
s. Re-trench-ment, *a lessening*
a. Ro-man-tic, *improbable, absurd, fanciful*

### Accented on the last.

v. Re-ad-mít, *to let in again*
v. Re-cog-nise, *to acknowledge*
v. Re-col-lect, *to call to mind*
v. Re-com-mend, *to praise to another*
v. Re-con-çile, *to settle disputes*
v. Re-em-bark, *to take shipping again*
v. Re-im-burse, *to repay*
v. Re-in-forçe, *to recruit*
v. Re-in-state, *to restore to possession*
s. Ren-dez-vous,* *a place of meeting*
s. Rep-ar-tee, *a witty reply*
v. Re-po$^z$s-sess, *to get again*
v. Rep-re-hend, *to censure*
v. Rep-re-$^z$sent, *to describe*

### S.

#### Accented on the first.

s. Sác-ra-ment, *the holy communion*
v. Sac-ri-fiçe, *to offer up: destroy*
s. Sac-ri-lege, *church robbery*
s. Sal-a-ry, *stated hire*
a. San-a-tive *healing*
v. Sanc-ti-ty, *to make holy*
s. Sanc-ti-on, *a decree ratified*
s. Sanc-ti-fy, *piety*
s. San-i-ty, *soundness of mind*
a. Sa-pi-ent, *wise, sage*
s. Sat-ir-ist, *a writer of satire*
v. Sa-tis-fy, *to content*
a. Sat-ur-nine, *melancholy*
a. Sa-vour-y, *pleasing to the smell or taste*

* *pr.* Ren-de-voo. (Ren-de-vooz.)

s. Scan-da-lous, *shameful*
s. Scar-çi-ty, *want of plenty*
v. Scar-i-fy, *to lance the skin*
s. Scav-en-ger, *a street cleaner*
s. Sce-ne-ry, *imagery*
s. Scep-ti-çi$^z$sm, *universal doubt*
s. Scriv-e-ner, *a notary*
a. Scru-pu-lous, *cautious, doubtful*
s. Scru-ti-ny, *inquiry*
a. Scur-ril-ous, *abusive*
s. Sec-ta-ry. *one of any sect*
a. Sec-u-lar, *worldly*
s. Sed-i-ment, *what settles at bottom*
a. Sed-u-lous, *industrious*
ad. Seem-ing-ly, *in show*
v. Seg-re-gate, *to set apart*
s. Sen-a-tor, *a member of parliament*
a. Sen-si-ble, *learned*
a. Sen-si-tive, *having perception*
a. Sen-su-al, *given to pleasure*
s. Sen-ti-ment, *opinion*
a. Sep-a-rate, *distinct*
s. Sep-ul-chre,† *a grave, a tomb*
s. Sep-ul-ture, *burial*
a. Se-ri-ous, *grave, solemn*
a. Ser-pen-tine, *winding*
a. Ser-rat-ed, *indented like a saw*
s. Ser-vi-tor, *the lowest rank in a college*
s. Ser-vi-tude, *slavery*
s. Set-tle-ment, *a jointure, colony*
v. Sig-nal-ize, *to make remarkable*
s. Sig-na-ture, *a singning one's name*
v. Sig-ni-fy, *to make known*
a. Sim-i-lar, *alike*
a. Sim-i-le, *a comparison*

† *pr.* Sep-pul-kur.

SPELLING ASSISTANT.  75

s. Sim-o-ny, *unlawful dealing in church preferment*
s. Si-ne-cure, *salary without employ*
a. Sin-gu-lar, *particular, odd*
a. Sin-is-ter, *unfair*
s. Skeleton, *the bones of a body arranged in order*
a. Slan-der-ous, *falsely abusive*
s. Slaugh-ter-house, *a house in which beasts are killed by the butcher*
s. So-journ-er, *a temporary dweller*
a. So-la-ry, *belonging to the sun*
s. Sol-e-çism, *an impropriety in speech*
v. Sol-emn-ize, *to celebrate*
s. Sol-i-tude, *lonely life*
a. Sol-va-ble, *that can be answer-* [ed
a. Sol-u-ble, *capable of separation*
s. Sor-çe-ry, *magic*
a. Sov-er-eign, *supreme, chief*
s. Spa-cious-ness, *roominess*
ad. Spa-ring-ly, *frugally* [larly
v. Spe″-çi-fy, *to mention particu-*
s. Spe″-çi-men, *an example*
ad. Spe-cious-ly, *with fair appearance*
s. Spec-ta-cle, *a remarkable show*
v. Spec-u-late, *to think on*
s. Spec-u-lum, *a looking glass*
a. Spher-i-cal,* *round*
s. Spi-çe-ry, *a repository of spices*
a. Splen-e-tic, *cross, peevish*
a. Spu-ri-ous, *false, pretended*
v. Stig-ma-tize, *to brand with disgrace*
v. Stim-u-late, *to spur on*
v. Stip-u-late, *to bargain*

\* *pr.* Sfer-re-kal.

s. Strat-a-gem, *an artful invention*
a. Stren-u-ous, *earnest, vigorous*
a. Stu-di-ous, *given to study*
s. Suav-i-ty,† *sweetness, pleasantness*
v. Sub-ju-gate, *to overcome*
a. Sub-se-quent, *following*
s. Sub-si-dy, *a tax or tribute*
s. Sub-stan-tive, *a noun*
v. Sub-sti-tute, *to put in the place of another*
s. Sub-ter-fuge, *shift pretence*
a. Suc-cu-lent, *juicy, moist*
s. Suf-fer-er, *one who suffers*
v. Suf-fo-cate, *to smother*
s. Su-i-çide, *self-murder*
a. Suit-a-ble, *agreeing, fit*
a. Sum-ma-ry, *short, concise*
a. Sump-tu-ous, *rich, costly*
s. Sup-ple-ment, *an addition*
s. Sup-pli-ant, *one who entreats*
v. Sup-pli-cate, *to beg*
s. Sur-ge-ry, *the art of healing wounds*
s. Sur-ro-gate, *a deputy* [food
s. Sus-te-nançe, *nourishment*
s. Syc-o-phant, *a flatterer*
s Sym-me-try, *proportion*
v. Sym-pa-thize, *to condole with*
s. Sym-pa-thy, *sincere affection*
s. Sym-pho-ny, *musical harmony*

*Accented on the second.*

s. Salt-pé-tre, *a mineral salt*
a. Scho-las-tic, *in the school line*
v. Se-ques-ter, *to separate*
a. Se-raph-ic, *angelic*

† *pr.* Swav-e-ta.

*v.* So-liç-it, *to urge to desire*
*a.* So-no-rous, *loud or high-sounding*
*a.* Spe-çif-ic, *peculiar to itself*
*s.* Spec-ta-tor, *a looker on*
*a.* Stu-pen-dous, *vast, wonderful*
*a.* Sub-mis-sive, *respectful, humble*
*s.* Sub-pœ-na, *a writ of summons*
*s.* Sub-scri-ber, *one who subscribes*
*s.* Sub-sist-ençe, *being: also food*
*a.* Sub-ver-sive, *tending to overturn*
*a.* Suc-cess-ful, *lucky* [order
*a.* Suc-çes-sive, *that follows in*
*s.* Suc-çes-sor, *one that immediately follows another in any employment*
*v.* Sur-ren-der, *to give up*
*s.* Sur-vey-or, *a superintendent: a measurer of land*
*s.* Sur-vi-vor, *the longest liver*
*s.* Sy-nop-sis, *a brief view*

*Accented on the last.*

*s.* Ser-e-náde, *night music*
*v.* Su-per-add, *to add over and above*
*a.* Su-per-fine, *eminently fine*
*v.* Su-per-scribe, *to write on the back*
*v.* Su-per-sede, *to set aside*
*v.* Super-vi²se, *to overlook*

## T.

*Accented on the first.*

*a.* Tán-gi-ble, *that may be touched*
*v.* Tan-ta-lize, *to balk*
*s.* Tap-es-try, *hangings wrought in figures*
*a.* Tech-ni-cal, *belonging to art*

*s.* Tel-e-scope, *a glass for distant objects*
*s.* Tem-per-ançe, *moderation*
*a.* Tem-per-ate, *sober, discreet*
*a.* Tem-po-ral, *worldly*
*a.* Ten-a-ble, *that may be held*
*s.* Ten-den-çy, *aim, drift*
*s.* Ten-e-ment, *a house*
*s.* Ter-ma-gant, *a scold*
*v.* Ter-mi-nate, *to limit, to end*
*a.* Ter-ri-ble,* *dreadful*
*v.* Ter-ri-fy, *to make afraid*
*a.* Ter-ti-an, *every third day*
*s.* Tes-ta-ment, *a will*
*v.* Tes-ti-fy, *to witness*
*s.* The-a-tre, *a building for public shows*
*s.* The-o-ry, *speculation*
*a.* Tim-o-rous, *fearful*
*a.* Tit-u-lar, *in name only*
*v.* Tol-er-ate, *to permit*
*a.* Trac-ta-ble, *easily managed*
*s.* Tra͝g-e-dy, *a mournful play*
*a.* Tra͝g-i-cal, *sad, mournful*
*a.* Trai-tor-ous, *traitor-like*
*a.* Tran-si-ent, *passing away*
*s.* Treaçh-e-ry, *breach of faith*
*s.* Trea²s-u-rer, *a keeper of treasure*
*s.* Trea²s-u-ry, *a place for money*
*a.* Trem-u-lous, *trembling*
*s.* Tri-an-gle, *a figure of three angles*
*a.* Trip-li-cate, *three-fold*
*a.* Triv-i-al, *of small consequence*
*a.* Tur-bu-lent, *violent, boisterous*
*s.* Tur-pi-tude, *inherent vileness*
*s.* Tu-te-lar, *one who protects*
*s.* Tym-pa-ny, *a dropsy*

* In this and the following word, ri takes the sound of re. It is erroneous to say *terrable*.

*a.* Typ-i-cal, *emblematical*
*a.* Tyr-an-nous, *cruel, oppressive*
*s.* Tyr-an-ny, *cruel government*

*Accented on the second.*

*s.* Tes-tá-tor, *one who leaves a will*
*a.* Tran-scen-dent, *very excellent*
*a.* Trans-pa-rent, *clear*
*a.* Tre-men-dous, *awful, dreadful*
*s.* Tri-bu-nal, *a judgment seat*
*a.* Tri-um-phant, *triumphing*

*Accented on the last.*

*a.* Trans-ma-rine,* *lying beyond sea*

## V

*Accented on the first.*

*s.* Vá-can-çy, *an empty place*
*s.* Vac-u-um, *space void of matter*
*ad.* Val-i-ant-ly, *courageously*
*s.* Vag-a-bond, *an idle stroller*
*s.* Va-ri-ançe, *disagreement*
*a.* Va-ri-ous, *different*
*s.* Vas-sal-a<sup>j</sup>ge *servitude*
*v.* Ve-<sup>j</sup>ge-tate,† *to cause growth*
*s* Ve-he-mençe, *earnestness*
*a.* Ve-he-ment, *fervent, eager*
*s* Ve-hi-cle, *that in which a thing is carried.*
*a.* Ven-di-ble, *saleable*
*a.* Ven-o-mous, *poisonous*
*v.* Ven-e-rate, *to esteem, reverence* [*heart*
*s.* Ven-tri-cle, *a cavity in the*
*v.* Ven-ti-late, *to air, to fan*
*a.* Ven-ture-some, *daring*
*v.* Ver-i-fy, *to prove true*

  \* *pr.* Trans-ma-reen.
  † *pr.* Ved-je-tate.

*a.* Ver-si-tile, *changeable*
*v.* Ver-si-fy, *so turn into verse*
*s.* Ver-te-bre, *a joint of the back*
*a.* Ver-ti-cal, *overhead*
*s.* Vet-er-an, *serving long*
*s.* Vic-er-a<sup>j</sup>ge, *the benefice of a vicar*
*a.* Viç-i-ous-ly, *wickedly*
*s.* Vic-to-ry, *the defeat of an enemy*
*s.* Vic-tu-al-ler, *one who provides victuals*
*s.* Vi<sup>j</sup>g-il-ançe, *watchfulness*
*a.* Vi<sup>j</sup>g-il-ant, *active, watchful*
*a.* Vig-or-ous, *lively, stout*
*v.* Vil-i-fy, *to abuse*
*a.* Vin-çi-ble, *that may be overcome*
*v.* Vin-di-cate, *to justify, to clear*
*v.* Vi-o-late, *to break or transgress*
*s.* Vi-o-lençe, *force, oppression*
*a.* Vi-o-lent, *furious, forcible*
*a.* Vir-tu-ous, *morally good*
*a.* Vir-u-lent, *hurtful, infectious*
*a.* Vi$^z$s-i-ble, *that may be seen*
*s.* Vis-i-tant, *one who goes to see another*
*a.* Vi$^z$s-u-al, *pertaining to the sight*
*v.* Vi-ti-ate, *to corrupt*
*a.* Vol-a-tile, *airy, light*
*a.* Vol-u-ble, *fluent of speech*
*s.* Vo-ta-ry, *one devoted*

*Accented on the second.*

*s.* Va-ca-tion, *leisure*
*s.* Ver-mil-ion, *a fine red colour*
*s.* Vex-a-tion, *acts of troubling*
*s.* Vi-bra-tion, *an alternate moving*
*a.* Vi-va-cious, *sprightly*
*s.* Vo-ca-tion, *employment*
*s.* Vo-li-tion, *the act of willing*
*a.* Vo-ra-cious, *ravenous*

*s.* Ut-ter-ançe, *speech*

*Accented on the second.*
*ad.* Ver-bá-tim, *word for word*
*s.* Ver-ti-go, *a giddiness*
*s.* Viçe-ge-rent, *one who acts for another*
*a.* Vin-dic-tive, *revengeful*
*s.* Vol-ca-no, *a burning mountain that emits flames, stones, &c.*
*a.* Un-daunted, *fearless*
*a.* Un-feign-ed, *real, sincere*
*a.* Un-time-ly, *unseasonable*
*a.* Un-wiel-dy, *unmanageable*
*a.* Un-wor-thy, *not deserving*

*Accented on the last.*
*s.* Vol-un-teér, *one who enters willingly: a soldier of his own accord*
*v.* Un-de-çeive, *to set right*
*v.* Un-der-go, *to suffer*
*v.* Un-der-mine, *to sap, to injure secretly*

## W

*Accented on the first.*
*s.* Wáp-en-take, *a division of a country*
*s.* War-ri-or, *a military man*
*s.* Wea-ri-ness. *fatigue*
*a.* Wea-ri-some, *fatiguing*
*a.* Whim-si-cal, *full of fancies*
*s.* Wi-dow-er, *a man whose wife is dead*
*s.* Wil-der-ness, *a desert*
*ad.* Wil-ful-ly, *on purpose*
*a.* Won-der-ful, *astonishing*
*s.* Wretch-ed-ness, *misery*

## Y.

*s.* Yeo-man-ry, *the body of yeoman*

## Z.

*ad.* Zeal-ous-ly, *with passionate ardour*
*s.* Zó-di-ac, *the twelve signs in the heavens*

---

# WORDS OF FOUR SYLLABLES.

Parts of Speech.

## A.

*Accented on the first.*
*a.* AC-ÇEP-TA-BLE,* *agreeable: seasonable*

Parts of Speech.
*s.* Ac-çes-sa-ry, *an abettor*
*s.* Ac-cu-ra-çy, *exactness*
*s.* Ac-ri-mo-ny, *sharpness: severity of temper or language*
*a.* Ad-mi-ra-ble, *excellent*

* Though *Mr. Walker* places the accent on the first, he notwithstanding gives a preference to its being on the second syllable, agreeably, to *Johnson* and *Baily.—Entick*, in his work, has the accent on the *first* syllable.

*s.* Ad-mi-ral-ty, *the supreme naval power*
*s.* Ad-ver-sa-ry, *an enemy*
*s.* Ag-ri-cul-ture, *husbandry*
*v.* A-li-en-ate, *to estrange from*
*s.* Al-le-go-ry, *a figure in rhetoric*
*a.* A-mi-a-ble, *lovely charming*
*a.* Am-i-ca-ble, *friendly*
*part.* An-i-mated, *spirited, lively*
*s.* Ap-o-plex-y, *a sudden deprivation of all sense and motion*
*a.* Ap-pli-ca-ble, *that may be applied*
*a.* Ar-bi-tra-ry, *not bound by law*
*s.* Arch-i-tec-ture, *the art of building*   [*hearers*
*s.* Au-di-to-ry, *the assembly of*

Accented on the second.

*v.* Ab-bré-vi-ate, *to shorten*
*v.* A-bom-i-nate, *to detest*   [*diet*
*a.* Ab-ste-mi-ous, *temperate in*
*s.* Ab-sur-di-ty, *foolishness*
*v.* Ac-cel-e-rate, *to hasten*
*a.* Ac-ces-si-ble, *approachable*
*v.* Ac-com-mo-date, *to adjust to fit*
*v.* Ac-com-pa-ny, *to join with*
*s.* Ac-com-plish-ment, *an acquirement: a completion*
*v.* Ac-cu-mu-late, *to heap up*
*s.* Ac-know-ledg-ment, *confession: gratitude*
*s.* Ac-tiv-i-ty, *nimbleness*
*v.* Ad-min-is-ter, *to give to*
*a.* Ad-mis-si-ble, *that may be admitted*
*s.* Ad-mis-si-on, *access*
*a.* A-do-ra-ble, *worthy of honour*
*s.* Ad-ver-si-ty, *affliction*
*s.* Ad-ver-ten-cy, *attention*

*s.* Ad-ver-ti$^z$se-ment, *intelligence*
*a.* Ad-vi-$^z$sa-ble, *fit to be done*
*v.* A-dul-te-rate, *to reduce in quality*
*s.* Af-fec-ti-on, *love, kindness*
*a.* Af-fir-ma-tive, *positive*
*s.* Af-flic-tion, *trouble, calamity*
*s.* A-gil-i-ty, *nimbleness*
*a.* A-gra-ri-an, *relating to land*
*a.* A-gree-a-ble, *pleasing*
*s.* A-lac-ri-ty, *willingness, readiness*
*s.* Al-le-gi-ançe, *duty of subjects*
*v.* Al-le-vi-ate, *to ease, to soften*
*s.* Al-ter-na-tive, *a choice of two things only*   [*sentative*
*s.* Am-bas-sa-dor, *a state repre-*
*a.* Am-big-u-ous, *doubtful*
*s.* Am-bi″-tion, *thirst after power*
*a.* Am-bi″-ti-ous, *greedy of honour: aspiring, proud*
*a.* A-me-na-ble, *subject to*
*a.* Am-phib-i-ous, *living by land and water*
*v.* Am-plif-i-cate, *to enlarge*
*s.* A-nal-o-gy, *relation*
*s.* A-nal-y-sis, *resolving into parts*
*s.* A-nat-o-my, *dissection*
*v.* An-ni-hi-late, *to destroy utterly*
*s.* An-nu-i-tant, *one who enjoys an annuity*
*s.* An-nu-i-ty, *a yearly allowance for life*
*a.* A-non-y-mous, *without a name, unknown*
*s.* An-tag-o-nist, *an opponent*
*v.* An-tic-i-pate, *to do before hand*
*s.* An-tip-a-thy, *a natural aversion*
*s.* An-ti″-qui-ty, *ancientness*

s. Anx-i-e-ty, *trouble of mind*
s. A-pol-o-gy, *a defence or excuse*
s. A-pos-tro-phe, *a figure in rhetoric: a comma*
v. Ap-pre-çi-ate, *to estimate*
v. Ap-pro-pri-ate, *to consign to any particular use*
a. Ap-prox-i-mate, *near to*
s. Ap-pur-te-nance, *an appendage* [numbers
s. A-rith-me-tic, *the science of*
a. Ar-tic-u-late, *distinct*
s. Ar-til-le-ry, *heavy cannon*
s. As-cen-den-çy, *influence*
a. As-pec-ta-ble, *visible*
s. As-pe-ri-ty, *roughness, harshness of speech*
v. As-sas-si-nate, *to murder secretly*
a. As-sid-u-ous, *diligent*
v. As-sim-i-late, *to make alike*
v. As-so-ci-ate, *to join with*
s. As-trol-o-gy, *foretelling by the stars*
s. As-tron-o-my, *the science of the heavenly bodies*
ad. A-tro-cious-ly, *wickedly*
v. At-ten-u-ate, *to lessen*
ad. Au-da-cious-ly, *boldly*
s. Au-re-li-a, *the chrysalis*
a. Au-ric-u-lar, *private, told in secret*
ad. Au-spi-cious-ly, *happily*
s. Aus-ter-i-ty, *severity, cruelty*
s. Au-thor-i-ty, *legal power*

*Accented on the third.*

a. Ac-çi-dén-tal, *happening by chance*
s. Ad-o-les-cençe, *state of youth*

s. Af-fi-da-vit, *a deposition on oath*
a. An-te-çe-dent, *going before*
a. Ap-o-plec-tic, *relating to apoplexy*
a. Ap-pre-hen-sive, *fearful, sensible*
s. Ar-bi-tra-tor, *a judge*

## B.

*Accented on the second.*

s. Bar-bár-i-ty, *cruelty*
s. Ba-rom-e-ter, *a weather-glass*
s. Be-at-i-tude, *blessedness*
a. Bel-lig-or-ent, *engaged in war*
s. Be-nef-i-çençe, *active goodness*
a. Be-nef-i-çent, *doing good*
s. Be-nev-o-lençe, *good will*
a. Be-nev-o-lent, *kind*
s. Be-nig-ni-ty, *sweetness of disposition*
a. Bi-en-ni-al, *lasting two years*
s. Bi-og-ra-phy, *a history of lives*
a. Bo-tan-i-cal, *belonging to herbs*

*Accented on the third.*

v. Bas-ti-ná-do, *to beat severely*
a. Be-a"-tif-ic, *that is blessed*

## C.

*Accented on the first.*

s. Çél-i-ba-çy, *single life*
s. Çer-e-mo-ny, *forms of civility*
a. Châr-i-ta-ble, *benevolent*
a. Com-men-ta-ry, *an interpretation or exposition*

s. Com-mis-sa-ry, *a civil officer*
s. Com-mon-al-ty, *the common people*
*s.* Com-pa-ra-ble, *that may be compared*
s. Com-pe-ten-çy, *sufficiency*
a. Com-pli-ca-ted, *intricate*
a. Con-quer-a-ble, *that may be conquered*
s. Con-tro-ver-sy, *dispute*
s. Con-tu-ma-çy, *stubbornness*
s. Con-tu-me-ly, *reproach*
s. Cor-ol-la-ry, *an inference*
s. Cor-pu-len-çy, *bulkiness of body*
a. Cor-ri-gi-ble *that may be amended*
a. Cred-it-a-ble *of good repute*
a. Cus-to-ma-ry, *usual*

*Accented on the second.*

a. Ca-dáv-er-ous, *ghastly*
s. Cal-am-i-ty, *misfortune*
s. Cal-id-i-ty, *great heat*
v. Cal-um-ni-ate, *to slander*
a. Ca-pa-cious-ness, *largeness*
v. Ca-paç-i-tate, *to enable*
s. Ca-paç-i-ty, *ability*
v. Ca-pit-u-late, *to surrender*
ad. Ca-pri-cious-ly, *whimsically*
s. Cap-tiv-i-ty, *imprisonment*
a. Car-niv-o-rous, *feeding on flesh*
s. Ca-tas-tro-phe, *a dreadful event or accident*
s. Çe-leb-ri-ty, *renown*
s. Çe-ler-i-ty, *swiftness*
a. Çe-les-ti-ally, *heavenly*
a. Çen-so-ri-ous, *apt to censure*
a. Çen-trif-u-gal, *flying from the centre* [*centre*
*e.* Çen-trip-e-al, *tending to the*

s. Çer-tif-i-cate, *a written testimony*
a. Ce-ru-le-an, *sky-coloured*
v. Cha-rac-ter-ize, *to describe*
s. Çhi″-ca-ne-ry, *cunning*
a. Chi-mer-i-cal, *imaginary*
a. Chi-rur-gi-cal, *relating to surgery*
s. Çir-cum-fer-ençe, *the measure round any circular body*
s. Çiv-il-i-ty, *kindness*
v. Co-ag-u-late, *to congeal*
s. Co-hab-i-tant, *an inhabitant of the same place*
s. Co-he-ren-çy, *agreement*
a. Co-in-çi-dent, *happening together*
a. Col-lat-er-al, *not direct*
ad. Col-lec-tive-ly, *in a body*
s. Co-loph-o-ny, *rosin*
s. Col-le-gi-an, *a member of a college*
a. Col-lo-qui-al, *relating to conversation*
a. Com-bus-ti-ble, *apt to take fire*
s. Co-me-di-an, *a stage player*
v. Com-mem-o-rate, *to celebrate*
a. Com-men-da-ble, *praise-worthy*
a. Com-men-su-rate, *of equal measure*
v. Com-mi$^z$s-e-rate, *to pity*
s. Com-mis-sion-er, *one empowered to act*
a. Com-mo-di-ous, *convenient*
s. Com-mod-i-ty, *merchandise*
s. Com-mu-ni-cant, *one who receives the sacrament*
v. Com-mu-ni-cate, *to impart*
s. Com-mu-ni-ty, *society in general*

*a.* Com-par-a-tive *implying comparison*
*s.* Com-par-i-son, *act of comparing*
*a.* Com-pas-sion-ate, *tender*
*a.* Com-pat-i-ble, *consistent with*
*a.* Com-pen-di-ous, *short*
*s.* Com-pen-di-um, *an abridgment*
*s.* Com-pet-i-tor, *a rival*
*s.* Com-pla-çen-çy, *pleasure, satisfaction*
*s.* Com-plex-ed-ness, *complication*
*s.* Com-pos-i-tor, *one who sets for the press*
*a.* Com-pul-so-ry, *forcing*
*a.* Com-pu-ta-ble, *capable of being numbered*
*v.* Con-çil-i-ate, *to reconcile*
*s.* Con-cin-ni-ty, *decency*
*a.* Con-com-i-tant, *united with*
*s.* Con-den-si-ty, *thickness*
*a.* Con-di-tion-al, *including turns*
*s.* Con-fec-tion-er, *a maker of sweetmeats*
*v.* Con-fed-e-rate, *to league*
*s.* Com-for-mi-ty, *compliance with*
*a.* Con-form-a-ble, *suitable*
*a.* Con-ge-ni-al, *agreeing in disposition*
*v.* Con-grat-u-late, *to rejoice with*
*s.* Con-gru-i-ty, *fitness*
*s.* Con-jec-tur-er, *a guesser*
*ad.* Con-nec-tive-ly, *in union*
*a.* Con-nu-bi-al, *belonging to marriage*
*a.* Con-sid-er-ate, *regardful*
*a.* Con-so-la-ble, *easily comforted*
*v.* Con-sol-i-date, *to harden*
*a.* Con-spic-u-ous, *easy to be seen*
*s.* Con-spir-a-çy, *a plot*
*s.* Con-stit-u-ent, *an elector*

*a.* Con-strain-a-ble, *liable to constraint*
*a.* Con-su-ma-ble, *susceptible of destruction*
*v.* Con-tab-u-late, *to floor with boards*
*a.* Con-ta-gi-ous, *infectious*
*v.* Con-tam-i-nate, *to corrupt*
*a.* Con-tem-pla-tive, *studious*
*a.* Con-temp-ti-ble, *mean*
*a.* Con-temp-tu-ous, *scornful*
*ad.* Con-ten-tious-ly, *perversely*
*a.* Con-tig-u-ous, *adjoining*
*s.* Con-tin-gen-çy, *accidental possibility*
*ad.* Con-tin-gent-ly, *accidentally*
*a.* Con-tin-u-al, *incessant*
*s.* Con-tin-u-ance, *duration*
*a.* Con-tin-u-ate, *united*
*a.* Con-tin-u-ous, *joined*
*a.* Con-ve-ni-ent, *suitable*
*a.* Con-vex-i-ty, *outside of an orb*
*a.* Con-viv-i-al, *social, festive*
*v.* Co-op-er-ate, *to act jointly*
*a.* Cor-nig-e-rous, *horned*
*a.* Cor-po-re-al, *bodily*
*v.* Cor-rob-or-ate, *to strengthen*
*a.* Cor-ro-di-ble, *possible to be consumed*
*s.* Cos-mog-ra-phy, *a description of the universe*
*s.* Cre-den-tials, *letters of recommendation*
*v.* Cre-du-li-ty, *easiness of belief*
*s.* Cri-te-ri-on, *a mark of judgment*

*Accented on the third.*

*a.* Çir-cum-já-çent, *lying round*
*v.* Co-a-les-çenҫe, *union*

# SPELLING ASSISTANT.

*a.* Co-e-ter-nal, *eternal with*
*a.* Co-ex-is-tent, *existing with*
*a.* Com-pre-hen-sive, *full*
*s.* Cor-re-spon-dençe, *intercourse*
*a.* Cor-re-spon-dent, *answerable*

## D.

### Accented on the first.

*s.* Dél-i-ca-çy, *neatness, niceness*
*a.* Des-pi-ca-ble, *worthless*
*a.* Des-ul-to-ry, *unsettled*
*a.* Dil-a-to-ry, *loitering*
*a.* Dis-pu-ta-ble, *liable to contest*
*a.* Dis-so-lu-ble, *admitting separation*
*s.* Dor-mi-to-ry, *a sleeping-place*
*s.* Dys-en-te-ry, *a looseness*

### Accented on the second.

*v.* De-cáp-i-tate, *to behead*
*a.* De-çen-ni-al, *lasting ten years*
*a.* De-cid-u-ous, *falling off*
*a.* De-ci-so-ry, *able to decide*
*a.* De-clar-a-tive, *explanatory*
*s.* De-cliv-i-ty, *descent*
*a.* De-coc-ti-ble, *that which may be boiled or prepared*
*v.* De-cor-ti-cate, *to divest of bark*
*s.* De-crep-i-tude, *old age*
*a.* De-du-çi-ble, *drawn from*
*ad.* De-duc-tive-ly *consequently*
*s.* De-fi-cien-cy *defect*
*a.* De-fi-na-ble *that may be explained*
*a.* De-fla-gra-ble, *apt to burn*
*a.* De-fin-i-tive, *decisive*
*a* De-gen-er-ous, *vile, base*
*s.* De-for-mi-ty, *uglinss*
*v.* De-gen-er-ate, *to grow worse*

*a.* De-lec-ta-ble, *delightful*
*v.* De-lib-er-ate, *to think*
*ad.* De-li-cious-ly, *sweetly*
*ad.* De-light-ful-ly, *with delight*
*v.* De-lin-e-ate, *to describe*
*s.* De-lin-quen-cy. *a fault*
*a.* De-lir-i-ous, *light-headed*
*s.* De-moc-ra-çy, *government by the people*
*s.* De-mol-ish-er, *a destroyer*
*a.* De-mon-stra-tive, *convincing*
*v.* De-nom-i-nate, *to give name to*
*v.* De-op-pi-late, *to clear a passage*
*a.* De-pec-ti-ble, *tough*
*a.* De-plo-ra-ble, *sad, lamentable*
*v.* De-pop-u-late, *to unpeople*
*s.* De-prav-i-ty, *corruption of manners*
*v.* De-pre-çi-ate, *to undervalue*
*v.* De-ra-cin-ate, *to root up*
*a.* De-riv-a-tive, *derived from*
*a.* De-rog-a-tive, *derogating*
*a.* De-sic-ca-tive, *drying*
*a.* De-si-ra-ble, *to be wished for*
*a.* De-spi-sa-ble, *contemptible*
*s.* De-spon-den-çy, *despair*
*ad.* De-struc-tive-ly, *ruinously*
*a.* De-ter-mi-nate, *limited*
*a.* De-tes-ta-ble, *odious*
*a.* De-trac-to-ry, *defamatory*
*a.* De-vo-ti-on-al, *pertaining to devotion*
*s.* Dex-ter-i-ty, *expertness*
*s.* Di-ag-o-nal, *a line from angle to angle*
*s.* Di-am-e-ter, *the line which divides a circle equally*
*s.* Di″-oç-e-san, *a bishop*
*s.* Di″-rec-to-ry. *a book directing*
*s.* Dis-com-fi-ture, *overthrow*
*a.* Dis-con-so-late. *comfortless*

v. Dis-coun-te-nançe, *to give a check to*
s. Dis-cre"-ti-on, *prudence*
v. Dis-crim-i-nate, *to distinguish between*
s. Dis-cus-si-on, *examination*
s. Dis-junc-ti-on, *a disjoining*
s. Dis-loy-al-ty, *unfaithfulness*
s. Dis-par-i-ty, *inequality*
s. Dis-pen-sa-ry, *a medicinal warehouse*
s. Dis-per-si-on, *the act of scattering*
v. Dis-qual-i-fy, *to make unfit*
s. Dis-qui-e-tude, *restlessness*
s. Dis-sec-ti-on, *anatomy*
v. Dis-sem-i-nate, *to scatter*
s. Dis-sen-si-on, *strife*
a. Dis-sim-i-lar, *unlike*
s. Dis-syl-la-ble, *a word of two syllables*
s. Dis-tinc-ti-on, *a difference*
s. Dis-tor-ti-on, *a twisting*
v. Di"-ver-si-fy, *to vary*
s. Di"-ver-si-ty, *variance*
s. Di"-vin-i-ty, *the Godhead*
a. Di"-vis-i-ble, *that may be divided*
s. Do-çil-i-ty, *readiness to learn*
s. Do-na-ti-on, *a gift*
s. Dox-ol-o-gy, *a song of praise*
s. Duc-til-i-ty, *pliancy*
s. Du-pliç-i-ty, *deceit*
s. Du-ra-ti-on, *length of continuance*

*Accented on the third.*

s. De-cli-ná-tor, *an instrument in dialling*

s. Des-pe-ra-do, *a desperate person*
a. Det-ri-men-tal, *injurious*
a. Dis-af-fec-ted, *averse from*
s. Dis-a-gree-ment, *a difference*
a. Dis-con-tent-ed, *dissatisfied*
v. Dis-con-tin-ue, *to leave off*
v. Dis-in-her-it, *to cut off by will*
a. Dis-re-spect-ful, *uncivil, irreverent*
s. Dis-si-li-tion, *act of bursting*
s. Dis-so-lu-tion, *a melting*
a. Dis-syl-la-bic, *consisting of two syllables only*
s. Dis-til-la-tion, *act of dropping*
s. Dis-tri-bu-tion, *sharing amongst*
s. Div-i-na-tion, *a foretelling*
s. Dom-i-na-tion, *power*
a. Dom-i-neer-ing, *overbearing*
s. Dul-co-ra-tion, *act of sweetening*
s. Du-pli-ca-tion, *act of doubling*

E.

*Accented on the first.*

a. Ed-i-fy-ing, *instructive*
s. Ef-fi-ca-çy, *ability, force*
a. El-i-gi-ble, *preferable*
s. Em-is-sa-ry, *a spy, a secret agent*
s. Ep-i-cu-rism, *luxury*
s. Ep-i-lep-sy, *a convulsive disease*
a. E-qui-ta-ble, *just, candid*
a. Ex-e-cra-ble, *hateful*
a. Ex-em-pla-ry, *worthy of imitation*

# SPELLING ASSISTANT.

a. Ex-o-ra-ble, *easy to be intreated*
a. Ex-pi-a-ble, *that may be atoned for*
a. Ex-pli-ca-ble, *explainable*
ad. Ex-qui-site-ly, *with great perfection*
a. Ex-tri-ca-ble, *that may be disentangled*

*Accented on the second,*

s. E-bri-e-ty, *drunkenness*
a. Ec-çen-tri-cal, *deviating from the centre*
s. E-con-o-my, *good management*
s. E-da-ci-ty, *greediness*
a. Ef-fec-ti-ble, *practicable*
ad. Ef-fec-tive-ly, *powerfully*
a. Ef-fec-tu-al, *efficacious*
a. Ef-fem-i-nate, *womanish*
ad. Ef-fi-cient-ly, *with effect*
s. Ef-fron-te-ry, *impudence*
a. E-gre-gi-ous, *remarkable*
v. E-jac-u-late, *to throw out*
a. E-lab-o-rate, *finished with elegance, labour and diligence*
ad. E-lec-tive-ly, *by choice*
a. E-lec-to-ral, *having the dignity of an elector*
a. E-lec-to-ry, *a form of medicine*
s. E-lec-to-rate, *a German principality*
v. E-lec-tri-fy, *to excite suddenly*
a. E-le-gi-ac, *plaintive*
v. E-lim-i-nate, *to thrust out*
a. E-lip-ti-cal, *oval like*
v. E-lu-ci-date, *to explain*

a. E-lu-di-ble, *possible to be eluded*
a. E-lu-so-ry, *tending to elude*
v. E-ma-çe-rate, *to make lean*
v. E-ma-ci-ate, *to waste away*
v. E-man-çi-pate, *to free from slavery*
s. Em-broi-de-ry, *variegated needlework*
s. E-mer-gen-çy, *sudden necessity*
a. E-met-i-cal, *provoking vomits*
a. E-mol-li-ent, *assuaging*
s. E-mol-u-ment, *profit*
a. Em-phat-i-cal, *forcible*
s. Em-pir-i-çism, *quackery*
v. Em-pov-er-ish, *to make poor*
s. En-co-mi-um, *praise*
s. E-nor-mi-ty, *heinousness*
s. En-thu-'si-a'sm, *false inspiration*
s. En-thu-'si-ast, *one who thinks himself inspired*
v. E-nu-mer-ate, *to reckon up*
v. E-nun-ci-ate, *to declare*
a. E-pis-co-pal, *belonging to a bishop*
s. E-pit-o-me, *an abstract*
v. E-pit-o-mise, *to abridge*
s. E-qual-i-ty, *likeness*
a. E-quiv-a-lent, *of the same value*
a. E-quiv-o-cal, *doubtful*
v. E-quiv-o-cate, *to dissemble*
v. E-rad-i-cate, *to root out*
s. Er-ro-ne-ous, *full of errors*
s. Es-tab-lish-ment, *settled form*
s. E-ter-ni-ty, *endlessness, duration*
a. E-the-re-al, *belonging to the air*

THE SCHOLAR'S

- E-vac-u-ate, to empty
- s. E-van-gel-ist, one who
- r. E-rup-e-rate, to steam out
- n. E-vel-u-ate, to unfold
- n. E-ven-tu-al, in the end
- a. E---, capable of proof
- r. *Exag-ge-rate, to enlarge
- r. *Ex-as-pe-rate, to enrage
- n. Ex-cru-ti-ate, to remove
- s. *Ex-ec-u-tor, one who exe-
  cutes a will
- r. *Ex-em-pli-fy, to illustrate
- r. *Ex-hil-a-rate, to make cheerful
- r. *Ex-on-e-rate, to ---
- s. *Ex-po-ri-ment, ---
- s. *Ex-tr-di-um, a ---
- - Ex-pa-ti-ate, to enlarge on
- a. Ex-pe-di-ent, proper
- s. Ex-pe-ri-ence, practical ---
  ledge
- ad. Ex-hi---, patient
- s. Ex-po-si-tion, an explanation
- r. Ex-pos-tu-late, to reason
- ad. Ex-tem-pore, without study
- r. Ex-tem-po-rize, to speak ex-
  tempore
- ad. Ex-ten-sive-ly, widely
- v. Ex-ten-u-ate, to lessen
- n. Ex-ter-i-or, outward
- r. Ex-ter-mi-nate, to cast out
- ad. Ex-ter-nally, outwardly
- a. Ex-tin-si-cal, external
- a. Ex-tra-ne-ous, foreign
- a. Ex-trav-a-gant, wasteful
- s. Ex-trem-i-ty, ---
  ---
- a. *Ex-u-ber-ant, over-abundant

Accented on the third.

- s. E-bul-li-tion, a boiling up
- s. Ed-u-ca-tion, instruction
  - pr. eggs

- F---a-cious, powerful
- s. E-e-va-tion, a lifting up
- s. Elo--- ---
- s. Em-a-na-tion, a flowing out
- s. Em-bar-ras-tion, a grasp or
  shipwreck
- s. Em-bro-ca-tion, a fomentation
- s. Em-en-da-tion, amendment
- s. Em-u-la-tion, rivalry
- s. En-er-va-tion, a weakening
- s. E-qui-noc-tial, a circle ---
  hea---
- s. Er-u-di-tion, learning
- s. Es-ti-ma-tion, esteem
- s. Ev-o-lu-tion, an unfolding
- s. *Ex-al-ta-tion, a lifting up
- s. Ex-cla-ma-tion, an outcry
- s. Ex-e-cra-tion, a curse
- s. Ex-ha-la-tion, vapor
- s. Ex-hi-bi-tion, a show
- s. Ex-hor-ta-tion, advice
- s. Ex-pec-ta-tion, a looking for
- s. Ex-pe-di-tion, enterprise
- a. Ex-pe-di-tious, quick, speedy
- s. Ex-pi-a-tion, atonement
- s. Ex-pi-ra-tion, the end
- s. Ex-pla-na-tion, a making plain
- s. Ex-por-ta-tion, a sending
  goods abroad
- s. Ex-po-si-tion, an explanation
- s. Ex-tir-pa-tion, a rooting out
- s. *Ex-ul-ta-tion, excessive joy

F.

Accented on the first.

- a. Fig-u-ra-tive, typical
- s. Flat-u-len-cy, windiness
- a. Fol-low-ed, loved
- a. For-mi-da-ble, terrible

Accented on the second.

- r. Fa-cil-i-tate, to make easy

## SPELLING ASSISTANT

s. Fa-çil-i-ty, *easiness*
ad. Fal-la-cious-ly, *sophistically*
ad. Fa-mil-iar-ly, *easily*
s. Fa-nat-i-çi²sm, *religious zeal*
a. Fan-tas-ti-cal, *whimsical*
a. Fas-tid-i-ous, *disdainful*
s. Fa-tal-i-ty, *destiny*
s. Fe-cun-di-ty, *fruitfulness*
s. Fe-liç-i-ty, *happiness*
a. Fe-lo-ni-ous, *villainous*
s. Fe-roç-i-ty, *fierceness*
s. Fer-til-i-ty, *abundance*
s. Fes-tiv-i-ty, *gayety*
ad. Fic-ti-tious-ly, *falsely*
s. Fi″-del-i-ty, *trustiness*
s. Flu-id-i-ty, *the state of flowing*
ad. For-bid-den-ly, *unlawfully*
s. For-mal-i-ty, *preciseness*
a. For-tu-i-tous, *accidental*
s. Fra-ǰgil-i-ty, *brittleness*
s. Fra-ter-ni-ty, *society*
s. Frau-du-len-cy, *deceitfulness*
s. Fri‴-ǰgid-i-ty, *coldness*
s. Fru-gal-i-ty, *thriftiness*
s. Fu-til-i-ty, *silliness*
s. Fu-tu-ri-ty, *the time to come*

### G.

*Accented on the second.*

s. Gar-rú-li-ty, *talkativeness*
s. Gen-til-i-ty, *good breeding*
s. Ge-og-ra-phy, *description of the earth*
s. Ge-om-e-try, *the art of measuring*
s. Gram-ma-ri-an, *one skilled in grammar*
a. Gra-niv-o-rous, *feeding on grain*
s. Gra-tu-i-ty, *a free gift*

### H.

*Accented on the first.*

a. Háb-i-ta-ble, *that may be inhabited*
a. Het-er-o-dox, *contrary to the established opinion*
a. Hon-our-a-ble, *worthy of honour*
a. Hos-pi-ta-ble, *friendly*

*Accented on the second.*

s. Ha-bíl-i-ment, *clothing*
a. Ha-bit-u-al, *customary*
v. Ha-bit-u-ate *to accustom to*
a. Har-mo-ni-ous, *musical*
a. He-ret-ti-cal, *addicted to 'eresy* [*feet*
s. Hex²-am-e-ter, *a verse of six*
s. Hi-lar-i-ty, *cheerfulness*
s. His-to-ri-an, *a writer of history* [*history*
a. His-tor-i-cal, *belonging to*
a. Ho-mol-o-ǰgous, *proportional*
s. Hos-til-i-ty, *open war*
s. Hu-man-i-ty, *fellow-feeling*
s. Hu-mid-i-ty, *dampness*
s. Hu-mil-i-ty, *meekness*
a. Hy-drop-i-cal, *dropsical*
s. Hy-per-bo-le, *beyond the truth*
s. Hyp-oc-ri-sy, *dissimulation*
s. Hy-poth-e-sis, *a supposition*
a. Hys-ter-i-cal, *troubled with fits*

*Accented on the third.*

s. He²s-i-ta-tion, *doubt*
a. Hor-i-zón-tal, *level*
a. Hy-me-ni-al, *pertaining to marriage*

I.

*Accented on the first.*

s. Id-i-o-ti°sm, *folly*
s. Ig-no-mi-ny, *dishonour*
a. Im-i-ta-ble, *that may be imitated*
s. Im-po-ten-çy, *feebleness*
s. In-ter-çes-sor, *a mediator*
a. In-ter-est-ed, *influenced*
s. In-ter-lo-per, *an intruder*
s. In-ti-ma-çy, *strict friendship*
s. In-tri-ca-çy, *perplexity*
s. In-ven-to-ry, *a list*

*Accented on the second.*

a. I-dén-ti-cal, *the same*
s. I-den-ti-ty, *sameness*
a. I-dol-a-trous, *tending to idolatry*
s. I-dol-a-try, *pagan worship*
a. I-do-ne-ous, *fit, proper*
a. Il-lib-er-al, *ungenteel*
a. Il-lim-it-ed, *unbounded*
a. Il-lit-er-ate, *ignorant*
v. Il-lu-mi-nate, *to enlighten*
a. Il-lus-tra-tive, *able to elucidate*
a. Il-lus-tri-ous, *noble*
a. Im-mac-cu-late, *spotless*
v. Im-man-a-cle, *to fetter*
s. Im-men-si-ty, *infinity*
a. Im-mod-er-ate, *beyond due bounds*
s. Im-mod-es-ty, *want of delicacy*
v. Im-mor-tal-ize, *to perpetuate*
s. Im-mu-ni-ty, *a grant*
a. Im-mu-ta-ble, *unalterable*
a. Im-pal-pa-ble, *that cannot be felt*
a. Im-pas-sa-ble, *that cannot be passed*
s. Im-ped-i-ment, *hinderance*

a. Im-pen-i-tent, *unrepenting*
a. Im-per-a-tive, *commanding*
a. Im-pe-ri-al, *royal*
a. Im-pe-ri-ous, *haughty*
a. Im-per-ti-nent, *silly, absurd*
a. Im-per-vi-ous, *impenetrable*
a. Im-pet-u-ous, *violent*
s. Im-pi-e-ty, *wickedness*
a. Im-plac-a-ble, *not to be appeased*
a. Im-pol-i-tic, *imprudent*
a. Im-por-tu-nate, *very urgent*
v. Im-pov-er-ish, *to make poor*
a. Im-preg-na-ble, *not to be taken*
s. Im-pri°s-on-ment, *confinement*
a. Im-prob-a-ble, *unlikely*
s. Im-prob-i-ty, *dishonesty*
a. Im-prov-i-dent, *void of foresight*
s. Im-pu-ni-ty, *freedom from punishment*
a. Im-pu-ta-ble, *chargeable*
a. In-ac-cu-rate, *not exact*
a. In-ad-e-quate, *disproportionate*
a. In-an-i-mate, *void of life*
s. In-an-i-ty, *emptiness*
v. In-au-gu-rate, *to consecrate*
a. In-ca-pa-ble, *unable, unfit*
ad. In-cau-tious-ly, *unwarily*
s. In-cer-ti-tude, *uncertainty*
ad. In-ces-sant-ly, *continually*
v. In-cin-e-rate, *to burn to ashes*
a. In-ci-so-ry, *cutting*
s. In-clem-en-çy, *severity*
a. In-cli-na-ble, *willing*
ad. In-cog-ni-to, *in secret*
a. In-com-pe-tent, *incapable*
a. In-con-gru-ous, *unfit*
a. In-con-ti-nent, *unchaste*
a. In-cor-po-ral, *immaterial*

## SPELLING ASSISTANT.

a. In-cred-i-ble, *surpassing belief*
a. In-cul-pa-ble, *innocent*
a. In-cu-ri-ous, *inattentive*
a. In-def-i-nite, *unlimited*
a. In-del-i-ble, *not to be blotted*
a. In-del-i-cate, *without decency*
v. In-dem-ni-fy, *to secure*
s. In-dem-ni-ty, *security*
a. In-dif-fer-ent, *neutral*
s. In-dig-ni-ty, *affront*
a. In-doç-i-ble, *unteachable*
a. In-du-bi-ous, *not doubtful*
a. In-dus-tri-ous, *diligent*
v. In-e-bri-ate, *to make drunk*
a. In-ef-fa-ble, *unspeakable*
a. In-el-e-gant, *unbecoming*
a. In-fal-i-ble, *certain*
a. In-fe-ri-or, *lower in degree*
s. In-fin-i-ty, *endlessness*
s. In-fir-ma-ry, *an hospital or residence for the sick*
s. In-fir-mi-ty, *feebleness*
a. In-flam-ma-ble, *apt to take fire*
s. In-flex-i-ble, *immoveable*
v. In-fo-li-ate, *to cover with leaves*
s. In-for-mi-ty, *shapelessness*
a. In-ge-ni-ous, *inventive*
a. In-gen-u-ous, *sincere*
a. In-glo-ri-ous, *dishonourable*
v. In-gra-ti-ate, *to get in favour*
s. In-gra-ti-tude, *unthankfulness*
s. In-gre-di-ent, *part of composition*
v. In-gur-gi-tate, *to swallow*
s. In-ha-bi-tant, *dweller*
s. In-her-i-tançe, *a right*
ad. In-hu-man-ly, *savagely*
a. In-i"-qui-tous, *sinful*
s. In-i"-qui-ty, *sin*
v. In-i"-ti-ate, *to instruct in*
a. In-ju-ri-ous, *hurtful*

v. In-oc-u-late, *to graft*
a. In-or-di-nate, *immoderate*
s. In-qui-e-tude, *restlessness*
a. In-qui$^z$s-i-tive, *prying*
a. In-sa-ti-ate, *not to be satisfied*
a. In-sen-si-ble, *without sense*
a. In-sid-i-ous, *treacherous*
v. In-sin-u-ate, *to hint*
s. In-teg-ri-ty, *honesty*
s. In-tel-li-genee, *news*
a. In-tel-li-gent, *well-instructed*
s. In-tem-per-ançe, *excess*
v. In-ter-ro-gate, *to question*
v. In-tim-i-date, *to frighten*
v. In-tox-i-cate, *to make drunk*
a. In-trac-ta-ble, *ungovernable*
s. In-tru-$^z$si-on, *a forcing in*
a. In-tu-i-tive, *perceiving immediately*
v. In-val-i-date, *to make void*
s. In-va-$^z$si-on, *a hostile entrance, an attack*
v. In-ves-ti-gate, *to examine into*
a. In-vet-er-ate, *obstinate*
a. In-vid-i-ous, *envious*
v. In-vig-or-ate, *to strengthen*
a. In-vin-çi-ble, *unconquerable*
a. In-vi-o-late, *unhurt*
a. In-vi$^z$s-i-ble, *not seen*
a. I-ras-çi-ble, *disposed to anger*
a. I-ron-i-cal, *by way of raillery*
v. Ir-ra-di-ate, *to brighten*
a. Ir-re$^z$s-o-lute, *unresolved*
a. Ir-rev-er-ent, *disrespectful*
a. I-tin-er-ant, *journeying*

*Accented on the third.*

s. Il-lus-tra-tion, *a making plain*
s. Im-i-ta-tion, *imitating*
s Im-per-fec-tion, *a blemish*
s. Im-pli-ca-tion, *an inferring*

s. Im-por-ta-tion, *bringing from abroad*
s. Im-po-si-tion, *a deceiving*
s. Im-pre-ca-tion, *an oath*
s. Im-pu-ta-tion, *an ascribing to*
s. In-ad-vér-tence, *carelessness*
a. In-ad-ver-tent, *heedless*
a. In-co-he-rent, *inconsistent*
a. In-con-sis-tent, *not suitable*
a. In-au-spi-cious, *unfortunate*
s. In-car-na-tion, *assuming flesh*
s. In-cli-na-tion, *tendency to a point*
a. In-de-pen-dent, *free*
s. In-cu-ba-tion, *a hatching*
s. In-cur-va-tion, *a bending*
a. In-ex-haust-ed, *unspent*
s. In-di-ges-tion, *the state of meats unconcocted*
s. In-dig-na-tion, *anger mingled with contempt*
s. In-dis-cre-tion, *imprudence*
a. In-of-fen-sive, *harmless*
s. In-flam-ma-tion, *a heat in the blood*
s. In-for-ma-tion, *intelligence*
s. In-hi-bi-tion, *a forbidding*
a. In-ju-di-ci-ous, *void of judgment*
s. In-no-va-tion, *a new custom*
a. In-stru-men-tal, *serviceable*
s. In-qui-si-tion, *strict inquiry*
s. In-spi-ra-tion, *supernatural grace*
s. In-sti-tu-tion, *an establishment*
a. In-ter-ja-cent, *lying between*
a. In-suf-fi-cient, *inadequate*
s. In-sur-rec-tion, *a rebellion*
s. In-ter-ces-sion, *entreating for another*
s. In-ter-dic-tion, *a forbidding*
s. In-ter-mis-sion, *a pause*
s. In-ter-mix-ture, *a mingling*

a. In-ter-mu-ral, *lying between walls*
s. In-ter-reg-num, *the vacancy of a throne*
s. In-ter-rup-tion, *hinderance*
s. In-ter-ven-tion, *a coming between*
s. In-ti-ma-tion, *a hint*
s. In-tro-duc-tion, *a preface*
s. In-tu-i-tion, *immediate knowledge*
s. In-vi-ta-tion, *act of inviting*
s. In-un-da-tion, *a flood*
s. In-vo-ca-tion, *a devout calling on*
s. Ir-re-li-gion, *impiety*

## L.

*Accented on the first.*

a. Lám-en-ta-ble, *to be lamented*
s. Lap-i-da-ry, *one skilled in jewels*
a. Le̯g-en-da-ry, *fabulous*
s. Lin-e-a-ment, *a feature*
a. Lit-e-ra-ry, *respecting learning*
s. Lit-e-ra-ture, *learning*
s. Lu-mi-na-ry, *a shining body*

*Accented on the second.*

a. La-bó-ri-ous, *toilsome*
s. Le-gal-i-ty, *lawfulness*
a. Lé-git-i-mate, *born in marriage*
ad. Li-cen-tious-ly, *immorally*
ad. Li-ti-gious-ly, *wranglingly*
s. Lo-cal-i-ty, *existence in place*
s. Lon-gev-i-ty, *length of life*
s. Lo-qua"-ci-ty, *talkativeness*
s. Lub-bri"-ci-ty, *slipperiness*
s. Lu-cid-i-ty, *brightness*
a. Lu-cif-er-ous, *giving light*

SPELLING ASSISTANT. 91

a. \*Lux-u-ri-ant, *abounding*
a. \*Lux-u-ri-ous, *voluptuous*
    *Accented on the third.*
s. Lam-en-ta-tion, *loud grief*
s. Leˈg-is-la-tion, *act of giving law.*
a. Leˈg-is-lá-tive, *law-giving*
s. Leˈg-is-la-tor, *a law-giver*
s. Leˈg-is-la-ture, *the power which makes laws*
s. Lim-it-a-tion, *restriction*
s. Li-que-fac-tion, *the act of melting*
s. Lit-e-ra-ti, *the learned*
s. Lit-i-ga-tion, *law suit*
s. Lu-cu-bra-tion, *study by night*

### M.

*Accented on the first.*

s. Máˈg-is-tra-çy, *office of a magistrate*
s. Mal-e-fac-tor,† *a criminal*
s. Man-u-fac-ture,† *work done by art*
s. Mat-ri-mo-ny, *marriage*
s. May-or-al-ty, *office of mayor*
s. Me-di-a-tor, *an intercessor*
s. Mel-an-cho-ly, *gloomy*
v. Me-li-o-rate, *to better*
a. Mem-o-ra-ble, *worthy of note*
s. Mer-çe-na-ry, *a hireling*
a. Mil-i-ta-ry, *warlike*
s. Min-i-a-ture, *small in size*
s. Mis-çel-la-ny, *a general collection*
a. Mo-men-ta-ry, *not lasting*

s. Mon-as-te-ry, *a convent*
    *Accented on the second.*
s. Ma-çhi-ne-ry,\* *workmanship*
a. Mag-nan-i-mous, *brave*
a. Mag-net-ic al, *attractive*
s. Mag-nif-i-çençe, *splendour*
a. Mag-nif-i-çent, *pompous*
a. Ma-jes-ti-cal, *august, stately*
s. Ma-jor-i-ty, *the greater number*
a. Ma-lev-o-lent, *bearing ill will*
ad. Ma-li-cious-ly, *with malignity*
s. Ma-lig-ni-ty, *malice*
a. Ma-te-rial, *important*
a. Ma-tu-ri-ty, *ripeness*
a. Me-chan-i-cal, *skilled in mechanics*
a. Me-diç-i-nal, *physical*
a. Me-lo-di-ous, *full of melody*
s. Me-mo-ri-al, *a memento*
s. Me-ri-di-an, *noon, mid-day*
a. Me-thod-i-cal, *agreeable to method* [*a country*
s. Me-trop-o-lis, *the chief city of*
s. Miˮ-nor-i-ty, *the smaller number* [*racle*
a Miˮ-rac-u-lous, *done by mi-*
a. Mo-nar-chi-cal, *belonging to a monarch*
s. Mo-nop-o-list, *one who engrosses a trade or business entirely to himself*
v. Mo-nop-o-lize, *to engross commodities*
s. Mo-nop-o-ly, *an engrossing of goods*
s. Mo-not-o-ny, *a sameness of tone*
a. Mu-niç-i-pal, *belonging to a city*

\* *pr.* Lugs.
† Walker accents these on the third.
\* *pr.* Ma-sheen-e-re.

s. Mu-nif-i-çençe, *liberality*
a. Mu-nif-i-çent, *generous*
a. Mys-te-ri-ous, *unaccountable*
s. My-thol-o-Jgy, *system of fables*

*Accented on the third.*

s. Mach-i-na-tion, *a malicious scheme*
s. Ma ni-fés-to, *a public declaration*
s. Man-u-mis-sion, *a releasing slaves*
s. Math-e-mat-ics, *the science of quantity*
s. Me-di-a-tion, *intercession*
s. Med-i-ta-tion, *deep thought*
s. Mem-o-ran-dum, *a note of remembrance*
s. Men-su-ra-tion, *act of measuring*
s. Met-a-phyᶻs-ics, *a science*
s. Mis-be-hav-iour, *ill conduct*
s. Mis-con-cep-tion, *a false opinion*
s. Mis-con-struc-tion, *a wrong interpretation*
s. Mis-de-mean-or, *an offence*
s. Mit-i-ga-tion, *abatement*
s. Mod-e-ra-tion, *temperance*
s. Mod-u-la-tion, *harmony*
s. Mol-es-ta-tion, *disturbance*
s. Mu-ne-ra-tion, *reward*
s. Mul-ti-la-tion, *a maiming*

N.

*Accented on the first.*

a. Ná″-ti-on-al, *concerning a nation* [*nature*
s. Nat-u-ral-ist, *one skilled in*
a. Na-vi-ga-ble, *passable for ships*
s. Nav-i-ga-tor, *a sea voyager*
a. Ne″-ces-sa-ry, *proper*

s. Nec-or-man-çy, *conjuration*
s. Nig-gard-li-ness, *covetousness*
a. Nu-ga-to-ry, *trifling*
a. Nu-mer-a-ble, *that may be numbered*

*Accented on the second.*

s. Na-ti″-vi-ty, *birth*
s. Ne-çes-sity, *obligation : also poverty, want*
a. Ne-ta-ri-ous, *wicked*
v. Ne-go-ti-ate, *to treat*
s. Neu-tral-i-ty, *of neither side*
v. No-bil-i-tate, *to make noble*
s. No-bil-i-ty, *high birth*
s. Non-en-ti-ty, *not existing*
a. No-to-ri-al, *taken by a notary*
a. No-to-ri-ous, *publicly known*
a. Nu-mer-i-cal, *denoting numbers*

*Accented on the third.*

s. Nav-i-ga-tion, *art of sailing*
s. Nid-u-la-tion, *the time of remaining on the nest*
s. Nom-i-na-tion, *an appointing*
s. Nu-me-ra-tion, *the art of numbering*

O.

*Accented on the first.*

s. Ob-sti-na-çy, *stubbornness*
s. Oc-cu-pi-er, *a possessor*
a. Op-er-a-tive, *effective*
s. Or-a-tory, *eloquence*
a. Or-di-na-ry, *common*

*Accented on the second.*

s. Ob-dú-ra-cy, *hardness of heart*
a. O-be-di-ent, *dutiful*
v. Ob-lit-er-ate, *to blot out*
s. Ob-liv-i-on, *forgetfulness*

s. Ob-scen-i-ty, *indecency*
s. Ob-scu-ri-ty, *privacy*
a. Ob-se-qui-ous, *obedient*
a. Ob-strep-er-ous, *clamorous*
a. Oc-ca-sion-al *usual*
v. Of-fi-ci-ate, *to act for another*
s. Of-fi-cious-ness, *overforward*
a. Om-ni-po-tent, *all-powerful*
s. Om-nis-ci-ence, *infinite knowledge*
a. Om-nis-ci-ent, *all-knowing*
a. Om-niv-or-ous, *all-devouring*
s. On-tol-o-gy, *metaphysics*
s. O-pa-ci-ty, *want of transparency*
s. O-pin-ion-ist, *one strongly attached to his own opinion*
a. Op-pro-bri-ous, *reproachful*
a. O-rac-u-lar, *uttering oracles*
a. Or-bic-u-lar, *spherical*
s. O-ri″-gi-nal,* *first copy*
s. Or-thog-ra-phy, *correct spelling*

Accented on the third.

s. Ob-li-ga-tion, *favour*
s. Ob-ser-va-tion, *remark*
s. Oc-cu-pa-tion, *trade or calling*
a. Om-ni-préˣs-ent, *present every where*
s. Op-er-a-tion, *action, effect*
s. Op-po-si-tion, *an opposing*
s. Or-di-na-tion, *an ordaining*
a. O-ri-en-tal, *eastern*
a. Or-na-men-tal, *serving to embellish*
s. Os-cil-la-tion, *a swinging*
s. Os-ten-ta-tion, *vain show*
v. O-ver-bur-den, *to overload*

* *pr.* O-rid-je-nal.

P

Accented on the first.

s. Pa-ci-fi-er, *one who pacifies*
s. Pag-e-an-try, *pomp, show*
a. Pal-a-ta-ble, *pleasant to the taste*
a. Pal-li-a-tive, *extenuating*
s. Pal-pa-ble-ness, *plainness*
v. Pan-e-gyr-ize, *to praise highly*
s. Par-al-lel-ism, *state of being parallel*
ad. Par-don-a-bly, *excusably*
s. Par-si-mo-ny, *sparingness*
s. Pas-sion-ate-ness, *aptness to be in a passion*
a. Pas-tur-a-ble, *fit for pasture*
s. Pa-tri-ar-chy, *jurisdiction of a patriarch*
s. Pat-ri-mo-ny, *an inheritance*
s. Pa-tri-ot-iˣsm, *public virtue*
s. Pec-u-la-tor, *robber of the public*
a. Pen-e-tra-ble, *that may be pierced*
a. Pen-e-tra-tive, *piercing*
v. Per-e-gri-nate, *to travel*
a. Per-emp-to-ry, *absolute*
s. Per-fo-ra-tor, *the instrument of boring*
ad. Per-il-ous-ly, *dangerously*
s. Per-il-ous-ness, *dangerousness*
a. Per-ish-a-ble, *liable to perish*
s. Per-i-win-kle, *a sea snail*
s. Per-ma-nen-cy, *duration*
s. Per-ri″-phe-ry, *circumference*
s. Per-se-cu-tor, *an oppressor*
ad. Per-son-al-ly, *in person*
ad. Per-ti-nent-ly, *appositely*
ad. Pes-ti-lent-ly, *destructively*
a. Pet-i-to-ry, *petitioning*
ad. Pil-fer-ing-ly, *filchingly*
ad. Pit-e-ous-ly, *sadly*

*a.* Pit-i-a-ble, *deserving pity*
*a l.* Pit-i-ful-ly, *mournfully*
*s.* Pla-gi-a-ry, *a thief in literature*
*a.* Pleas-ur-a-ble, *delightful*
*s.* Plen-te-ous-ness, *abundance*
*a.* Pli-a-ble-ness, *flexibility*
*a.* Prac-ti-ca-ble, *that may be done* [*a prebend*
*s.* Preb-en-da-ry, *he who holds*
*a.* Pred-a-to-ry, *plundering*
*s.* Pred-e-ces-sor,\* *one going before*
*a.* Pref-er-a-ble, *better*
*s.* Pres-by-te-ry, *priesthood*
*a.* Prof-it-a-ble, *useful*
*s.* Prof-li-ga-cy, *abandoned conduct*
*s.* Prom-on-to-ry, *a head land*
*s.* Pros-e-cu-tor, *one who sues at law*
*s.* Pur-ga-to-ry, *a fictitious place of punishment after death*

*Accented on the second.*

*a.* Pa-ro-chi-al, *belonging to a parish*
*v.* Par-ti-ci-pa-te, *to partake*
*s.* Pen-in-su-la, *almost an island*
*a.* Pe-nu-ri-ous, *niggardly*
*v.* Per-am-bu-late, *to walk about*
*a.* Per-cep-ti-ble, *easily perceived*
*a.* Per-en-ni-al, *continued*
*a.* Per-fid-i-ous, *false, treacherous*
*a.* Per-pet-u-al, *endless* [*petual*
*v.* Per-pet-u-ate, *to make per-*
*a.* Per-spic-u-ous, *clear*
*s.* Phe-nom-e-non, *a natural appearance*
*s.* Phil-an-thro-py, *love of mankind*

\* *Accented on the third.*

*s.* Phil-ol-o-gy, *grammatical learning*
*s.* Phil-o-so-phy, *knowledge, natural or moral*
*s.* Phle-bot-o-my, *blood-letting*
*s.* Plu-ral-i-ty, *more than one*
*a.* Po-et-i-cal, *pertaining poetry*
*a.* Po-lit-i-cal, *relating to politic*
*a.* Pos-te-ri-or, *latter*
*s.* Pos-te-ri-ty, *after age*
*a.* Prag-mat-i-cal, *impertinent*
*a.* Pre-ca-ri-ous, *uncertain*
*a.* Pre-cip-i-tate, *very hasty*
*v.* Pre-des-ti-nate, *to fore-ordain*
*s.* Pre-dic-a-ment, *condition*
*a.* Pre-dom-i-nant, *prevailing*
*s.* Pre-em-i-nence, *superiority*
*v.* Pre-med-i-tate, *to think beforehand*
*v.* Pre-oc-cu-py, *to possess first*
*a.* Pre-par-a-tive, *serving to prepare*
*v.* Pre-pon-der-ate, *to outweigh*
*a.* Pre-pos-te-rous, *absurd*
*s.* Pre-rog-a-tive, *special right*
*s.* Pre-ser-va-tive, *a safeguard*
*s.* Pro-fun-di-ty, *depth*
*s.* Pro-gen-i-tor, *a forefather*
*v.* Prog-nos-ti-cate, *to foretell*
*s.* Pro-lix-i-ty, *tediousness*
*a.* Pro-mis-cu-ous, *mixed*
*s.* Pro-pen-si-ty, *inclination*
*s.* Pro-pri-e-tor, *an owner*
*s.* Pro-pri-e-ty, *justness*
*s.* Pros-per-i-ty, *good success*
*s.* Pro-tu-ber-ance, *a swelling out*
*a.* Pro-ver-bi-al, *relating to proverbs*
*a.* Pro-vin-ci-al, *of a province*
*s.* Prox-im-i-ty, *nearness*
*s.* Punc-til-i-o, *a trifling formal-*

*Accented on the third.*

s. Pal-li-a-tion, *an extenuation*
s. Pal-pi-ta-tion, *a parting*
s. Pan-e-gyr-ic, *encomium*
s. Pen-e-tra-tion, *sagacity*
a. Pen-i-ten-ti-al, *sorrowful*
s. Per-fo-ra-tion, *a boring through*
s. Per-se-cu-tion, *oppression*
s. Per-se-ve-rance, *constancy*
a. Per-spi-ca-cious, *quick sighted*
s. Per-spi-ra-tion, *a sweating*
a. Per-ti-na-cious, *obstinate*
s. Per-tur-ba-tion, *trouble of mind*
s. Pes-ti-len-tial, *infectious*
s. Pet-ri-fac-tion, *any thing changed into stone*
s. Pol-i-ti-cian, *one skilled in politics*
s. Pop-u-la-tion, *the number of people*
s. Pre-con-cep-tion, *conceiving beforehand*
a. Pre-ju-di-cial, *hurtful*
s. Pre-pos-ses-sion, *prejudice*
s. Pre-sen-ta-tion, *a presenting*
s. Pres-er-va-tion, *a preserving*
s. Proc-la-ma-tion, *a public notice*
s. Proc-u-ra-tor, *an agent*
s. Prof-a-na-tion, *a profaning*
s. Pro-hi-bi-tion, *a forbidding*
s. Prol-on-ga-tion, *a lengthening*
s. Pro-mul-ga-tion, *a making public*
s. Prop-a-ga-tion, *increase*
s. Pros-e-cu-tion, *a suit at law*
s. Prot-es-ta-tion, *an assurance*
a. Prov-i-den-tial, *effected by Providence*
s. Prov-o-ca-tion, *cause of anger*
s. Pub-li-ca-tion, *edition of a book*
s. Punc-tu-a-tion, *art of pointing in writing*
s. Pu-tre-fac-tion, *rottenness*

Q.

*Accented on the second.*

s. Qua-ter-ni-on, *the number four*
a. Quo-tid-i-an, *daily*

R.

*Accented on the first.*

a. Rea-son-a-ble, *just*
a. Rep-u-ta-ble, *of good repute*
a. Rev-o-ca-ble, *that may be recalled*

*Accented on the second.*

s. Ra-pac-i-ty, *excessive greediness*
s. Ra-pid-i-ty, *swiftness*
s. Re-al-i-ty, *truth*
s. Re-cep-ta-cle, *a place to receive*
a. Re-cip-ro-cal, *mutual*
s. Re-cog-ni-sance, *a bond*
v. Re-crim-i-nate, *to accuse in return*
s. Re-dun-dan-cy, *superfluity*
a. Re-frac-to-ry, *obstinate*
s. Re-gal-i-ty, *royalty*
v. Re-gen-er-ate, *to renew*
v. Re-it-er-ate, *to repeat again*
a. Re-mark-a-ble, *observable*
v. Re-mu-ner-ate, *to reward*
v. Re-nu-mer-ate, *to pay back*
s. Re-pub-li-can, *a subject of a republic*
v. Re-pu-di-ate, *to divorce*

*a.* Re-ˣsis-ti-ble, *that may be resisted* [spect
*a.* Re-spec-ta-ble, *worthy of re-*
*a.* Re-spon-si-ble, *answerable*
*a.* Re-sto-ra-tive, *that recruits*
*v.* Re-sus-ci-tate, *to renew*
*v.* Re-tal-i-ate, *to return*
*v.* Re-ver-ber-ate, *to rebound*
*a.* Rhe-tor-i-cal, *pertaining to rhetoric*
*a.* Ri-dic-u-lous, *silly*
*s.* Ro-tun-di-ty, *roundness*
*s.* Rus-tic-i-ty, *clownishness*

Accented on the third.

*s.* Ra-re-fác-ti-on, *expansion of parts*
*s.* Re-can-ta-ti-on, *an unsaying*
*s.* Re″-ci-ta-ti-on, *a repeating*
*s.* Re″-cog-ni-ti-on,* *a calling to mind*
*s.* Rec-ol-lec-ti-on, *remembrance*
*v.* Rec-on-nói-tre,* *to view*
*s.* Rec-re-a-ti-on, *amusement*
*s.* Ref-or-ma-ti-on, *amendment of life*
*s.* Ref-u-ta-ti-on, *a disproving*
*s.* Reg-u-la-ti-on, *method, rule*
*s.* Reg-u-la-tor, *that regulates*
*s.* Re-im-burse-ment, *repayment*
*s.* Re-en-force-ment, *supply fresh assistance*
*s.* Re-lax-a-ti-on, *respite from study*
*s.* Rep-ar-a-ti-on, *a repairing*
*s.* Re-per-cus-si-on, *a rebounding*
*s.* Rep-e-ti″-ti-on, *a repeating*
*s.* Rep-re-hen-si-on, *reproof*
*s.* Rep-u-ta-ti-on, *honour*
*s.* Reˣs-er-va-ti-on, *a keeping in store*

* pr. Rek-kog-nish-an.
* pr. Reck-on-noi-tur

*s.* Reˣs-ig-na-ti-on, *a resigning*
*s.* Reˣs-o-lu-ti-on, *design, courage*
*s.* Res-pi″-ra-ti-on, *a breathing*
*s.* Res-ti″-tu-ti-on, *a restoring*
*s.* Res-to-ra-ti-on, *a recovery*
*s.* Reˣs-ur-rec-ti-on, *a rising from the dead*
*s.* Re-tri″-bu-ti-on, *repayment*
*s.* Ret-ro-spec-ti-on, *a reviewing or looking backwards*
*s.* Rev-e-la-ti-on, *a revealing*
*a.* Rev-er-en-ti-al, *respectful*
*s* Rev-o-ca-ti-on, *a recalling*
*s.* Rev-o-lu-ti-on, *change in government*

S.

Accented on the first.

*a.* Sál-u-ta-ry, *wholesome*
*s.* Sanc-ti-mo-ny, *holiness*
*s.* Sanc-tu-a-ry, *a holy place*
*a.* San-gui-na-ry, *bloody* [time
*a.* Sea-ˣson-a-ble, *at a proper*
*a.* Sec-on-da-ry, *second*
*s.* Sec-re-ta-ry, *one who writes for another*
*a.* Sed-en-ta-ry, *sitting much*
*s* Sem-i-cir-cle, *half a circle*
*s.* Sem-i-na-ry, *a school*
*a.* Ser-vice-a-ble, *useful*
*a.* So-ci-a-ble, *friendly*
*a.* Sol-i-ta-ry, *retired*
*s.* Sov-er-eign-ty, *supreme power*
*a.* Spec-u-la-tive, *contemplative*
*s.* Spec-u-la-tor, *a theorist*
*s.* Stat-u-a-ry, *one who carves images*
*a.* Sump-tu-a-ry, *relating to expense*

*Accented on the second*

- a. Sab-bat-i-cal, *resembling the sabbath*
- ad Sa-ga-cious-ly, *acutely*
- s. Sa-ga″-çi-ty, *quickness of understanding*
- a. Sal-u-bri-ous, *healthful*
- s. Sal-u-bri-ty, *wholesomeness*
- s. Sa-ti-e-ty,* *fulness*
- v. Sa-tir-i-cal, *censorious*
- s. Sa-tu-ri-ty, *fulness*
- a. Sa-tur-ni-an, *happy, golden*
- s. Sce-nog-ra-phy, *the art of perspective*
- a. Schiˣs-ma-ti-cal, *separating from the church*
- a. Scho-las-ti-cal, *belonging to a school*
- a. Scor-bu-ti-cal, *diseased with the scurvy*
- s. Scu-ril-i-ty, *low abuse*
- ad. Se-di-tious-ly, *tumultuously*
- s. Se-di-tious-ness, *turbulence*
- s. Se-du-li-ty, *diligent assiduity*
- a. Seig-neu-ri-al,† *independent*
- a. Se-mip-e-dal, *containing half a foot*
- s. Sen-so-ri-um, *the seat of sense*
- ad. Sen-ten-tious-ly, *with striking brevity*
- s. Sen-ten-tious-ness, *pithiness of sentences*
- a. Sep-ten-ni-al, *lasting seven years*
- s. Sep-ten-tri-on, *the north*
- a. Se-raph-ic-al, *angelic*
- s. Se-ren-i-ty, *calmness*
- s. Ser-vil-i-ty, *meanness*
- s. Se-ver-i-ty, *rigour*

† *pr.* Sa-ti-e-ty, *not* Sa-si-e-ty.
† *pr.* Se-nu-re-al.

- a. Sex-en-ni-al, *lasting six years*
- s. Short-sight-ed-ness, *defect of sight.*
- a. Si-de-re-al, *starry*
- a. Sig-nif-i-cant, *expressive*
- s. Sim-il-i-tude, *likeness*
- s. Sim-pliç-i-ty, *plainness*
- s. Sin-çer-i-ty, *purity of mind*
- s. So-bri-e-ty, *temperance*
- s. So-ci-e-ty, *company*
- s. So-dal-i-ty, *fraternity*
- s. So-lem-ni-ty, *gravity*
- a. So-li″-çit-ous, *anxious*
- s. So-li-ci-tress, *a woman who solicits for another*
- s. So-li″-ci-tude, *anxiety*
- s. So-lid-i-ty *firmness*
- s. So-lil-o-quy, *a talking to one's self*
- a. Som-nif-e-rous, *causing sleep*
- a. So-nif-er-ous, *bringing sound*
- ad. So-no-rous-ly, *with high sounds*
- a. So-phis-ti-cal, *deceitful*
- a. Spon-ta-ne-ous, *voluntary*
- s. Sta-bil-i-ty, *firmness*
- s. Ster-il-i-ty, *barrenness*
- s. Stu-pid-i-ty, *dulness*
- s. Sub-lim-i-ty, *height*
- a. Sub-or-di-nate, *inferior*
- a. Sub-ser-vi-ent, *instrumental*
- v. Sub-stan-ti-ate, *to establish*
- ad. Suc-çes-sive-ly, *in succession*
- a. Sul-phu-re-ous, *containing sulphur*
- a. Su-per-flu-ous, *overmuch*
- a. Su-pe-ri-or, *greater, prefferable*
- a. Su-per-la-tive, *highest degree*
- s. Su-pre-ma-çy, *sovereignty*
- a. Sur-mount-a-ble, *conquerable*
- a. Sus-çep-ti-ble, *capable of impression*
- a. Sym-bol-i-cal, *typical*

9

*a.* **Sy-non-y-mous,** *of the same signification*

*Accented on the third.*

*a.* Sac-er-dó-tal, *priestly*
*a.* Sac-ra-men-tal, *relating to the sacrament*
*a.* Sac-ri-li-gious, *violating things sacred*
*s.* Sal-u-ta-tion, *a greeting*
*s.* Sat-is-fac-tion, *content, pleasure*
*a.* Sci-en-tif-ic, *containing knowledge*
*s.* Scin-til-la-tion, *a sparkling*
*s.* Seg-re-ga-tion, *separation from others*
*a.* Sem-i-cir-cled, *half round*
*s.* Sem-i-co-lon, *this mark* [;]
*s.* Sem-i-flu-id, *imperfectly fluid*
*a.* Sem-i-lu-nar, *like a half moon*
*s.* Sem-i-na-tion, *art of sowing*
*s.* Sep-a-ra-tion, *disjunction*
*s.* Se-ques-tra-tion, *a confiscation*
*s.* Se-ques-tra-tor, *one who deprives a man of property, a confiscator*
*s.* Sit-u-a-tion, *place or office*
*s.* Spec-u-la-tion, *scheming*
*s.* Spo-li-a-tion, *a plundering*
*s.* Ster-nu-ta-tion, *act of sneezing*
*s.* Stim-u-la-tion, *motive*
*s.* Stip-u-la-tion, *an agreement*
*s.* Stu-pe-fac-tion, *insensibility*
*s.* Sub-ju-ga-tion, *a subduing*
*s.* Suf-fo-ca-tion, *a smothering*
*s.* Su-per-car-go, *manager of a ship's cargo*
*a.* Su-per-fi-cial, *shallow, imperfect*
*s.* Su-per-fi-cies, *the surface*
*s.* Su-per-scrip-tion, *a direction*
*s.* Su-per-sti-tion, *mistaken piety*
*a.* Su-per-sti-tious, *bigoted*

*s.* Su-per-struc-ture, *what is built on another*
*s.* Su-per-vi-sor, *an inspector*
*s.* Sup-pli-ca-tion, *earnest prayer*
*s.* Sup-po-si-tion, *imagination*
*s.* Sup-pu-ra-tion, *formation of matter*
*a.* Sur-rep-ti-tious, *false*
*s.* Sus-ci-ta-tion, *a raising up*
*a.* Sym-pa-thet-ic, *compassionate*

*Accented on the last.*

*v.* Su-per-a-bóund, *to be superfluous*
*v.* Su-per-in-duçe, *to add*
*v.* Su-per-in-tend, *to oversee*

**T.**

*Accented on the first.*

*s.* Tab-er-na-cle, *a place of worship*
*a.* Tab-u-la-ted, *having a flat surface*
*ad.* Te-di-ous-ly, *in such a manner as to weary*
*s.* Te-di-ous-ness, *wearisomeness by continuance*
*s.* Tem-per-a-ment, *constitution*
*ad.* Tem-per-ate-ly, *moderately*
*s.* Tém-pe-ra-ture, *state or situation*
*a.* Tem-po-ra-ry, *for a time*
*s.* Tem-po-ri-zer, *a time server*
*a.* Ten-ant-a-ble, *inhabitable*
*s.* Ter-ri-to-ry, *a district or country*
*s.* Tes-ti-mo-ny, *evidence*
*a.* Tol-er-a-ble, *passable*
*a.* Tran-si-to-ry, *passing away*
*a.* Trea-son-a-ble, *guilty of treason*
*a.* Trib-u-ta-ry, *paying tribute*

*Accented on the second.*

s. Tau-tól-o-gy, *repetition of words*
s. Te-mer-i-ty, *rashness*
a. Tem-pes-tu-ous, *stormy*
a. Te-ne-bri-ous, *dark, gloomy*
s. Te-nu-i-ty, *smallness*
s. Te-pid-i-ty *lukewarmness*
a. Ter-ra-que-ous, *consisting of land and water*
a. Ter-res-tri-al, *earthly*
a. Te-trag-o-nal, *square*
a. The-at-ri-cal, *belonging to the stage*
s. The-oc-ra-cy, *divine government*
s. The-od-o-lite, *an instrument for measuring land*
s. The-ol-o-gist, *a divine*
s. The-ol-o-gy, *divinity*
a. Thra-son-ic-al, *boastful*
s. Tim-id-i-ty, *fearfulness*
s. To-pog-ra-phy, *description of particular places*
s. To-tal-i-ty, *whole quantity*
a. Tra-di-tion-al, *delivered by tradition*
s. Tra-ge-di-an, *a writer of tragedy*
s. Tran-quil-li-ty, *peace of mind*
s. Tran-scen-den-cy, *excellence*
a. Trans-la-to-ry, *transferring*
s. Trans-pa-ren-cy, *that which will transmit light*
a. Tri-an-gu-lar, *having three angles*
a. Tri-en-ni-al, *lasting three years*
s. Tri-syl-la-ble, *a word of three syllables*
a. Tu-mul-tu-ous, *disorderly*
a. Ty-ran-ni-cal, *like a tyrant*

U

s. U-bi"-qui-ty, *a being in all places*
a. U-nan-i-mous, *of one mind*
a. Un-ten-a-ble, *uninhabitable*
a. Un-wea-ri-ed, *not tired*
s. Ur-ban-i-ty, *good breeding*
a. *Ux-o-ri-ous, *submissively fond of a wife*

V

*Accented on the first.*

a. Vál-u-a-ble, *precious*
a. Va-ri-a-ble, *changeable*
v. Va-ri-e-gate, *to diversify*
s. Ve-ge-ta-ble,† *a plant*
a. Ve-ge-ta-tive,‡ *producing vegetation*
a. Ven-er-a-ble, *respectable*
s. Ven-ti-la-tor, *an instrument to air houses*
a. Vis-ion-a-ry, *ideal*
a. Vol-un-ta-ry, *perfectly free*
a. Vul-ner-a-ble, *that may be wounded*

*Accented on the second.*

s. Va-cu-i-ty, *emptiness*
a. Vain-glo-ri-ous, *vain without merit*
s. Va-lid-i-ty, *efficacy, certainty*
s. Va-ri-e-ty, *change*
s. Ve-loç-i-ty, *quick motion*
s. Ve-raç-i-ty, *truth*
a. Ver-ti-gi-nous,§ *whirling, giddy*

\* *pr.* Ugs.
† *pr.* Ved-je-ta-bl.
‡ *pr.* Ved-je-ta-tiv.
§ *pr.* Ver-tid'-jin-us.

s. Vi-cin-i-ty, *neighbourhood*
s. Vic-is-si-tude, *change*
a. Vic-to-ri-ous, *conquering*
s. Vi-vac-i-ty, *liveliness*
a. Vo-cif-er-ous, *noisy*
a. Vo-lu-mi-nous, *of many volumes*
a. Vo-lup-tu-ous, *luxurious*

*Accented on the third.*

s. Val-u-a-tion, *a set value*

s. Va-ri-a-tion, *a change*
s. Veg-e-ta-tion, *growth*
s. Ven-er-a-tion, *reverence*
s. Ven-ti-la-tion, *a cooling*
s. Ver-ber-a-tion, *a beating*
s. Vin-di-ca-tion, *defence*
s. Vi-o-la-tion, *infringement*
s. Vis-it-a-tion, *a visiting*

## WORDS OF FIVE SYLLABLES.

Parts of Speech.

### A.

*Accented on the first.*

s. Ad-mi-ra-ble-ness, *the quality of being admirable*
s. A-mi-a-ble-ness, *lovliness*
s. Ap-pli-ca-ble-ness, *fitness to be applied*
ad. Ar-bi-tra-ri-ly, *despotically*

*Accented on the second.*

a. A-bol-ish-a-ble, *that which may be abolished*
a. A-bom-i-na-ble, *detestable*
a. Ab-sol-u-to-ry, *that which absolves*
a. Ab-ste-mi-ous-ly, *without indulgence*
s. Ab-ste-mi-ous-ness, *the quality of being abstemious*
a. Ac-com-mo-da-ble, *that which may be fitted*
ad. Ac-com-mo-date-ly, *suitably fitly*
a. Ac-com-pa-na-ble, *sociable*

Parts of Speech.

a. Ad-min-is-tra-tive, *that which administers*
s. A-po″-the-ca-ry, *one who compounds and sells*
a. Au-thor-i-ta-tive, *having authority*
a. Aux-il-i-a-ry,* *helping*

*Accented on the third*

a. Ac-a-de-mi-cal, *relating to an academy*
s. Ac-a-de-mi-an, *a scholar*
a. Ac-a-dem-i-cal, *belonging to an academy*
ad. Ac-ci-den-tal-ly, *casually*
s. Ac-ci-den-tal-ness, *the quality of being accidental*
a. A-di-aph-o-rous, *neutral*
s. A-di-aph-o-ry, *neutrality*
a. Ad-mi-nic-u-lar, *that which gives help*
a. Ad-van-ta-ge-ous, *profitable*
s. Af-fa-bil-i-ty, *easiness of manners*

* pr. Awg-zil-ya-re.

## SPELLING ASSISTANT. 101

*a.* Al-i-men-ta-ry, *nourishing*
*a.* Al-le-go-ri-cal, *figurative*
*a.* Al-pha-bet-i-cal, *belonging to the alphabet*
*s* Am-phi-the-a-tre, *a Roman building for public sports*
*v.* A″-na-them-a-tize, *to pronounce accursed by ecclesiastical authority*
*s.* An-i-mos-i-ty, *hatred*
*s.* An-ni-ver-sa-ry, *a yearly celebration*
*s.* Arch-i-pel-a-go, *part of the Mediterranean*
*s.* Ar-gu-men-ta-tive, *reasoning*
*s.* A″-ris-toc-ra-çy, *government by the nobility*
*a.* A″-rith-met-i-cal, *belonging to arithmetic*
*s.* As-sa-foet-i-da, *a gum of an offensive smell*
*s.* As-si-du-i-ty, *diligence*
*a.* As-tro-nom-i-cal, *belonging to astronomy*
*s.* Au-then-tiç-i-ty, *genuineness*

*Accented on the fourth.*

*s.* Ab-bre-vi-a-tion, *shortening*
*s.* Ab-bre-vi-a-tor, *one who abridges*
*s.* Ab-la-que-a-tion, *opening the ground about the roots of trees*
*s.* A-bom-i-na-tion, *a detestable thing*
*s.* Ac-cel-er-a-tion, *the act of quickening*
*s.* Ac-cen-tu-a-tion, *the act of placing the accent*
*s.* Ac-com-mo-da-tion, *provision of conveniencies*
*s.* Ac-cu-mu-la-tion, *a heaping up*
*s.* Ad-ju-di-ca-tion, *act of granting something to a litigant*

*s.* Al-le-vi-a-tion, *an easing*
*s.* Am-pli-fi-ca-tion, *an enlargement*
*s.* An-i-mad-ver-sion, *censure*
*s.* An-ni-hi-la-tion, *reducing to nothing*
*s.* An-ti-ci-pa-tion, *foretaste*
*s.* Ap-pro-pri-a-tion, *claiming to one's self*
*s.* Ap-prox-i-ma-tion, *a coming nearer*
*s.* A-rith-me-ti-cian, *one skilled in arithmetic*
*s.* Ar-tic-u-la-tion, *the act of forming words*
*s.* As-sas-si-na-tion, *a murdering*
*s.* As-sev-er-a-tion, *an earnest vouching*
*s.* As-sim-i-la-tion, *a making like*
*s.* As-so-ci-a-tion, *a union*
*s.* At-ten-u-a-tion, *a making less*

### B.

*Accented on the third.*

*s.* Bac-cha-na-li-an, *a drunkard*
*s.* Ben-e-fi-cial-ness, *profit*
*s.* Bib-li-og-ra-pher, *a transcriber*
*a.* Bib-li-oth-e-cal, *belonging to a library*
*a.* Bi-o-graph-i-cal, *relating to biography*
*s.* Brag-ga-do-çi-o, *a boaster*

### C.

*Accented on the second.*

*a.* Ca-lam-i-tous-ness, *misery*
*s.* Ce-le-bri-ous-ness, *fame*
*ad.* Cen-so-ri-ous-ly, *in a severe reflecting manner*

s. Cen-so-ri-ous-ness, *disposition to reproach*
s. Cen-tu-ri-a-tor, *one who distinguishes times by centuries*
ad. Chi-mer-ic-al-ly, *vainly*
s Cir-cu-lar-i-ty, *a circular form*
v. Cir-cum-am-bu-late, *to walk round about*
a. Co-ag-u-la-ble, *that which is capable of concretion*
s Co-ef-fi-ca-cy, *power of acting together*
ad. Col-lat-er-al-ly, *side by side*
a. Com-mem-o-ra-ble, *deserving commemoration*
a. Com-men-da-to-ry, *praiseworthy*
a. Com-men-su-ra-ble, *equal in measure*
a. Com-mu-ni-ca-tive, *sociable*
s. Com-mo-di-ous-ness, *convenience*
a. Com-mu-ni-ca-ble, *that which may be imparted*
a. Com-pan-ion-a-ble, *fit for good fellowship*
ad. Com-par-a-tive-ly, *in a state of comparison*
ad. Com-pas-sion-ate-ly, *tenderly*
ad. Com-pen-di-ous-ly, *shortly*
a. Con-sid-e-ra-ble, *great*
a. Con-sol-a-to-ry, *giving comfort*
a. Con-tem-po-ra-ry, *of the same time*

*Accented on the third.*

a. Cab-a-lis-tic-al, *mysterious*
a. Cal-e-fac-to-ry, *heating*
s. Ca-pa-bil-i-ty, *capacity*
s. Car-a-van-sa-ry, *an inn*
a. Car-ti-lag-i-nous, *gristly*

a. Cas-u-is-tic-al, *relating to cases of conscience*
a. Cat-e-gor-i-cal, *positive*
a. Cen-ti-fo-li-ous, *having a hundred leaves*
a. Cer-e-mo-ni-al, *formal*
a. Cer-e-mo-ni-ous, *full of ceremony*
a. Char-la-tan-ic-al, *quackish*
s. Chris-ti-an-i-ty, *the religion of Christians*
a. Chro-no-log-i-cal, *relating to time*
a. Cir-cum-am-bi-ent, *surrounding*
v. Cir-cum-nav-i-gate, *to sail round* [equal
s. Co-e-qual-i-ty, *state of being*
a. Com-pli-men-ta-ry, *polite*
s. Con-san-guin-i-ty, *relationship*
s. Con-ti″-gu-i-ty, *nearness*
s. Con-ti″-nu-i-ty, *connexion*
a. Con-tra-dic-to-ry, *inconsistent with*
s. Con-tra-ri-e-ty, *oppositeness*
a. Con-tro-ver-ti-ble, *disputable*
s. Cor-nu-co-pi-a, *the horn of plenty*
s. Cred-i-bil-i-ty, *likelihood*
s. Crim-i-nal-i-ty, *guilt*
s. Cu-ri-os-i-ty, *inquisitiveness*

*Accented on the fourth.*

s. Ca-lum-ni-a-tion, *slander*
s. Can-on-i-za-tion, *act of declaring a saint* [render
s. Ca-pit-u-la-tion, *terms of sur-*
a. Char-ac-ter-is-tic, *peculiar to*
s. Cir-cum-lo-cu-tion, *a circuit or compass of words*

\* Or, pr. Kar-ak-ʼer-risʼ-tik

s. Cir-cum-val-la-tion, *a trenching round*
s. Cir-cum-vo-lu-tion, *the act of rolling round*
s. Civ-il-i-za-tion, *the art of civilizing*
s. Clar-i-fi-ca-tion, *a making clear*
s. Co-ag-gu-la-tion, *a curdling*
s. Com-mem-o-ra-tion, *a public celebration*
s. Com-men-su-ra-tion, *equality of measure*
s. Com-mis-er-a-tion, *sympathy*
s. Com-mu-ni-ca-tion, *intercourse*
s. Con-cat-e-na-tion, *a linking together*
s. Con-cil-i-a-tion, *a reconcilement*
s. Con-fed-er-a-tion, *alliance*
s. Con-grat-u-la-tion, *a wishing of joy*
s. Con-sid-e-ra-tion, *reason, thought*
s. Con-tam-i-na-tion, *a corrupting*
s. Con-tin-u-a-tion, *progression*
s. Con-tra-dis-tinc-tion, *an opposite distinction*
s. Con-tra-val-la-tion, *a trenching against*
s Co-op-er-a-tion, *joint exertion*
s. Cor-rob-or-a-tion, *a confirmation*

### D.

*Accented on the first.*

a. Ded-i-ca-to-ry, *complimental*
s Dil-a-to-ri-ness, *slowness*
a Dis-çip-li-na-ry, *relating to discipline*

*Accented on the second.*

a. De-bíl-i-ta-ted, *enfeebled.*

a. De-clam-a-to-ry, *full of declamation*
a. De-clar-a-to-ry, *serving to declare*
s. De-clin-a-to-ry, *an instrument in dialing*
a. De-fam-a-to-ry, *slandered*
s. De-gen-e-ra-çy, *a growing worse*
ad. De-lib-er-ate-ly, *advisedly*
a. De-lib-er-a-tive; *apt to consider*
a. De-nom-i-na-tive, *that which gives a name*
a. Den-tic-u-la-ted, *set with small teeth*
a. De-rog-a-to-ry, *detracting from*
a. De-ter-min-a-ble, *that which may be decided*
ad. De-ter-min-ate-ly, *resolutely*
a. De-ter-min-a-tive, *conclusive*
ad. Di-ag-o-nal-ly, *in a diagonal direction*
s. Di-min-u-tive-ness, *smallness*
a. Dis-cre-tion-a-ry, *unlimited*
a. Dis-cu-bi-to-ry, *fitted to the posture of leaning*
a. Diˢs-hon-our-a-ble, *shameful*
a. Dis-in-ter-est-ed, *impartial*
a. Dis-pir-it-ed, *want of vigour*
a. Dis-pun-ish-a-ble, *without penal restraint*
a. Dis-ser-vice-a-ble, *injurious*
a. Dis-til-la-to-ry, *belonging to distillation*
ad. Dis-tri-bu-tive-ly, *by distribution*
ad. Dra-mat-ic-al-ly, *by representation*

*Accented on the third.*

a. Del-e-te-ri-ous, *deadly*

a. Dem-o-cra-ic-al, *pertaining to democracy*
a. Des-ul-to-ri-ous, *unsettled*
a. Di-a-bol-i-cal, *highly wicked*
s. Di-a-co-di-um, *syrup of poppies*
a. Di-a-lec-tic-al, *logical*
a. Di-a-met-ri-cal, *describing a diameter*
a. Dic-ta-to-ri-al, *authoritative*
s. Dis-a-bil-i-ty, *want of power*
a. Dis-a-gree-a-ble, *unpleasing*
a. Dis-al-low-a-ble, *not allowable*
a. Dis-com-mo-di-ous, *inconvenient*
n. Dis-in-car-ce-rate, *to set at liberty* [duty
s. Dis-o-be-di-ence, *breach of*
a. Dis-in-gen-u-ous, *insincere*
ad. Dis-o-bli-ging-ly, *in an offensive manner*
a. Dis-pro-por-tion-ate, *unsuitable*
ad. Dis-re-spect-ful-ly, *irreverently*
a. Dis-son-ta-ne-ous, *inconsistent*
s. Dis-sim-il-i-tude, *unlikeness*
s. Di-u-tur-ni-ty, *length of duration*
a. Du-o-dec-i-mo, *12 leaves to a sheet*
s. Du-ra-bil-i-ty, *power of lasting*

Accented on the fourth.

s. De-bil-i-ta-tion, *the act of weakening*
s. De-com-po-si-tion, *act of compounding things already compounded* [noise
. De-crep-i-ta-tion, *a crackling*
. De-fat-i-ga-tion, *weariness*
s. De-gen-er-a-tion, *the act of degenerating*
s. De-i-fi-ca-tion, *making a God of a mortal*
s. De-lib-e-ra-tion, *deep thought*
s. De-lin-e-a-tion, *a sketch*
s. De-nom-i"-na-tion, *a name*
s. De-nom-i-na-tor, *the giver of a name*
s. De-nun-ci-a-tion, *a public threat*
s. De-nun-ci-a-tor, *a denouncer*
s. De-pop-u-la-tion, *a dispeopling*
s. Des-poi-li-a-tion, *act of despoiling or stripping*
s. De-ter-mi"-na-tion, *decision*
s. De-ter-mi-na-tor, *one who determines*
s. Dig-ni-fi-ca-tion, *exaltation*
s. Di-la-cer-a-tion, *act of rending in two*
s. Di"-lap-i-da-tion, *a falling to decay* [dicial
s. Di-lu-ci-da-tion, *the act of making clear*
s. Di-nu-me-ra-tion, *act of numbering out singly* [dicial
a. Dis-ad-van-ta-ge-ous, *preju-*
s. Dis-ap-pro-ba-tion, *censure*
s. Dis-crim-i"-na-tion, *a distinction*
s. Dis-fig-u-ra-tion, *deformity*
s. Dis-in-cli"-na-tion, *dislike*
s. Dis-in-gen-u-i-ty, *insincerity*
s. Dis-ob-li-ga-tion, *offence*
s. Dis-rep-u-ta-tion, *ill character*
s. Dis-sat-is-fac-tion, *displeasure* [ing
s. Dis-sem-i"-na-tion, *a scatter-*
s. Dis-sem-i-na-tor, *a spreader*
s. Dis-sim-u-la-tion, *hypocrisy*
s. Dis-so-ci-a-tion, *a disunion*
s. Di-var-i"-ca-tion, *a branching out*

## E.

*Accented on the second.*

s. Ef-fém-i-na-çy, *unmanly delicacy*
s. E-lec-tu-a-ry, *a soft compound medicine*
a. E-ma-çi-a-ted, *wasted away*
s. E-pis-co-pa-çy, *office of a bishop*
a. E-pis-to-la-ry, *by letter*
a. Ex-plan-a-to-ry, *containing explanation*

*Accented on the third.*

s. Ec-çen-triç-i-ty, *deviation from a centre, irregular*
a. E-co-nom-i-cal, *frugal*
s. E-las-tiç-i-ty, *a springiness*
a. El-e-men-ta-ry, *simple, pure*
a. Em-ble-mat-i-cal, *allusive*
a. E-nig-mat-ic-al, *obscure*
a. Ep-i-dem-i-cal, *universal*
s. Ep-i-gram-ma-tist, *a writer of epigrams*
a. Ep-i-sod-ic-al, *contained in an episode*
s. E-qua-bil-i-ty, *evenness*
s. E-qua-nim-i-ty, *evenness of mind*
s. E-qui-for-mi-ty, *uniform equality*
a. E-qui-lat-e-ral, *of equal sides*
s. E-qui-lib-ri-um, *equal balance*
s. E-qui-pon-der-ance, *equality of weight*  [gospel
a. Ev-an-gel-ic-al, *agreeable to*
s. Et-y-mol-o-gy, *derivation of words*  [up
s. Ex-ag-ge-ra-tion,* *act of heaping*
v. Ex-com-mu-ni-cate, *to exclude from the church*

Ex. * pr. egs.

*Accented on the fourth.*

s. Ed-i-fi-ca-tion, *improvement*
s. E-jac-u-la-tion, *a short fervent prayer*
s. E-lu-çi-da-tion, *explanation*
s. E-man-çi-pa-tion, *a setting free*
s. E-nu-mer-a-tion, *a counting*
s. E-quiv-o-ca-tion, *a double meaning*
s. E-rad-i-ca-tion, *a rooting up*
s. E-vac-u-a-tion, *an emptying*
s. E-vap-o-ra-tion, *a fuming away*
s. Ex-ag-ger-a-tion,* *an enlarging*
s. Ex-am-i-na-tion, *a trial*
s. Ex-as-per-a-tion, *provoking to anger*
s. Ex-hil-ar-a-tion, *a making merry*  [ing
s. Ex-on-er-a-tion, *a disburthen-*
s. Ex-pec-to-ra-tion, *clearing the breast*
s. Ex-pos-tu-la-tion, *a reasoning with*
s. Ex-ten-u-a-tion, *palliation*
s. Ex-ter-mi-na-tion, *a rooting out*
a. Ex-tra-ju-di-cial, *out of the course of law*

## F.

*Accented on the third.*

a. Fa-ci-ne-ri-ous, *wicked*
s. Fal-li-bil-i-ty, *liableness to be deceived*
s. Fem-i-nal-i-ty, *female nature*
s. Flam-ma-bil-i-ty, *the quality of admitting to be set on fire*
s. Flex-i-bil-i-ty, *pliancy*

* pr. Egz-aj-e-rú-shun.

s. Fu-si-bil-i-ty, *capacity of being melted*
s. Fus-ti-la-ri-an, *a low fellow*

## G.

*Accented on the third.*

s. Ge-ne-ál-o-gy, *pedigree*
s. Gen-e-ral-i-ty, *the bulk*
s. Gen-e-ros-i-ty, *liberality*
a. Ge-o-graph-ic-al, *relating to geography*
a. Ge-o-met-ric-al, *pertaining to geometry*
s. Grad-u-al-i-ty, *regular progression*
a. Gram-i-niv-o-rous, *grass-eating*

## H.

*Accented on the second and third.*

a. Hem-is-pher-ic-al, *half round*
a. He-réd-i-ta-ry, *descending by heirship*
a. Her-e-mit-ic-al, *solitary*
s. Hip-po-pot-a-mus, *the river horse*
a. His-tri-on-ic-al, *befiting the stage*
a. Hom-i-let-ic-al, *social, conversible*
a. Ho-mo-ge-ne-ous, *similar in kind*
Hos-pi″-tal-i-ty, *kindness to strangers*
s. Hy-dro-pho-bi-a, *dread of water*
a. Hy-per-bol-i-cal, *beyond the truth*
a. Hy-per-bo-re-an, *northern*
a. Hy-per-crit-i-cal, *too critical*
s. Hyp-o-chon-dri-ac, *affected with melancholy*
a. Hyp-o-crit-i-cal, *dissembling*
a. Hy-po-thet-i-cal, *supposed*

## I. J.

*Accented on the first.*

a. I'm-pre-ca-to-ry, *containing wishes of evil*
s. Ju-di-ca-to-ry, *court of justice*

*Accented on the second.*

a. Im-ág-in-a-ble, *possible to be conceived*
a. Im-a-gin-a-ry, *ideal*
a. Im-pen-e-tra-ble, *not to be pierced*
a. Im-prac-ti-ca-ble, *that cannot be done*
s. In-ac-cu-ra-cy, *want of exactness*
a. In-ap-pli-ca-ble, *unsuitable*
s. In-çen-di″-a-ry, *an inflamer; a house burner*
a. In-com-pa-ra-ble, *matchless*
a. In-cor-ri-gi-ble, *past amendment*
a. In-dis-pu-ta-ble, *not to be disputed*
a. In-dis-so-lu-ble, *that cannot be broken*
a. In-du-bi-ta-ble, *certain*
a. In-es-ti-ma-ble, *invaluable*
a. In-ev-i-ta-ble, *not to be avoided*
a. In-ex-o-ra-ble, *not to be prevailed with*
a. In-ex-pli-ca-ble, *not to be explained* [cleared
a. In-ex-tri-ca-ble, *not to be*
a. In-fat-u-a-ted, *bewitched*
a. In-flam-ma-to-ry, *apt to inflame* [inhabited
a. In-hab-i-ta-ble, *that may be*

## SPELLING ASSISTANT.

*s.* In-hos-pi-ta-ble, *unkind*
*a* In-im-i-ta-ble, *above imitation*
*a* In-nu-me-ra-ble, *numberless*
*a.* In-sa-ti-a-ble, *not to be satisfied*
*a.* In-sep-a-ra-ble, *not to be parted* [*be borne*
*a.* In-suf-fer-a-ble, *which cannot*
*a.* In-su-per-a-ble. *not to be overcome* [*stood*
*a.* In-tel-li-gi-ble, *easily understood*
*s.* In-tem-per-a-ture, *excess of some quality*
*a.* In-tol-er-a-ble, *insufferable*
*a.* In-val-u-a-ble, *above value*
*a.* In-va-ri-a-ble, *unchangeable*
*s.* In-vet-e-ra-çy, *extreme obstinacy*
*a.* In-vi-o-la-ble, *not to be broken*
*a.* In-vol-un-ta-ry, *unwilling*
*a.* In-vul-ne-ra-ble, *that cannot be wounded*
*a.* Ir-rep-a-ra-ble, *not to be repaired*
*a.* Ir-rev-o-ca-ble, *that cannot be recalled*
*s.* I-tin-e-ra-ry, *a book of travels*

Accented on the third.

*a.* Ig-no-min-i-ous, *disgraceful*
*s.* Il-le-gal-i-ty, *unlawfulness*
*a.* Il-le-git-i-mate, *unlawful*
*s.* Im-be-çil-i-ty, *feebleness*
*a.* Im-mar-ces-si-ble, *unfading*
*a.* Im-ma-te-ri-al, *trifling*
*s.* Im-ma-tu-ri-ty, *unripeness*
*a.* Im-me-mo-ri-al, *time out of mind*
*d.* Im-me-thod-ic-al, *confused*
*s.* Im-mo-bil-i-ty, *want of motion*
*s.* Im-mo-ral-i-ty, *vice*
*s.* Im-mor-tal-i-ty, *a never dying*

*a.* Im-per-cep-ti-ble, *not to be perceived*
*s.* Im-por-tu-ni-ty, *strong entreaty*
*s.* Im-pro-pri-e-ty, *unfitness*
*s.* In-a-bil-i-ty, *want of power*
*a.* In-ac-çes-si-ble, *which cannot be come at*
*s.* In-ac-tiv-i-ty, *idleness*
*s.* In-ad-ver-ten-çy, *inattention*
*a.* In-ar-tic-u-late, *not distinct*
*s.* In-ca-paç-i-ty, *inability*
*s.* In-çi-vil-i-ty, *rudeness*
*ad.* In-co-he-rent-ly, *inconsistently*
*s.* In-co-lu-mi-ty, *safety, security*
*a.* In-com-bus-ti-ble, *not to be consumed by fire*
*a.* In-com-mo-di-ous, *inconvenient* [*with*
*a.* In-com-pat-i-ble, *inconsistent*
*a.* In-com-pas-sion-ate, *void of compassion*
*a.* In-con-çeiv-a-ble, *not to be imagined*
*a.* In-con-di-tion-al, *without exception*
*s.* In-con-gru-i-ty, *absurdity*
*a.* In-con-sid-e-rate, *thoughtless*
*s.* In-con-sis-ten-cy, *absurdity*
*a.* In-con-so-la-ble, *not to be comforted*
*a.* In-con-sum-a-ble, *not to be wasted*
*a.* In-con-tes-ta-ble, *sure, certain*
*s.* In con-ve-ni-ençe, *disadvantage*
*a.* In-con-ver-sa-ble, *unsocial*
*a.* In-con-vin-ci-ble, *not to be convinced*
*a.* In-cor-po-re-al, *spiritual*
*a.* In-cor-rup-ti-ble *not admitting decay*

s. In-cre-du-li-ty, *unbelief*
a. In-de-fea-²si-ble, *that cannot be annulled* [*decay*
a. In-de-fec-ti-ble, *not liable to*
a. In-de-lib-er-ate, *rash*
s. In-de-pen-den-cy, *freedom*
a. In-de-ter-mi-nate, *uncertain*
a. In-dis-crim-i-nate, *altogether*
a. In-dis-pen-sa-ble, *absolutely necessary*
s. In-di-vid-u-al, *a single person*
a. In-di-vi²s-i-ble, *which cannot be divided*
a. In-ef-fec-tu-al, *without effects*
s. In-e-qual-i-ty, *unevenness*
a. In-ex-haus-ti-ble, *that cannot be spent*
a. In-ex-pe-di-ent, *improper*
a. In-ex-pres-si-ble, *not to be expressed*
s. In-fe-liç″-i-ty, *unhappiness*
s. In-fer-til-i-ty, *unfruitfulness*
s. In-fi-del-i-ty, *unfaithfulness*
s. In-ᴶge-nu-i-ty, *genius*
a. In-har-mo-ni-ous, *not musical*
s. In-hu-man-i-ty, *cruelty*
a. In-sig-nif-i-cant, *trifling*
s. In-sin-çer-i-ty, *falsehood*
s. In-si″-pid-i-ty, *tasteiessness*
s. In-sta-bil-i-ty, *unsteadiness*
a. In-stan-ta-ne-ous, *immediate*
a. In-sup-pòrt-a-ble, *not to be endured* [*rable*
a. In-sur-mount-a-ble, *unconquerable*
a. In-tel-lec-tu-al, *belonging to the mind*
a. In-ter-me-di-ate, *between*
s. In-tre-pid-i-ty, *courage*
s. In-va-lid-i-ty, *want of force*
s. In-u-til-i-ty, *unprofitableness*
a. Ir-refᷧ-ra-ga-ble,* *not to be denied*

* pr Ir-refʹ-fra-ga-bl.

a. Ir-re-pròach-a-ble, *free from blame* [*be resisted*
a. Ir-re-²sis-ti-ble, *which cannot*
a. Ir-re-trie-va-ble, *irrecoverable*

*Accented on the fourth.*

s. Il-lu-mi-na-tion, *an enlightening*
s. Im-aᴶg-in-a-tion, *fancy*
s. In-au-gu-ra-tion, *investing with a dignity*
s. In-dis-po-si-tion, *illness*
s. In-e-bri-a-tion, *drunkenness*
a. In-ef-fi-ca-tious, *of no force*
s. In-fat-u-a-tion, *folly*
s. In-oc-u-la-tion, *a grafting*
s In-sin-u-a-tion, *a sly hint*
s. In-ter-lo-cu-tion, *a dialogue*
s. In-ter-po-la-tion, *a false insertion*
s. In-ter-po-si-tion, *mediation*
s. In-ter-pre-ta-tion, *an explanation*
s. In-ter-ro-ga-tion, *a question*
s. In-tim-i-da-tion, *terror*
s. In-tox-i-ca-tion, *drunkenness*
s. In-ves-ti-ga-tion, *an examining*
s. Ir-ra-di-a-tion, *strong brightness*
s. Ir-res-o-lu-tion, *want of courage*

M.

*Accented on the third.*

a. Maᴶg-is-te-ri-al, *imperious*
s. Mag-na-nim-i-ty, *bravery*
s. Man-u-fac-tu-rer, *an artificer*
a. Mat-ri″-mo-ni-al, *nuptial*
s. Me-di″-oc-ri-ty, *middle state*
a. Mer-it-o-ri-ous, *deserving*
s. Met-a-mor-pho-sis, *change of shape*
a. Met-a-phor-i-cal, *figurative*

2. Met-a-phys-i-cal, *belonging to metaphysics* [*shop*
s. Me-tro-pol-i-tan, *an arch-bi-*
a. Min-is-te-ri-al, *of a minister*
a. Mis-çel-la-ne-ous, *mixed*
s. Mon-o-syl-la-ble, *a word of one syllable*
a. Mu-çil-a″-gi-nous, *slimy*
a. Mul-ti″-fa-ri-ous, *of various sorts* [*riety*
s. Mul-ti″-pliç-i-ty, *a great va-*
s. Mu-ta-bil-i-ty, *changeableness*
a. My-tho-loj-g-i-cal, *fabulous*

*Accented on the fourth.*

s. Man-i-fes-ta-tion *discovery*
s. Math-e-ma-ti-cian, *one versed in mathematics*
s. Me-li-o-ra-tion, *improvement*
s. Me-temp-sy-chó-sis, *transmigration of souls*
s. Mod-i-fi-ca-tion, *a qualifying*
s. Mor-ti-fi-ca-tion, *vexation*
s. Mul-ti-pli-ca-tion, *act of multiplying*

### N.
*Accented on the third.*

s. Non-con-for-mi-ty, *non-agreement*
s. No-to-ri-e-ty, *public knowledge*

*Accented on the fourth.*

s. Ne-go-ti-a-tion, *a treaty of business* [*treat*
s. Ne-go-ti-a-tor, *one employed to*
s. No-ti-fi-ca-tion, *a making known*

### O.
*Accented on the second.*

s. Ob-zsér-va-to-ry, *a look out house*

s. Of-fiç-i-ous-ness, *over forwardness*
ad. O-rij-g-i-nal-ly, *primarily*

*Accented on the third.*

a. O-do-rif-e-rous, *sweet-scented*
s. Op-por-tu-ni-ty, *fit time*
a. O-ra-tor-i-cal, *becoming an orator*
a. Or-tho-grap-i-cal, *relating to spelling*

*Accented on the fourth.*

s. Ob-lit-er-a-tion, *a blotting out*
s. Or-gan-i-za-tion, *a regularity of parts*

### P.

*Accented on the second.*

v. Par-tic-u-lar-ize, *to mention expressly*
a. Pe-cu-ni-a-ry, *relating to money*
a. Pre-lim-i-na-ry, *introductory*
a. Pre-par-a-to-ry, *previous*
a. Pro-fes-si-on-al, *belonging to a profession*
s. Pro-fiç-i-en-çy, *progression in any art*

*Accented on the third.*

a. Pan-e-gyr-i-cal, *praising*
a. Par-a-dox-i-cal, *contradictory*
s. Par-al-lel-o-gram, *a figure whose sides are parallel*
a. Par-si″-mo-ni-ous, *sparing*
a. Pat-ri-mo-ni-al, *derived from ancestors*
a. Pe-ri-od-i-cal, *at stated times*
a. Per-pen-di-cu-lar, *upright*
s. Per-pe-tu-i-ty, *duration*
a. Per-spi″-ca-çi-ous, *quick-sighted*

s. Per-spi″-cu-i-ty, *clearness*
a. Per-ti″-na-çi-ous, *obstinate*
a. Phil-o-soph-i-cal, *belonging to philosophy*
s. Phra-ᶻse-o-lo-gy, *diction*
s. Phyᶻs-i″-og-no-my, *knowledge of nature*
s. Plau-ᶻsi″-bil-i-ty, *seeming fairness*
s Pol-y-syl-la-ble, *a word of many syllables*
s. Pos-si′-bil-i-ty, *a being possible*
a. Pre-ter-nat-u-ral, *not natural*
a. Pri-mo-ⁱge-ni-al, *first born*
s. Pri-mo-ⁱgen-i-ture, *eldership*
s. Prin-çi″-pal-i-ty, *a prince's domain*
s. Prob-a-bil-i-ty, *likelihood*
a. Prob-le-mat-i-cal, *uncertain*
s. Prod-i″-gal-i-ty, *extravagance*
a. Prov-i-den-ti-al, *effected by Providence*
s. Pu-er-il-i-ty, *childishness*
a. Py-ra-mid-i-cal, *like a pyramid*

*Accented on the fourth.*

s. Pa-ci-fi-ca-tion, *peace making*
s. Par-ti-ci-pa-tion, *a taking part of*
s. Per-am-bu-la-tion, *a walking through*
s. Per-e-gri-na-tion, *a travelling*
s. Pre-cip-i-ta-tion, *hurry*
s. Pre-des-ti-na-tion, *a fore ordaining*
s. Pre-med-i-ta-tion, *forethought*
s. Pre-va-ri-ca-tion, *double dealing*
s. Pro-cras-ti-na-tion, *delay*
s. Prog-nos-ti-ca-tion, *aforetelling*
s. Pro-nun-ci-a-tion, *mode of utterance*
s. Pro-pi-ti-a-tion, *an atonement*

s. Pu-ri-fi-ca-tion, *a making clear*

Q.

*Accented on the third.*

a. Qua-dri-lat-e-ral, *having four sides*
s. Quin-qua-ⁱges-i-ma, *Shrove Sunday*

R.

*Accented on the second.*

a. Re-me-di-a-ble, *that may be remedied*
s. Re-poᶻs-i-to-ry, *a store-room*
ad. Re-çip-ro-cal-ly, *mutually*
a. Re-cov-er-a-ble, *that may be regained*

*Accented on the third.*

v. Re-ca-pit-u-late, *to sum up*
s. Reg-u lar-i-ty, *good order*
a. Re-pre-hen-si-ble, *deserving reproof*
s. Rep-re ᶻsen-ta-tive, *a deputy*
s. Rev-o-lu-tion-ist, *a supporter of a revolution*
s. Riᶻs-i″bil-i-ty, *power or propensity to laugh*

*Accented on the fourth.*

s. Ram-i-fi-ca-tion, *a branching out*
s. Rat-i-fi-ca-tion, *a confirming*
s. Re-cip-ro-ca-tion, *an interchanging*
s. Rec-om-mend-a-tion, *character*
s. Re-crim-i-na-tion, *a charge retorted*
s. Re-gen-er-a-tion, *a new birth*
s. Re-mu-ner-a-tion, *a reward*
s. Re-nun-ci-a-tion, *a renouncing*
s. Re-pre-sen-ta-tion, *image, figure*
s. Re-pu-di-a-tion, *a divorce*

s. Re-sus-cit-a-tion, *a reviving*
s. Re-tal-i-a-tion, *a doing like for like*
s. Ret-ro-gra-da-tion, *a going backward*
s. Re-ver-be-ra-tion, *a beating back*

### S.
#### Accented on the first.
a. Stá-ti-on-a-ry, *fixed*

#### Accented on the second.
s. Sub-sid-i-a-ry, *adding*
s. Suf-fiç-i-en-çy,* *enough*
s. Sig-nif-i-can-çy, *meaning*

#### Accented on the third.
a. Sal-u-tif-e-rous, *wholesome*
a. Sat-is-fac-to-ry, *giving content*
s. Se-ni″-or-i-ty, *eldership*
s. Sen-si-bil-i-ty, *feeling*
s. Sin-gu-lar-i-ty, *oddity*
a. Sub-ter-ra-ne-ous, *underground*
a. Su-per-çil-i-ous, *very haughty*
a. Su-per-em-i-nent, *very eminent*
a. Su-per-ex-çel-lent, *very excellent*
s. Su-per-flu-i-ty, *excess*
a. Sys-te-mat-i-cal, *methodical*

#### Accented on the fourth.
a. Su-per-a-bún-dant, *more than enough*
s. Su-per-in-ten-dent, *an overlooker*

#### Accented on the fourth.
s. Sanc-ti-fi-ca-tion, *a making holy*
s. Scar-i-fi-ca-tion, *a slight cut*
s. Sig-ni-fi-ca-tion, *meaning*

✻ *pr.* Suf-fish-en-se.

s. Sol-em-ni-za-tion, *celebration*
s. So-li-ci-ta-tion, *importunity*
s. Spe-ci-fi-ca-tion, *a particularity*
s. Sub-or-di-na-tion, *inferiority*
s. Sub-til-i-za-tion, *a making thin*

### T.
#### Accented on the third.
s. Taç-i″-túr-ni-ty, *habitual silence*
s. Tes-ti″-mo-ni-al, *a certificate*
a. The-o-lojg-i-cal, *belonging to divinity*
a. The-o-ret-i-cal, *speculative*
a. Typ-o-graph-i-cal, *relating to printing*

### U.
#### Accented on the second.
a. Un-al-ter-a-ble, *unchangeable*
a. Un-an-swer-a-ble, *not to be refuted*
a. Un-au-tho-ri-zed, *not supported by authority*
a. Un-char-i-ta-ble, *unkind*
a. Un-çiv-i-li-zed, *barbarous*
a. Un-cul-ti-va-ted, *waste, desert*
a. Un-dis-çi-pli-ned, *untrained*
a. Un-fath-om-a-ble, *not to be sounded*
a. Un-fa-vour-a-ble, *not promising*
a. Un-gov-ern-a-ble, *unruly*
a. Un-oc-cu-pi-ed, *not inhabited, unpossessed*
a. Un-par-al-lel-ed, *unequalled*
a. Un-par-don-a-ble, *not to be forgiven*
a. Un-prof-i-ta-ble, *useless*
a. Un-qual-i-fi-ed, *unfit*
a. Un-ser-viçe-a-ble, *of no use*

*a.* Un-ut-ter-a-ble, *inexpressible*
*a.* Un-war-rant-a-ble, *not justifiable*

*Accented on the third.*

*a.* Un-ac-cep-ta-ble, *displeasing*
*a.* Un-ac-coun-ta-ble, *inexplicable*
*a.* Un-ac-cus-tom-ed, *not used to*
*s.* U-na-nim-i-ty, *general consent*
*a.* Un-at-tain-a-ble, *not to be acquired* [*shunned*
*a.* Un-a-void-a-ble, *not to be*
*a.* Un-con-trôl-la-ble, *not to be governed*
*a.* Un-de-ni-a-ble, *most certain*
*a.* Un-en-light-en-ed, *uninstructed : dark*
*a.* Un-e-quiv-o-cal, *plain, direct*
*s.* U-ni″-for-mi-ty, *sameness*

*a.* Un-in-hab-i-ted, *empty*
*s.* U-ni-ver-si-ty, *a place where the liberal arts are taught and studied*
*a.* Un-per-çeiv-a-ble, *not to be seen*

V

*Accented on the first.*

*s.* Vá-ri-a-ble-ness, *changeableness* [*accord.*
*ad.* Vol-un-ta-ri-ly, *of one's own*

*Accented on the second.*

*part.* Ver-mic-u-la-ted, *inlaid*
*s.* Vo-cab-u-la-ry, *a little dictionary*
*s.* Vo-lup-tu-a-ry, *a luxurious person*
*s.* Vol-u-bil-i-ty, *fluency of speech*

---

## WORDS OF SIX SYLLABLES.

Parts of Speech.

### A.

*a.* An-te-di″-lu-vi-an, *existing before the flood*
*a.* An-ti″mo-nar*ch*-i-cal, *against monarchy*

### C.

*Accented on the fourth.*

*s.* Com-pat-i″-bil-i-ty, *suitableness*

### D.

*Accented on the second and third.*

*a.* Dis-cre″-ti-on-a-ry, *optional*
*a.* Dis-pro-pôr-ti-on-al. *unequal*

Parts of Speech.

### E.

*Accented on the second and third.*

*s.* E-láb-o-ra-to-ry, *a workshop*
*a.* Ex-tra-or-di-na-ry, *uncommon.*

*Accented on the fourth.*

*a.* Ec-cle-²si-ás-ti-cal, *relating to the church*

### F.

*Accented on the fourth.*

*s.* Fa-mil-i″-ár-i-ty, *intimacy*

### G.

*Accented on the fourth.*

*s.* Gen-e-ral-ís-si-mo, *a commander in chief*

# SPELLING ASSISTANT.

## H.

*Accented on the fourth.*

a. Het-er-o-gé-ne-ous, *unlike*
a. Hi-e-ro-glyph-i-cal, *emblematical, allusive*
s. His-to-ri″-og-ra-pher, *a writer of history*

## I.

*Accented on the third.*

s. Il-le-git-i-ma-çy, *illegality of birth*
a In-com-men-su-ra-ble, *that cannot be measured*
a. In-com-mu-ni-ca-ble, *not to be told*
a. In-con-sid-er-a-ble, *unimportant*
a. In-de-fat-i-ga-ble, *unwearied with labour*
s. In-sig-nif-i-can-çy, *worthlessness*
ad. In-stan-ta-ne-ous-ly. *in a moment*
s. In-suf-fiç-i-en-çy, *incapacity*
s. In-ter-rog-a-to-ry, *a question*
s. Ir-re-cov-er-a-ble, *not to be recovered*
a. Ir-re-me-di-a-ble, *incurable*

*Accented on the fourth.*

s. Il-lib-e-rál-i-ty, *meanness*
s. Im-mu-ta-bil-i-ty, *constancy*
s. Im-par-ti-al-i-ty, *justice*
s. Im-pet-u-os-i-ty, *violence*
s. Im-pos-si-bil-i-ty, *that cannot be done*
s. Im-pla-ca-bil-i-ty, *that cannot be reconciled*
s. Im-prob-a-bil-i-ty, *unlikelihood*

a. In-ar-ti-fiç-i-al, *without art*
a. In-com-pre-hen-si-ble, *not to be conceived*
a. In-con-tro-ver-ti-ble, *indisputable*
s. In-cred-i-bil-i-ty, *difficulty of belief*
s. In-fal-li-bil-i-ty, *freedom from error*
s. In-fe-ri-or-ity, *lower degree*
s. In-flex-i-bil-i-ty, *obstinacy*
s. In-hos-pi-tal-i-ty, *unkindness to strangers*
s. In-sen-si-bil-i-ty, *want of feeling*
a. Ir-rec-on-çi-la-ble, *not to be reconciled*
s. Ir-reg-u-lar-i-ty, *disorder*

## M.

*Accented on the fourth.*

a. Mach-i″-a-vé-li-an, *crafty*
s. Ma-te-ri″-al-i-ty, *bodily existence*
s. Med-i″-ter-ra-ne-an, *sea enclosed by land: the sea that divides Europe from Africa and part of Asia*
s. Me-te-o-rol-o-gy, *the doctrine of meteors*

## P.

*Accented on the fourth.*

a. Pa″-çi″-fi-ca-to-ry, *peaceful*
a. Par-li″-a-men-ta-ry, *belonging to parliament*
s. Par-tic-u-lar-i-ty, *something odd*
s. Pe-cu-li″-ar-i-ty, *oddness*
s. Pu-sil-la-nim-i-ty, *cowardice*

R.

*Accented on the third.*
a. Rec-om-mén-da-to-ry, *recommending*
a. Re͡s-i″-den-ti-a-ry, *holding residence*

*Accented on the fourth.*
s. Rat-i-o-nal-i-ty, *the power of reason*

S.

*Accented on the third.*
a. Su-per-án-nu-a-ted, *disqualified by age*
a. Su-per-nu-mer-a-ry, *above the usual number*

*Accented on the fourth.*
s. Spir-i-tu-al-i-ty, *devotion*
s. Su-per-in-ten-den-çy, *an overseeing*

s. Su-pe-ri-or-i-ty, *advantage*
s. Sus-çep-ti-bil-i-ty, *quality of admitting*

T.

*Accented on the second and fourth.*
a. Tra-di″-ti-on-a-ry, *descending with posterity*
a. Trig-o-no-met-ri-cal, *belonging to trigonometry*

V U.

*Accented on the third.*
a. Val-e-tú-di-na-ry, *sickly*
a. Un-in-hab-i-ta-ble, *unfit for habitation*
a. Un-in-tel-li-ji-gi-ble, *not to be understood*

*Accented on the fourth.*
s. U-ni-ver-sal-i-ty, *generality*
a. Un-jus-ti-fi-a-ble, *base*

## WORDS OF SIX AND SEVEN SYLLABLES.

*Accented on the fifth.*

Parts of Speech.

A.
s. AN-TI-TRIN-I-TA′-RI-ANS, *those who deny the doctrine of the Christian Trinity*

C.
s. Çir-cum-am-bu-lá-tion, *walking round*
s. Çir-cum-nav-i-ga-tion, *a sailing round*

D.
s. Dis-con-tin-u-á-tion, *a leaving off*
s. De-te-ri-o-ra-tion, *a making worse*
s. Di″-ver-si-fi-ca-tion, *change, variation*

E.
s. Ex-com-mu-ni-cá-tion, *a sentence of the church.*

# SPELLING ASSISTANT.

*a.* **Ex-em-pli-fi-ca-tion,** *an illustrating*

### I.
*s.* I-den-ti-fi-cá-tion, *an identifying*
*s.* Im-ma-te-ri-al-i-ty, *immaterial quality*
*s.* Im-mea-su-ra-bil-i-ty, *not admitting measure*
*a.* Im-par-i-syl-lab-i-cal, *unequal in syllables*
*s.* Im-pen-e-tra-bil-i-ty, *extreme hardness*
*s.* In-com-pat-i-bil-i-ty, *incongruity*
*s.* In-con-sid-e-ra-tion, *want of thought*
*s.* In-cor-rup-ti-bil-i-ty, *incorruptible quality*
*s.* In-dem-ni-fi-ca-tion, *security against loss*
*s.* In-de-ter-mi-na-tion, *indecision*
*s.* In-dis-sol-u-bil-i-ty, *void of dissolution*
*s.* In-di-vi$^z$s-i-bil-i-ty, *which cannot be divided*
*s.* In-sa-ti-a-bil-i-ty, *never to be satisfied*
*s.* In-ter-lin-e-a-tion, *an interlining*
*s.* Ir-ra″-ti-o-nal-i-ty, *want of reason*

### L.
*s.* Lat-i-tu-di-ná-ri-an, *one who departs from orthodoxy*

### M.
*s.* Mal-ad-min-is-trá-tion, *bad management*
*s.* Mis-rep-re-sen-ta-tion, *representing wrong*

### N.
*s.* Nat-u-ral-i-zá-tion, *admitting aliens to the rights of subjects*

### P.
*s.* Plen-i-po-tén-ti-a-ry, *a national negotiator*
*s.* Pre-de-ter-mi-na-tion, *a determining beforehand*

### R.
*s.* Ra-ti-oç-i-ná-tion,\* *the art of reasoning*
*s.* Re-ca-pit-u-la-tion, *a summing up*
*s.* Rec-on-çil-i-a-tion, *a reconciling*
*s.* Re-ex-am-i-na-tion, *a second examination*

### S.
*s.* Su-per-an-nu-á-tion, *disqualification by age*
*s.* Su-per-er-o-ga-tion, *doing more than is required*

### T.
*s.* Tran-sub-stan-ti-á-tion, *the doctrine of the real presence*

### V
*s.* Val-e-tu-di-ná-ri-an, *a sickly or infirm person*
*s.* Vol-a-til-i-za-tion, *a making volatile*

\* *pr.* Rash-e-os-e-na′-chun.

*Words spelt alike, but which, in different Parts of Speech, change their pronunciations; being accented on the first Syllable when Nouns, and the last when Verbs.*

| NOUNS. Accented on the first. | VERBS. Accented on the last. |
|---|---|
| A'bsent, *not present* | To Abse'nt, *to keep away* |
| An Abstract, *an abridgment* | To Abstract, *to shorten* |
| A Collect, *a short prayer* | To Collect, *to gather together* |
| A Compound, *a mixture* | To Compound, *to mingle* |
| A Contest, *a quarrel* | To Contest, *to dispute* |
| A Contract, *a deed* | To Contract, *to bargain* |
| Converse, *conversation* | To Converse, *to discourse* |
| A Convert, *a reformed person* | To Convert, *to change* |
| A Convict, *a criminal* | To Convict, *to prove guilty* |
| A Convoy, *a guard* | To Convoy, *to protect* |
| A Desert, *a wilderness* | To Desert, *to forsake* |
| An Extract, *a quotation* | To Extract, *to select* |
| A Ferment, *a tumult* | To Ferment, *to work like beer* |
| Frequent, *occurring often* | To Frequent, *to resort to* |
| Import, *meaning* | To Import, *to bring from abroad* |
| An Insult, *an affront* | To Insult, *to ill use* |
| An Object, *any thing presented to our senses* | To Object, *to oppose* |
| A Present, *a gift* | To Present, *to give* |
| Produce, *the thing produced* | To Produce, *to bring forth* |
| A Project, *a scheme or design* | To Project, *to contrive* |
| A Rebel, *a traitor* | To Rebel, *to revolt* |
| A Record, *a public register* | To Record, *to enrol* |
| Refuse, *waste* | To Refuse, *to deny* |
| A Subject, *he who owes obedience* | To Subject, *to subdue* |
| A Torment, *a great pain* | To Torment, *to torture* |

*Grammatical Terms, with their respective Marks or Notes and Explanation.*

| Used in Writing. | | Used in Print. | |
|---|---|---|---|
| Apostrophe - - | ' | Single Accent - - - | ' |
| Brace - - | { | Double Accent - | " |
| | | Asterisk - - | * |

SPELLING ASSISTANT.    117

| Caret       | ʌ   | Index     | ☞ |
| Ellipsis    | ——  | Obelisk   | † |
| Hyphen      | -   | Paragraph | ¶ |
| Parenthesis | ( ) | Parallel  | ‖ |
| Quotation   | " " | Section   | § |
| Crotchet    | [ ] |           |   |

A Comma, a Semicolon; a Colon: a Period or Full Stop a Note of Interrogation ? a Note of Admiration !

An Apostrophe is used to shorten a word: as I'll, for I will.

A Brace is used to couple Lines together, whether in poetry or prose; as,

  Religion only can our wants restrain,  ⎫
  The mind support beneath corporeal pain, ⎬
  Make life more sweet, and death eternal gain. ⎭
  To a year's Rent from Christmas, 1809, ⎫
    to Christmas, 1810    ⎭

A Caret is placed where a word is left out in writing; as, I.ive mutual.
    in ʌ love.

An Ellipsis supplies the place of a letter or letters in a word, when the writer does not choose to write the word at length; as J——s T—ms—n, James Thomson.

Asterisks, *** are sometimes used for the same purpose.

The Hyphen is used to part syllables; as, Ab-ba.

A Parenthesis serves to include a sentence in the body of another; as, This act of cruelty (for such it certainly was) is almost the only stain in the character of, &c.

A Quotation " signifies that the words so marked are transcribed from the writings of another in his own words. The end of a Quotation is marked thus," and shows that the passage quoted is finished.

Single accent denotes the stress to be laid upon a particular syllable in a word.

Double Accent serves to mark a short sound in a syllable.

Crotchets enclose short sentences or references, that have no connexion with the subject treated of.

An Asterisk,  ⎫ Are all used as references to the bottom of the
An Index,   ⎬ page or margin of a book. Figures, also, as
An Obelisk, and ⎭ 1, 2, 3, &c. are used in like manner, and have,
A Parallel     in general, the same signification.

N. B. A Paragraph ¶ and Section § are not always used like the other marks, as references to the margin or bottom of a page. They are chiefly used to mark the divisions and separate heads of a discourse. The former character is to be met with in many parts of the Old and New Testament; and in Locke's Essay this mark § is prefixed to the Sections of the discourse.

*Contractions used in Writing and Print; (but it is to be remembered that except in Addresses and Accompts, such Contractions in the body of a letter are improper.)*

## IN WRITING.

Acct. *Account*
Ansr. *Answer*
Apl. *April*
Aug. *August*
Bart. *Baronet*
Capt. *Captain*
Per { Cent. *by the hundred*
      { Cwt. *by the* 100 *weight*
Co. *Company*
Cr. *Creditor*
Dr. *Debtor*
Dec. *December*
Ditto *or* Do *as before*
Dwts. *pennyweights*
Edmd. *Edmund*
Edwd. *Edward*
Eliz. *Elizabeth*
Esq. *Esquire*
Feb. *February*
Fred. *Frederick*
Gab. *Gabriel*
Gent. *Gentlemen*
Genl. *General*
Geo. *George*
Govr. *Governor*
Greg. *Gregory*
Gr. *Gross*
Grs. *Grains*
Gs. *Guineas*
Hanh. *Hannah*
Hhd. *Hogshead*
Honble. *Honourable*
Hond. *Honoured*
Inst. *Instant*
Ian. *January*

Jno. *John*
Jos. *Joseph*
Knt. *Knight*
£. Libræ, *Pounds*
S. Solidi, *Shillings*
D. Denarii, *Pence*
Lieut. *Lieutenant*
lb. *a pound weight*
Mr. *Master*
Mrs. *Mistress*
Madm. *Madam*
Messrs. *Masters*
Michs. *Michaelmas*
Midsr. *Midsummer*
Monr. *Monsieur*
Mo. *Month*
Nat. *Nathaniel*
No. *Number*
Nov. *November*
Ob. *Obedient*
Oct. *October*
Oz. *Ounce*
Pd. *Paid*
P. S. *Postscript*
Qrs. *Quarters*
Qt. *Quart, or* **Quantity**
Recd. *Received*
Rev. *Reverend*
Richd. *Richard*
Robt. *Robert*
Rt. Hon. *Right Honourable*
Rt. Worp. *Right Worshipful*
Rt. Rev. *Right Reverend*
Sr. *Sir*
St. *Saint*

SPELLING ASSISTANT. 119

Servt. *Servant*
Sept. *September*
Thos. *Thomas*
Ult. ultimus, *the last*
Viz. videlicet,* *that is to say*
Vide, *see*

Wk. *Week*
Wt. *Weight*
Xmas. *Christmas*
&, *and*
&c. et cetera,† *and so forth*

† *pr.* Et-set'-e-ra.

* *pr.* Ve-del'-e-set.

## IN PRINT.

A. B. artium baccalaureus, *Bachelor of Arts*
A. D. anno Domini, *in the year of our Lord*
A. M. ante-meridiem, *before noon*
A. M. artium magister, *Master of Arts*
A. M. anno mundi, *in the year of the world*
B. D. baccalaureus divinitatis, *Bachelor of Divinity*
D. D. doctor divinitatis, *Doctor of Divinity*
F. R. S. *Fellow of the Royal Society*
G. R. Georgius Rex, *King George*
J. H. S. Jesus Hominum Salvator, *Jesus the Saviour of Men*
L. C. J. *Lord Chief Justice*
LL. D. utriusque legis doctor, *Doctor of Laws*
M. A. magister artium, *Master of Arts*
M D. medicinæ doctor, *Doctor of Medicine*

M. S. memoriæ sacrum, *Sacred to the Memory*
M. S. *Manuscript*
MSS. *Manuscripts*
N. B. nota bene, *take notice*
N. S. *New Style*
P M. post meridiem, *afternoon*
Q. E. D. quod erat demonstrandum, *which was to be demonstrated*
Q. E. I. quod erat inveniendum, *which was to be discovered*
R. rex aut regina, *King or Queen*
dele, *expunge*
e. g. exempli gratia, *for example*
q. d. quasi dicat, *as if he should*
i. e. id est, *that is*        [*say*
id. idem, *the same*
v. *verse*
yn. *then*
yr. *your*
yt. *that*
Also, fol. *folio*, 4to. *quarto.* 8vo. *octovo.* 12mo. *duodecimo.*— And 1st. *first*, 2d. *second*, 3d. *third* ; and *th* over the other *ordinal numerals, as* 4th *fourth* 5th. *fifth, &c.*

## SYNONYMOUS WORDS.

*Viz. Such as agree in the general sense, but differ in the application.*

To Abandon *iniquity*
   Leave *a place*
   Forsake *in resentment or neg-*
   Relinquish *a claim* [*lect*
   Desert *treacherously*
   Quit *business*
To Abdicate *a crown*
   Renounce *error*
   Resign *an office*
To Abate *in eagerness*
   Diminish *in number*
   Decrease *in quantity*
   Lessen *in value*
   Relax *in effort*
   Impair *in vigour or intellect*
To Abhor *a crime*
   Hate *affectation*
   Detest *treachery, meanness*
   Loathe *food*
To Abolish *customs*
   Disannul *a contract*
   Abrogate *a law*
   Revoke *a promise*
   Repeal *a statute*
   Take *any thing*
To Accept *services*
   Receive *favours*
To Accost *a person*
   Approach *a place*
To Acquiesce *under authority*
   be Resigned *from a sense of duty*
   Agree *in disposition or opinion*
   Consent, *by persuasion*

To Augment *in number*
   Add *together*
To Adjust *matters*
   Reconcile *animosities*
To affirm *a position*
   Assert *a right or opinion*
   Aver *a sentiment*
   Attest *in evidence*
   Declare *openly*
   Swear, *by oath* [*ledg'*
   Avouch, *from positive know-*
   Protest, *from conscience*
   Maintain, *by argument*
To Fear *any thing*
   Dread *punishment*
To be apprehensive *of loss*
   Afraid *of danger*
To Ask *a favour*
   Inquire *for Information*
   Interrogate *for truth*
To Assist *those in want*
   Help *in labour*
   Relieve *in distress*
   Succour *in danger*
To Avoid *disputes*
   Shun *bad company*
   Fly *from danger*
To Awake *from sleep*
   Awaken *curiosity*
Abilities, *mental powers*
   Ingenuity *of invention*
   Cleverness *to perform*
   Parts, *natural talents*

Sagacity *to discern*
Capacity *to grasp*
Acuteness *to distinguish*

Subtlety *to refine*
Ability *to execute*
Capacity *to comprehend*
Abject *in thought or resolution*
Mean, *a defect of generosity*
Low *in situation*
Beggarly *in circumstances*
A Learned Lawyer (Learned Gentleman in the House of Commons, or Learned Lord in the other House) implies a Lawyer
Skilful *in practice*
Profound *in theory*

An Acute *reasoner*
A Judicious *historian*

A Subtle *sophist*
An Enlightened *philosopher*

Abstemiousness *in eating or drinking* [*pleasures*
Temperance, *moderation in all*
Sobriety, *self-government and serious discipline of the soul*
Absent *in company from inadvertency*
Inattentive *from indolence or indifference*
Absurd, *ridiculously opposite to reason*
Unreasonable *in one's request*
Inconsistent, *contradictory*

Abundance, *overflowing, plenty*
Competency, *adequate sufficiency*

Abuse, *scurrilous language*
Affront, *wilful rudeness*
Insult, *by scornful reproof*

Acid, *sour, sharp*
Poignant, *keen, piercing*
Sour, *sullen, morose*

Caustic, *acrimoniously severe and cutting*
Sharp, *quick at repartee*
Acknowledgment *of mistake*
Confession *of guilt*

Acquainted, *by a slight knowledge of*
Familiar, *by long habit*
Intimate, *closely connected with*
Act, *action, deed*
Exploit, *successful exertion*
Action, *the performance of any thing*
Deed, *any thing performed*

Address, *mode of intercourse, manner of conversation*
Air, *quality of appearance*
Mien, *turn of countenance*
Behaviour, *conduct in company*
Deportment, *external demeanour*
Manners, *general habits*
Carriage *of the body*

Adjacent, *lying near to*
Contiguous, *close, adjoining*
Administration *of justice*
Management *of public concerns*
Conduct *of business*
Government *of the country*
Direction, *order with instruction*
Admonition, *to reprove*
Advice *of a friend*
Counsel, *deliberate instruction*

Advantageous, *subservient to our temporal interest*
Profitable, *conducive to our general welfare*
Beneficial, *useful in any respect*

Affairs, *circumstances or transactions in general*
Business, *particular employment*
Agreeable *conversation*
Pleasing *address*

Agreement *in verbal promise*
Contract, *in written testimony*
Bargain, *in relation to sale*
Aim, *endeavour*
View, *object proposed*
Design, *intention*
All *men*
Every *man*
Allurements *to entice*
Attractions *to engage*
Charms, *to fascinate*
Alone, *in solitude*
Only, *one*

Also, *in addition*
Likewise, *in comparison*

Always. *God is always present*
Ever. *Man is ever regardless*
Continually. *Death approaches without cessation*
Perpetually. *The good shall rejoice perpetually*

Amazed *at what is marvellous*
Astonished *at what is grand*
Surprised *at what is unexpected*
Consternation. *Struck with consternation at scenes of horror*
Ambiguity, *uncertainty of signification* [city
Equivocation, *intentional duplicity*

Amusement *in reading*
Diversion *in playing*

Ancient *date*
Old *age*
Antique *piece of art*

Angry, *resenting a provocation*
In a Passion, *actually irritated*
Passionate, *very apt to be irritated*
Choleric, *surly and ill-tempered*

Apartment *to dwell in*
Chamber *to sleep in*
Room *of a house*

Apartments, *suite of rooms*
Lodgings, *hired apartments*
Apparition, *to the senses*
Vision, *of the imagination*
Arrogance, *undue self-importance*
Pride *of heart*
Vanity, *silly affectation*
Haughtiness *of behaviour*
Presumption, *audacity*
Artifice, *to deceive*
Stratagem, *to disguise*
Trick, *to elude*
Device, *contrivance*
Cunning, *crafty*

Ashamed *of our faults*
Bashful *when spoken to*
Assiduous, *diligently employed in business*
Expeditious *in our business*
Quick *in our motions*

Attachment, *from esteem*
Passion, *vehement love*
Devoted to, *from reverence or* **af-**
*fection*
Audaciousness, *daring*
Effrontery, *shameless*
Impudence, *vulgar sauciness*
Boldness, *undaunted courage*

Austerity *of living*
Severity *of thinking*
Rigour *of punishing*

Authority, *of a Governor*
Jurisdiction, *of a Magistrate*
Dominion, *of a Prince*

Avaricious, *unwilling to part with money*
Covetous, *eager to obtain it*
Niggardly, *mean, saving*

To Be *healthy*
Exist, *and not to be only imaginary*
Subsist, *continue still*

To Beat *for a long time*
Strike *a blow*

To behold *with attention*
Look *at a distant object*
View *with exactness*
See *distinctly*

To Bid, *invite*
Order, *command*

To Bind *the hands*
Tie *him to a stake*

To Bring *what one has with him*
Fetch *what he is sent for*

Bad, *not good*
Vile, *base, hateful*

Battle, *a general engagement*
Combat, *between two persons*
Fight, *to conquer*

Beams *of the sun*
Rays *of light*

Beautiful *woman*
Handsome *house*
Pretty *cottage*

Benediction *of the priest*
Blessing *of God*

Beneficence, *actual goodness*
Benevolence, *the desire of doing good*

Bias, *partiality*
Inclination *to aid the unfortunate*
Propensity *to vice*

Big, *in bulk*
Large, *in extent*
Great, *exalted*

Bliss, *eternal*
Happiness, *high prosperity*
Felicity, *exalted state of happiness*

Boggy *quagmires*
Marshy *lands*

Bounds *of moderation*
Limits *of a kingdom*
Confines *of the grave*

Bounty, *in acts of giving*
Generosity, *in acts of greatness*
Liberality, *in candid sentiment*

Bravery, *in battle to face danger*
Courage, *to make us advance*
Intrepidity, *coolly daring certain danger*
Resolution, *steady firmness*

Brightness *of the moon*
Light *of the stars*
Splendour *of the sun*
Brilliancy *dazzles*
Radiancy *glitters*
Lustre *shines*

Broad *cloth*
Wide *room*

Brook, *a small stream*
Rivulet, *between banks*
Stream, *a running water*

Burden *carried*
Load *drawn*

Buttress, *to support laterally*
Prop, *to stand under*
Support, *to prevent falling*

To Call *for help.*
Name, *to distinguish*
To Cease *from labour*
Finish *his business*
Leave off *work*

To Chastise *a child*
Punish *a malefactor*
Discipline *a regiment*
Correct, *for amendment*

To Elect *a candidate*
Make choice *of a wife*
Choose *what pleases us*
Prefer *what pleases us best*

To Compel, *by authority*
Constrain, *by fear*
Oblige, *by necessity*
Force, *by strength*

To Complete *a piece of mechanism*
Conclude *an oration*
End *a journey*
Finish *any undertaking*

To Comprehend *sciences*
Understand *languages*
Conceive, *to imagine*

To Conceal *our designs*
Dissemble *our thoughts*
Disguise *our intentions*

To Concern *our interests*
Touch *our feelings*

To Conduct *an affair*
Lead *the helpless*
Guide *a traveller*

To Conquer *our enemies*
Subdue *our passions*
Overcome *any obstacle*

To Cry *like children*
Weep *like grown persons*
Calamity, *deep distress*

Misfortune, *loss of friends, &c.*
Disaster, *deplorable incident*
Cannot, *personal inability*
Impossible, *not in nature practicable*

Care, *thought*
Caution, *in acting warily*
Discretion, *in governing or directing* [*practice*
Prudence, *in applying wisdom to*
Case, *particular situation*
Circumstance, *accidental*
Conjuncture, *concurrence of things* [*gency*
Occasion, *opportunity or exi*
Occurrence, *an event or incident*

A Cave *is dug*
A Cell *is built*
Celebrated *for his abilities*
Famous *for his great exploits*
Renowned *in history*
Illustrious *family*

Chance, *accident*
Fortune, *events of war*

Change *our dress*
Vary *our opinions*
Alter *our manner of living*
Changeable *in appearance*
Inconstant *in resolution*
Fickle *in his attachments*
Unsteady *in his pursuits*

Charm, *fascinating influence*
Enchantment, *preternatural control* [*craft*
Spell, *power of magic or witch-*
Charms *of virtue*
Graces *of a Christian spirit*
Chief *commander*
Head *boy*

Choked *by eating too greedily*
Suffocated *by smoke*
Smothered *by violence*
Church, *body of Christians*
Temple *for public worship*
Circumspection *in speaking to strangers*
Regard *to truth*
Consideration *for people of ability*

Clearness, *distinctness of idea*
Precision, *accuracy of language*

Clergyman, *a man in holy orders*
Parson,* *a beneficed clergyman*
Clothes *which cover the body*
Dress *which makes us gay*

Clock *strikes the hour*
Dial *shows it*

Clownish, *from want of education*
Unpolite, *owing to a bad one*

Colours *of a regiment*
Flag *of a ship*

Commerce *with other nations*
Trade *among ourselves*
Traffic, *exchange of merchandise*

Compassion, *general concern for all who are wretched*
Commiseration, *joining in the sorrows of others*
Pity, *the distress of another: sometimes used in contempt*

Complaisant *in address*
Gallant *lover*
Polite *courtier*
Well-bred *gentleman*
Complete *design*
Perfect *beauty*
Finished *workmanship*

Complete, *in wanting nothing*
Entire, *in not being broken*

Complicated *affairs*
Involved *in such misery*

Conclusion, *the close*
Sequel, *the succeeding part*

Condition *of a thing*
State *of health*
Situation *of affairs*

Constancy *in affection*
Resolution *against obstacles or dangers*
Steadiness *in continuance*

Content *of mind*
Satisfaction, *in obtaining what we desire*

Contented *in our station*
Satisfied *with our possessions*

Continual *noise*
Continued *stream*

Continuance *in any office*
Continuation *of the same subject*

Conversation *on general subjects*
Discourse *on any particular topic*

Copy *of a writing or painting*
Model *of a building*
The Coward *is unwilling to face danger*
A Poltroon *will basely avoid it*

Crime *against the laws*
Vice *against morality*
Sin *against religion*

---

* "The appellation of a *parson*," says Judge Blackstone, Comm. vol. i. p. 284 "(however it may be depreciated by familiar, clownish, and indiscriminate use,) is the most legal, most beneficial, and most honourable title that a parish priest can enjoy; because such a one (as Sir Edward Coke observes) and he only, is said *vicem seu pe sonam ecclesiæ gerere*."

11*

Crooked *tree*
Deformed *in shape*
Hump-backed *by a local protuberance*

Cure *performed*
Remedy *procured*

Current *of air*
Stream *of light*

Customs, *the general practice of the people*
Manners, *their way of life*
Fashions *of their dresses*

To Detain *what he has taken*
Keep *what he possesses*

To Disclose *intrigues*
Reveal *something unknown*
Divulge *a secret*
Tell *for information*

To Disguise *by false appearance*
Mask, *to hide*

To Disperse *separate*
Scatter *loosely*

To Dwell *in a large house*
Live *in London*

Danger, *real appearance of mischief*
Hazard, *fortuitous loss*
Risk, *exposure to misfortune*
Venture, *trial for loss or gain*

Darkness, *want of light*
Obscurity, *unknown*
Death, *extinction of life*
Decease, *a law term signifying death*
Departure *from one life to another*
Defamation, *false report*
Detraction, *from deserved good fame*

Defect *of character*
Imperfection *of human nature*
Fault *of the workman*

Dejected, *sad from apprehension*
Dull, *stupid, heavy*
Low-spirited, *from bodily infir-*  [mity
Melancholy *from disappointment or sorrow*

Delicate, *not vulgar*
Fine, *excellent*
A delicate *compliment*
A fine *poem*

Delight *in doing good*  [senses
Pleasure, *gratification of the*
Derision, *sportive insult*
Ridicule, *contemptuous merriment*

Design *is the soul of action*
Intention *is the effect of reflection*
Design, *what we propose to execute*
Project, *often chimerical*
Destiny *ordains*
Lot *decides*

Determination *of a point*
Resolution *of a difficulty*

Detriment, *implies loss of property*
Harm, *a small degree of hurt*
Injury, *malignant wrong*
Hurt, *a great degree of harm (generally applied to bodily pain)*
Mischief, *much damage*

Devotion, *fervent prayer*
Religion, *forms of public faith and worship*
Piety, *to set God always before us*

Difference, *we make up the difference*
Dispute, *we end the dispute*
Quarrel, *we appease the quarrel*

Discerning (*sensible*) *mind*
Knowing (*cunning*) *man*
Discernment, *to distinguish*
Judgment, *to compare*
Discovery *of the properties of the magnet*
Invention *of the art of printing*
Disdain *of others*
Haughtiness, *self-importance*
Sickness *is called indisposition*
Disease, *in man*
Distemper *in brutes*

Disgraceful *as an object of reproach* [*fence*
Scandalous, *as giving public of-*
Ditch, *usual boundary of a field*
Trench *for carrying off the water*

Diversity, *of colours*
Variety *of amusements*
Divination *brings to light*
Prediction *foretells*

Doubt, *requires consideration*
Uncertainty, *caution*
Suspense, *patience*

Dregs *of wine*
Sediment *of water*

Drunk, *by too much liquor*
Fuddled, *stupidly drunk*
Intoxicated, *over-animated by drinking*
Duty, *that which ought to be done*
Obligation, *that which binds us to*
Duty *of life* [*do it*
Obligation *of conscience*

To Found *an hospital* [*support*
Endow, *give property for its*
Institute *a law*
Establish *on a lasting bas*

To Enlarge *a town*
Increase *our expenses*
To Excel *all others* [*sirely so*
Be Excellent, *but not exclu-*
To Expect, *with little doubt*
Hope, *but not so certainly*
To Extol, *human ability*
Praise, *human conduct*
Easy *to perform*
Ready *to come at*
Effectual *stop*
Efficacious *remedy*
Effigy, *representation by picture or sculpture*
Image, *molten or graven*
Statue, *resemblance effected by the chisel*
Effort, *attempt*
Endeavour, *striving to accomplish*
Elegant, *implies superior taste*
Genteel, *above the vulgar*
Emolument *of office*
Gain *of trade*
Lucre, *dishonourable gain*
Profit *of labour*
End *of life*
Extremity *of a kingdom*
Enormous *crime*
Immense *expanse*
Huge *giant*
Vast *tract of land*
Enough *to have*
Sufficient *to employ*
Epistle *of St. Paul*
Letter *of correspondence*
Erudition, *depth of knowledge*
Literature, *polite instruction*
Learning, *school instruction*

Esteem *him who does good*
Regard *a quiet neighbour*
Veneration *for his eminent quali-* [ties
Respect *to his rank and dignity*

Excuse *a fault*
Pardon *an offence*
Forgive *an injury*

Experiment, *to prove*
Trial, *to choose*
Proof, *the effect of experiment*

Faded, *decayed in brilliancy of colour*
Withered, *shrivelled by the loss of juices*

To Find *what we sought after*
  Meet *with things unsought for*
To Feel *a blow*
  Handle *a staff*

Falsehood, *a civil term of reprobation applied to an untruth*
Lie, *an uncivil and vulgar one*

Fashion, *shape, pattern*
Figure, *carved or painted*
Form, *outline*

Fatigued *with walking*
Wearied *with standing*
Tired *with success*

Fervency *of mind*
Warmth *of devotion*

Flat, *deficient in spirits*
Insipid, *tasteless*

Frankness, *without disguise*
Plainness, *without dissimulation*
Ingenuousness, *artlessness*
Sincerity, *without deceit*

Frequently, *many times*
Often, *still more frequently*

To Give *to our servants*
  Present *to princes*
  Offer *to God*

Gaiety, *lightness of spirit*
Joy *of the heart*
Mirth, *excited by humour*

Gallantry, *complimentary attention to the ladies*
Love, *affection founded on esteem*

General, *most men*
Universal, *all mankind*

Genius, *for poetry*
Talent *for speaking*

Gentle, *animals gentle from nature*
Tame, *made so by discipline*

Glory *to God*
Honour *to good men*

Good-fortune *is the effect of chance*
Prosperity *is the success of conduct*

Good-humour, *cheerful pleasing manner*
Good-nature *a disposition to promote the good of others*

Grave, *through humour*
Serious, *from reflection*

Great *knowledge*
Sublime *expressions*

To Hanker after, *desire with great eagerness* [or not
  Wish for *things at a distance*
  Long for, *with great desire*
  Lust after, *with unjustifiable desires*

To Have *an estate*
  Possess *riches*

Hasty *in his actions*
Passionate *in his words*

eadstrong, *not to be advised*
bstinate, *not convinced*
pinionated *in his notions*
repossessed *in his affections*
ıfatuated, *foolishly misled*

[owever *he was an excellent au-thor* ·
[evertheless *he was a bad liver*
et *he acquired fame*
ı the mean while *he lost esteem*

o Instruct *in science*
  Learn *an animal to play tricks*
  Teach *to read*

nagination, *brilliant* imagination
[otion, *singular* notion

nmediately, *without delay*
ıstantly, *without intervention of time*
'resently, *soon after*
[ow, *at the very instant*

ınpediment *stays*
)bstacle *resists*
)bstruction *puts an entire stop to*

mpertinent, *implies intrusion*
mpudent, *want of modesty*
aucy, *pert familiarity*

ndigence, *a situation where the necessaries of life are scantily supplied*
'overty, *where its conveniences are wanting*
Ieed, *pressing urgency*
Vant, *scarcity*
iecessity, *accidental but urgent want*

ndolent, *averse to exertion*
ᴀzy, *averse to labour*

Ineffectual *unable to complete*
In vain, *useless*
To no purpose, *having wholly failed*
Joining *of streams*
Union *of families and states*
Justice, *by authority*
Right *of disposal*
To Learn *to read*
  Study *science*

To Let down *the lid of a trunk*
  Lower *a building*
Level *country*
Smooth *marble*

Little *man*
Small *twig*
Lover, *a professed suitor to a lady*
In Love, *truly loving ner*
Luxury, *love of pleasure, extravagant indulgence*
Voluptuousness, *sensual gratification*

To Manifest, *to show openly*
  Publish *to the world*
  Proclaim *it to all men*

To Muse *deeply, intensely*
  Think, *to consider of any thing*
  Study, *to acquire learning*

Methodical *in our affairs*
Regular *in our conduct*
Modest *in our dress*
Reserved *in our words and actions*

Near *relation*
Nigh *the brink*
It is Necessary, *not to be neglect-* [ed

We Ought *it is our duty*
    Should, *it is proper*

New *clothes*
Fresh *butter*
Recent *events*

No, *he has* no *patience at all*
Not, *he has* not *enough*

To Observe *what is doing*
    Remark *what is said*

Opinion, *a favourable* opinion *of*
Sentiment, *a just* sentiment

Thought, *a chimerical* thought
To Permit *by consent*
    Suffer *abuse*
    Tolerate *evil*

Peace *among the nations*
Quiet *family*
Tranquil *mind*

Prerogative *of a ruler*
Privilege *of a subject*
Prospect, *a confined* prospect
View, *an extensive* view

Qualities, *good or bad*
Talents, *abilities*

To Restore *what we have taken*
    Return *what has been lent us*
    Surrender *what we have in*
        [*trust*

Riot *of a mob*
Uproar *of a drunken man*
Tumult *of the people*

Road, *the beaten way of travel-*
    *lers* [*place*
Way, *the passage from place to*

Robust *constitution*
Stout *made*

To Reprimand *a child*
    Reprove *a friend*
    Check *a servant*

The Rogue *steals in secret*
    Sharper *steals by finesse*
    Thief *steals by every method*

To Shake *with cold*
    To Tremble *with fear*

Servitude *of a hired servant*
    Slavery *of the negroes*

Sociable *qualities*
Social *virtues*

Value, *price*
Worth, *desert*

# APPENDIX.

## TABLE. I.

List *of* French *and other* Foreign Words *and* Phrases *in common Use, with their* Pronunciation *and* Explanation.

Aid-de-camp (*aid-de-cóng.*) Assistant to a general.

A-la-mode (*al-a-mode.*) In the fashion.

Antique (*antéek.*) Ancient, or Antiquity.

A propos (*ap-ro-pó.*) To the purpose, Seasonably, or By the bye.

Auto da fe (*auto-da-fá.*) Act of faith (burning of heretics.)

Avant courier (*a-vaun-koo-re-ay.*) A messenger sent forwards to announce the approach of some great personage.

Bagatelle, (*bag-a-tél.*) Trifle.

Beau (*bo.*) A man dressed fashionably.

Beau monde (*bo-mónd.*) People of fashion.

Beaux esprits (*boze-esprée.*) Gay fellows; men of wit.

Belle (*bell.*) A woman of fashion or beauty.

Belles lettres (*bell-lettre.*) Polite literature.

Billet doux (*bil-le-dóo.*) Love letter.

Bon mot (*bon-mo.*) A piece of wit.

Bonne bouche (*bonn-boosh.*) A nice or sweet morsel.

Bon ton (*bon-tóng.*) Fashion.

Bon-vivant (*bon-ve-vong.*) A luxurious person.

Boudoir (*boo-dwor.*) A small private apartment.

Carte blanche (*cart-blansh.*) Unconditional terms.

Chateau (*shat-ó.*) Country seat.

Chef d'œuvre (*shef-deuvre.*) Master-piece.

Ci-devant (*see-de-vang.*) Formerly.

Comme il faut (*com-el-fó.*) As it should be.

Con amore (*con-a-mo-rer.*) Gladly.

Conge d'elire (*congec-da-leér.*) Permission to choose.

Corps (*core.*) Body.

Corps Diplomatique (*cor-de-ploma-teke.*) The diplomatic body.

Coup de grace (*coo-de-grás.*) Finishing stroke.

Coup de main (*coo-de-main.*) Sudden enterprise.

Coup d'œil (*coo-deil.*) View, or glance.

Debut (*de-bu.*) Beginning.

Denouement (*de-no-móng.*) Finishing, or winding up.

Dernier ressort (*dern-yair-ressór.*) Last resort.

Depôt (*de-pó.*) Store, or magazine.

Dieu et mon droit (*dew-a-mon-drwau.*) God and my right.

Douceur, (*doo-seur.*) Present or bribe.

Double entendre (*doo-ble on-ten-der.*) An obscene allusion in disguise.

Eleve (*a-lave.*) Pupil.

Eclaircissement (*ec-lair-cis-móng.*) Explanation.

Eclat (*ec-lá.*) Splendour, or sudden and violent noise.

En bon point (*on-bon-poain.*) Jolly.

Encore (*en-kor.*) Again.

En flute (*on-flate.*) Carrying guns on the upper deck only, the hold being filled with stores.

En masse (*on-máss.*) In a body.

En passant (*on-pas-sang.*) By the way.

Ennui (*on-wée.*) Tiresomeness.

Entree (*on-tráy.*) Entrance.

Entre-nous (*on-tre-nou.*) Between ourselves, in secrecy.

Etude (*a-tud.*) Study.

Faux pas (*fo-pá.*) Fault, or misconduct.

Fete champetre (*fait-sham-paiter.*) A rural entertainment.

Femme couverte (*fem-koo-veyrte.*) A married woman.

Femme sole (*feme-sole.*) An unmarried woman.

Fille de chambre (*fill-de-shambre.*) A chambermaid.

Honi soit qui mal y pense (*ho-née-swau kee mal e panss*) May evil happen to him who evil thinks.

Hors de combat (*hor-de-com-bad.*) Unfit for battle.

Ich dien (*ich-dena.*) I serve.

Incognito. In disguise, or unknown.

In petto. Hid, or in reserve.

Je ne scais quoi (*zhe-ne-say-kwau.*) I know not what.

Jet d'eau (*zha-do.*) An artificial water spout.

Jeu de mots (*zheu-de-mó.*) Play upon words.

Jeu d'esprit (*zheu-des-pree.*) Play of wit.

L'argent (*lar-zhung.*) Money or silver.

Mal a propos (*mal-ap-ro-pó.*) Unseasonable or unseasonably.

Manege (*man-azh.*) A place for training horses, a riding school.

Mauvaise honte (*mo-vaiz-honte.*) Unbecoming bashfulness.

Nom de guerre (*nomg-de-gáir.*) Assumed name.

Nonchalance (*nong-shal-ance.*) Indifference.

Outre (*oo-tráy.* Preposterous.

Penchant (*pong-shong.*) Inclination, desire.

Per due. Concealed.

Petit maitre (*pé-tee-maitre.*) A fop, or coxcomb.

Protege (*pro-te-zhay.*) A person patronised and protected.

Rouge (*rooje*) Red, or red paint, for the face.

Ruse de guerre (*ruz-de-gair.*) A trick of war, stratagem.

Sang froid (*sang-froau.*) Coolness, indifference, apathy.

Sans (*sang.*) Without.

Savant (*sav-ang.*) A learned man.

Soi disant (*swau-dee-zang.*) Pretended.

Table d'hote (*tabl-d'ot'.*) A public table.

Tapis (*tap-ée.*) Carpet.

Tact (*tact.*) Quick perception.

Tête a Tête (*tait-a-tait.*) Face to face, a familiar discourse.

Tocsin (*tok-sin.*) Alarm-bell.
Unique (*you-néek.*) Singular.
Valet de chambre (*va-la-de-shambr.*) Footman.

Vive la bagatelle (*veev-la-bag-a tél.*) Success to trifles.
Vive le roi (*veev-ler-wau.*) Long live the king.

## TABLE II.

EXPLANATION *of* LATIN WORDS *and* PHRASES *in Common Use among English Authors.*

*N. B. The pronunciation is the same as if the words were English; but divided into distinct syllables, and accented as below.—In all these words, a ending a syllable, has the sound of a as in* father—*t before i and another vowel, and after the accent, is. as in* English, *pronounced like c soft, or like sh.—æ and œ are pronounced like e long.*

Ab' in-i'-ti-o, *from the beginning*
Ad ar-bit'-ri-um, *at pleasure*
Ad cap-tan'-dum, *to entrap*
Ad-den'-da, *things to be added*
Ad in-fin-i'-tum, *to infinity*
Ad lib'-it-um, *at pleasure*
Ad ref-er-end'-um, *for consideration*
Ad va-lo'-rem, *according to value*
A for-ti-o'-ri, *with strong reason*
A'-li-as, *otherwise*
Al'-ib-i, *elsewhere, or proof of having been elsewhere*
Al'-ma ma'-ter, *university*
A men'-sa et tho'-ro, *from bed and board*
A'-mor pa'-tri-æ, *the love of one's country*
Ang'-li-ce. *in English*
An'-no ur'-bis con'-di-tæ, *or* A. U. C. *in the year of the city* (Rome) *being built*
A pos-te-ri-o'-ri, *from a latter reason, or behind*
A pri-o'-ri, *from a prior reason*
Ar-ca'na, *secrets*
Ar-ca'-num, *secret*

Ar-gu-men'-tum ad hom'-in-em, *personal argument*
Ar-gu-men'-tum bac-u'-li-num, *argument of blows*
Au'-di al'-ter-am par'-tem, *hear both sides*
Bo'-na fi'-de, *in reality*
Cac-o-e'-thes scri-ben'-di, *passion for writing* [*is wanting*
Cæ'-te-ra de'-sunt, *the remainder*
Ca'-pi-as ad res'-pon-den'-dum, *a writ issued to take the defendant, that he may be answerable to the plaintiff*
Ca'-pi-as ad sa-tis-fa'-ci-en'-dum, *a writ issued, after judgment, to arrest the defendant, until he shall satisfy the plaintiff*
Cer'-ti-o-ra'-ri, *a writ to order the record of a cause to be brought before a superior court*
Com-mu'-ni-bus an'-nis, *on the annual average*
Com'-pos men'-tis, *in one's senses*
Co'-ram non ju'-di-ce, *before an improper tribunal*
Cre'-dat Ju-dæ'-us, *a Jew may believe it* (*but I will not*)

Cre-den'-da, *things to be believed; articles of faith*

Cui bono, (ki bo'-no) *what advantage is intended?*

Cui malo (ki ma'-lo) *what mischief will result?*

Cum mul'-tis a'-li-is, *with many others*

Cum priv-i-le'-gi-o, *with privilege*

Da'-tum, or Da'-ta, *point or points settled or determined*

De fac'-to, *in fact*

De'-i gra'-tia, *by the grace or favour of God*

De ju'-re, *by right*

De no'-vo, *afresh, over again*

De'-sunt cæt'-er-a, *the rest is wanting*

Di'es non, *a day on which no legal proceedings can take place, or on which public offices are shut*

Div'-i-de et im'-pe-ra, *divide and govern—the monarchical maxim*

Dom'-in-e di'-ri-ge nos, *O Lord direct us*

Dram'-a-tis per-so-næ, *characters represented*

Du-ran'-te vi'-ta, *during life*

Du-ran'-te be'-ne pla"-ci-to, *during pleasure*

Ec-ce hom'-o, *behold the man*

Ec-ce sig'-num, *behold the sign or mark*

Er'-go, *therefore*

Er-ra'-ta, *errors*—Er-ra'-tum, *error*

Est'-o per-pet'-u-a, *may it last for ever*

Ex, *late. As, the ex-minister, means the late minister*

Ex-cerp'-ta, *extracts*

Ex-em'-pli gra ti-a, *as an example; for instance*

Ex of-fi'-ci-o, *by virtue of his office*

Ex par'-te, *on the part of, or one side*

Ex post fac'-to, *for and after an act done; affecting an act previously committed*

Fac sim i-le, *exact copy or resemblance*

Fas'-ces, *a bundle of twigs*

Fe'-lo de se, *self-murderer*

Fi'-at, *let it be done*

Fi'-er-i fa'-ci-as, *a writ empowering a sheriff to levy the amount of a debt, or of damages*

Gen'-e-ra, *classes*

Gra'-tis, *for nothing*

Ib-i'-dem, *in the same place*

I'-dem *the same*

Id est, *that is*

Im-per'-i-um in im-per'-i-o, *one government within, or subject to, another; [as the several states and federal government]*

Im-pri-ma'-tur, *let it be printed*

Im-pri'-mis, *in the first place*

In cœ'-lo qui'-es, *there is rest in heaven*

In-cog'-ni-ta, *unknown: applied to the singular, feminine, and neuter plural*

In-cog'-ni-to, *a concealment of the proper person or rank*

in for'-ma pau'-per-is, *as a pauper, or poor person*

In com-men'-dam, *for a time*

In pro'-pri-a per-so'-na, *in person*

In-stant'-er, *instantly*

In sta'-tu quo, *in the former state*

In ter-ro'-rem, *as a warning*

In trans'-i-tu, *on the passage*

Ip'-se dix-it, *mere assertion*

Ip'-so fac'-to, *by the mere fact*

Item, *also; individual thing*

Ju'-re di-vi'-no, *by divine right*

Ju'-re hu-ma'-no, *by human law*

Lex na-tu'ræ, *the law of nature*

Lex non scrip'-ta, *unwritten law; the common law*

Lex scrip'-ta, *written or statute law*

Lex tal'-i-o'-nis, *the law of retaliation*

Lo'-cum te'-nens, *deputy*

Lu'-sus na-tu'-ræ, *an irregular production of nature*

Mag'-na char'-ta, (*kar-ta*) *the great charter of England*

Mal'-a fi'-de, *with a design to deceive*

Mal'-um in se, *evil in itself, as murder*

Mal'-um pro-hib'-i-tum, *evil prohibited by laws, as the killing of game*

Max'-i-mum, *the highest rate*

Me-men'-to mo'-ri, *remember thou must die*

Me'-um and tu'-um, *mine and thine*

Min'-i-mum, *the lowest rate*

Mo'-dus op-er-an'-di, *the method or manner of operating*

Mul'-tum in par'-vo, *much in a small space*

Mu-ta'-tis mu-tan'-dis, *after making the necessary changes*

Nem. con. *an abbreviation of* nemine contradicenté; *no person opposing or disagreeing*

Ne'-mo me im-pu'-ne la-ces'set, *nobody shall provoke me with impunity*

Ne plus ul'-tra, *no farther or greater extent*

Ni-si pri' us, *a judicial writ, by which a sheriff is to assemble a jury on a certain day*

No'-lens vo'-lens, *willing or not*

Non com'-pos, *or* Non com-pos men'-tis, *out of one's senses*

Nol'-le pros'-e-qui, *no cause of prosecution*

Non as-sump'-sit, *he did not assume, or undertake*

Non est in-ven'-tus, *in law signifies, he has not been found; sudden disappearance*

No'-vus ho'-mo, *a man recently emerged from obscurity*

Ob'-it, *he (or she) died*

O'-nus pro-ban'-di, *the burden of proving*

O tem'-po-ra, O mo'-res, O *the times, O the manners*

Om'-nes, *all*

O'-nus, *burden*

Par'-i pas'-su, *with an equal pace: by a similar gradation*

Pas'-sim, *every where*

Per se, *alone, or by itself*

Pen-den'-te li'-te, *whilst the suit or contest is pending and undetermined*

Per di'-em, *by the day*

Plus, *more; opposed to* minus

Pos'-se com-i-ta'-tus, *the inhabitants of the country, which the sheriff is authorized to call forth*, when opposed in his official duties

Post mor'-tem, *after death*

Post ob'-it, *a post-obit bond is that which promises payment of money after the death of a certain person; generally by his heir.*

Pri'-ma fa'-ci-e, *the first view; not referring to any thing subsequently*

Pri'-mum mob'-i-le, *that which gives motion to all the parts*

Prin-cip'-i-a, non homines, *principles, not men*

Pro bo'-no pub'-li-co, *for the public benefit*

Pro and con, *for and against*

Pro for'-ma, *for form's sake*

Pro hac vi'-ce, *for this time*

Pro re na'-ta, *for the occasion*

Pro tem'-po-re, *for the time, not permanently*

Quam'-di-u se be-ne ges'-ser-it, *as long as he shall conduct himself properly; during good behaviour* [sufficient

Quan'-tum suf'-fi-cit, *as much as is*

Qua'-re im-pe'-dit, *a writ which lies for a patron of a church-living, against the disturber of his right of advowson*

Quid nunc, *a news hunter*

Quis sep-ar-a'-bit, *who shall separate us?*

Qui tam, *an action in the manner of an information on a penal statute*

Quo'-ad hoc, *as far as this*

Quo an'-im-o, *intention*

Quo-ad, *as to*

Quo war'-ran-to, *by what warrant, or authority*

Quon'-dam, *former*

Re-qui-es'-cat in pa'-ce, *may he rest in peace*

Re-sur'-gam, *I shall rise again*

Rex, *king*

Sanc'-tum sanc-to'-rum, *the holy of holies*

Scan'-da-lum mag-na'-tum, *scandal against the nobility*

Sci'-re fa'-ci-as, *a writ ordering the defendant to show cause, why the execution should not be made out of a judgment which has passed*

Se-cun'-dum ar-tem, *according to art*

Se-ri-a'-tim, *in regular order*

Si'-ne di'-e, *without mentioning any particular day*

Si'-ne qua non, *indispensable requisite, or condition*

Spec'-tas et tu spec-tab'-e-re, *you see and you will be seen*

Sta'-tu quo, *in its (his, her, or their) former state*

Sub si-len'-ti-o, *in silence*

Sta'-tus quo, *the " status quo ante bellum," the state in which [the several belligerents were] before the war*

Su'-i gen'-e-ris, *singular, or unparalleled*

Sum'-mum bo'-num, *greatest good*

Tæ'-di-um vi-tæ, *weariness of life*

To'-ga vir-i'-lis, *the manly robe; wore by the Roman youth*

Tri'-a junc'-ta in u'-no, *three joined in one*

Ul-ti-ma'-tum, *ultimate or last offer or decision*

U'-ti-le dul'-ci, *utility with pleasure*

U'-na vo'-ce, *unanimously*
U'-ti pos-si-de'-tis, *as you possess*
Va'-de me'-cum, *constant companion*
Ver'-sus, *against*
Vel'-u-ti in spec'-u-lum, *as in a looking-glass*
Ven-di'-ti-o'-ni ex-po'-nas, *a writ empowering a sheriff to sell certain property therein described*
Ve-ni'-re fa'-ci-as, *a writ by which a sheriff is empowered to summon a jury*

Ver-ba'-tim et lit-er-a'-tim, *word for word, and letter for letter*
Vi'-a, *by the way*
Vi'-ce, *in the room of*
Vi'-ce ver'-sa, *the reverse*
Vi'-de, *see*
Vi et ar'-mis, *by force and arms, not lawful*
Vis in'-er-ti-æ, *sluggishness*
Vi'-va vo'-ce, *by word of mouth*
Vi'-vant rex et re-gi'-na, *long live the king and queen*
Vul'-go, *commonly*

## PREPOSITIVE PARTICLES.

As a great number of Latin, Greek, and French verbs, verbalized nouns, or adjectives, are adopted into our language, composed of verbs, verbalized nouns, or adjectives, and prepositions, retaining in English the compound senses, or those analogous to them, which they have in those languages; and as many of the prepositions are often combined with words purely English, it was thought important to prepare for the use of English scholars the following lists of Greek, Latin, and French prepositions with their meanings in composition. A simple root, in many instances, (so numerous indeed as to make at least a fifth part of our language,) is found combined with most of the prepositions: so, that with a knowledge of the various meanings of the prepositions and terminations, a scholar may learn the orthography and precise meanings of the fifth part of his language, by simply learning those of the roots, which it is probable do not constitute one-twentith part even of these. A collection of roots, with their meanings, follows the exercises on the *Tables of Terminations*: And directions for using them may be found in the *Exercises*, —Quest. 22, &c.

The following general observations on the nature of compound verbs seem to be worthy of notice:—

1. A compound verb active, formed from an active verb, ought to be followed by two objects, one for the verb, the other for the preposition.
2. A verb active, formed from a neuter verb, has one object for the preposition.
3. A verb neuter, formed from an active verb, ought to govern like the first; but it has in English only an object for the preposition.
4. A verb neuter, formed from a neuter verb, has only an object for the preposition, or else the preposition takes the nature of an adverb.
5. Prepositions in verbs or adjectives, formed from nouns, spend their force on them, but connect them with the objects in active verbs, or with the subjects in neuter verbs, and with the nouns to which the adjective refers in adjectives.

6. But, most *generally*, the effect of the preposition is apparently confined to the verb, and may be considered as an adverb, though in almost every case, a mental allusion to an object is undoubtedly made. Of more than 3000 verbs, combined with four different prepositions, not the 25th part were found to be followed, in their ordinary use, by the prepositions and their objects. And even when the preposition is expressed, it is not always translated by the correspondent English preposition, the general substitute *to* and others being often used instead, as appears from the tables.

7 With nouns not verbal, the prepositions perform the office of adjectives; as *ex-minister, e-pi-dermis, up-land, &c.*

8. Some of the prefixes are adverbs and some prepositions in the languages to which they belong; as the Latin *di, dis, intro, re, retro, se,* the Greek *a,* and the English *un.* But most of them, however, are translated by an English preposition, which therefore must have an object expressed or implied.

Note.—Words beginning with *re*, ought not to be followed by *back*, or *again*.

9. The most usual signs of contrariety, in Greek words is *a*, in Latin and English *dis, in,* and *un,* (the last two varied doubtless from the vulgar sign of negation.)

## TABLE III.

*Latin Prepositions.*

*a, ab, abs.*—1. from, away, off; 2. imperfection; 3. intension; 4. difference; 5. taking from the substance of; 6. privation, or contrariety; as, 1. avert, turn from or away, ab-solve, loose from, ab-scission, cutting off; 2. ab-ortion, imperfect birth; 3. ab-negation, positive denying; 4. ab-sonant, sounding harshly; 5 abuse, wear away by using, treat ill; 6. ab-lactate, take from milk, wean.

Note.—*a* is used before *m, v; ab* before *d, h, j, , n, r, s; abs* before *c, t* These prepositions denote the point where motion begins, and are opposed to *ad* which denotes where it must end.

*ad,* (ac, af, ag, al, am, an, ap, ar, as, at.)—1. to; 2. towards; 3. together; 4. agreeably to; 5. hostilely to; 6. against; 7. next to, or by; 8. at; 9 at the end, or after; 10. upwards; 11. intension: as, 1. ad-ject, cast to; 2. ad-vesperate, draw towards evening; 3. at-trition, rubbing together; 4. as-sent, assonant, think, sounding, agreeably to; 5. af-front, displease to the face intentionally; 6. af-flict, dash against; 7. ad-jacent, lying next to; 8. ad-mire, wonder at; 9. af-fix, put after; 10. ac-clivity, slope upwards; 11. ad-ult, quite grown

Note.—*d* in *ad*, becomes *c, f, g, l, m, n, p, r, s, t,* before these letters, and is omitted before *sp. st.*

*am.*—Round: as, am-b-ient, extending round; am-b-ition, (going round;) electioneering, desire of office, or power.

*ante*—Before: as, ante-cedent, going before; ante-past, fore-taste; ante diluvian, before the flood; anti-cipate, take before.

Note.—*Ante* sometimes becomes *an* as, ancestors for antecessors. It is opposed to *post.—See pro.*)

*circum.*—1. round, or about ; 2. expletive : as, 1. circum volve, roll roun 1; 2. circum-ambient, surrounding.

Note.—*Circum* is a separable, and *am* an inseparable preposition. *Remark*—As *inter* requires more than one governed object, so *circum* implies more than one correlative object.

*con, co,* (col, com, cor.)—1 with, together ; 2. within or back ; 3. for contra, against ; 4. exchange ; 5. round, (ends together:) as, 1. co-oqual, equal with; co-exist, exist with ; 2. co-erce, keep within or back, curb ; 3. con tend, stretch or struggle with ; 4. commute, change one (punishment) for another ; 5. com-pass, surround, distance round.

Note.—*Co* is used before vowels, *h* silent, and English words generally ; *con* before *l, m, r,* changes *n* into those letters : becomes *com* before *b, p,* and even *cog* before *n* in cognomination, cognation, with cognition and words of the same root.

*contra.*—1. against ; in the opposite part ; or by opposite qualities : as 1. con-tradict, say the contrary ; 2. contra-fissure, fissure in the opposite part ; 3. con-tra-distinguish by opposite qualities.

Note.—The meanings of *contra* are but figures of those of *con,* its root.

*de.*—1. from out of; 2. simply from, down ; 3. forth ; 4. for ; 5. against ; 6. priva-tion ; 7. decrease ; 8. intension ; 9 contrariety ; 10. expletive : as, 1. de-duct, draw out ; 2 de-spise, look from (with dislike ;) de-pend, hung from or down ; deject, cast down ; 3. de-ambulate, walk abroad ; 4 de-plore, weep for ; 5. de-precate, pray (to be delivered) from ; 6. de-capitate, behead ; 7. de-fame, de-tract from the fame of ; 8. claim, cry out vehemently ; 9. de-tect, uncover; de-scend, come down ; de-merit, ill-deserving ; de-decorous, disgraceful, 10. de-clare, make clear; de-albate, whiten ; de-nude, strip ; de-prave, make vi-cious.

Note.—*De* unites the powers of *a* and *e*; and denotes the separation of one body from an-other, to which it had been contiguous, by which it had been contained, or of which it had formed a part. It is opposed to *ad* and *in*, and differs from *a* in that the correlative object of *a* is extraneous to its governed object ; while that of *de* may be contained in its governed ob-ject. Hence the separation suggested by *de* is held more difficult than that suggested by *a*, as either a barrier, or the coherence of a mass, is to be overcome.

*di dis.*—1. asunder, apart ; 2. aside ; 3. ahroad ; 4. difference ; 5. contrariety : as, 1. di-lacerate, tear apart ; 2. di-vert, turn aside ; 3. dif-fuse, pour, scatter abroad, disseminate ; 4. dis-sent, think differently ; 5. dis-junct, dis-joined, diffident, distrusting.

Note.—*Di* seems to be but a variation of *de*, as its meanings show ; *s* in *dis* being assumed for euphony.—*Di* is used before *d, g, l, m, n, v* ; *dis* before *c, l, p, g, t.* Before *r, j,* either *di* or, *ais* is used : before *sp, st,* only *di.* *F.* is doubled after *di* ; and *di* before a vowel inserts *r,* as di-remption.

*ex.*—1. out of, forth ; throughout, thoroughly : 3. privation ; 4. intensive or expletive : 5. out of office : as, 1 e-ject, cast-out ; exclaim, cry out ; expel, drive out ; 2. elaborate, thoroughly laboured ; 3. ex-animate, deprived of life, ex-uccous, deprived of juice ; 4. ex-asperate, irritate greatly ; 5. ex-minister, former minister ; ex-president.

Note.—*e* is used before *b*, *d*, *g*, *l*, *m*, *n*, *r*, *j*, *v* : *ex* before vowels and *h*, *p*, *q*, *t*, *s* Before *f*, *s* becomes *f*; and *s* disappears sometimes after *ex* : as, exist for ex-sist.

*extra.*—1. without, or not within ; 2. outwards ; 3. beyond ; 4. for *ex*, out of : as, 1. extra-provincial, without the province ; 2. extra-mission, sending out or outwards ; 3. extra-ordinary, beyond ordinary ; 4. extra-vagant, wandering beyond just limits.

Note.—*Extra* differs from *ex*, its root, in that its correlative object may, or may not, be contained in its governed object : while *ex* supposes its correlative to be contained in its governed.

*in*, (ig, il, im, ir)—1. in or within ; 2. into ; 3. inwards ; 4. towards ; 5. against ; 6. over ; 7. upon ; 8. intension ; 9. privation ; 10. negation : as, 1. in-habit, dwell in ; in-hibit, hold in, curb ; 2. in-duct, lead in ; 3. in-flect, bend inwards ; 4. in-cline, lean towards ; 5. inflict, dash upon or against ; 6. im-pend, hang over ; 7. insist, stand on ; 8 in-durate, harden in or thoroughly ; 9. in-capacitate, deprive of capacity ; 10. im-pure, not pure ; ignorant, not knowing ; ir-rational, not rational.

Note.—*n*. before *b*, *m*, *p*, becomes *m* ; and *s*, *l*, *r*, before these letters, and even *g* before *n* in ignoble, ignominy, ignorance, ignoscible. (See note under *con*.)

*intro.*—1. inwards ; 2. into : as, 1. intro-spect, look inwards ; 2. intro-duce, bring into company or acquaintance.

*inter.*—1. between, among ; 2. on the way between ; 3. together ; 4. reciprocation : as, 1. inter-vene, come between ; 2. inter-vert, turn on the way between ; 3. inter-mingle, mingle together ; 4. inter-change, change reciprocally ; inter-marry, to marry some of one family with some of another.

Note.—*Inter* differs from its root *in*, in that its governed objects are separated by its correlative object, while *in* denotes that the correlative is enclosed by the parts of the governed.

*juxta.*—Nigh, or besides : as, juxta-position, placing by.

Note.—Though *juxta* is from *jungere*, to join, it does not imply actual contact.

*ob*, (oc, of, op.)—1. in the way of ; 2. against ; 3. to ; 4. towards ; 5. over ; 6. about ; 7. inversion : as, 1. ob-ject, throw in the way ; ob-trude, thrust in the way ; oblate, extended in the way of the motion ; 2. ob-loquy, speaking against ; ob-durate, hardened against ; 3. of-fer, bring in the way, present to ; 4. ob-vert, turn towards ; 5. ob-duce, draw or spread over ; 6. ob-ambulation, walking about ; 7. ob-cordate, obovate.

Note.—*Ob* differs from *ad* in that *ad* denotes the point at which motion end : while *ob* denotes the object which must obstruct it. B in *ob* becomes *c*, *f*, *p*, before these letters, *s* in ostentation ; and is sometimes omitted, as in the word o-mit.

*per.*—1. through ; 2. thoroughly, throughout : 3. intension ; as, 1. per-form, form, through, finish ; 2. per-fect, make thoroughly complete ; 3. per-durable, very durable.

Note.—*Per* denotes the relation which a moving body bears to the surface which supports ; to the mediu through which it passes, and to the obstacle it overcomes. *Per* sometimes changes *r* to *l*, as in pel-lucid.

*nt.*—1. behind ; 2. after: as, post-diluvian, after the flood ; post-meridian, after noon ; post-humous, after burial ; post-scrip., written at the end or after.

*e.*—1. before ; 2. beforehand ; 3. superiority: as, 1. pre-fix, fix before ; pre-cursor, forerunner ; present, being before ; pre-mature, before ripe, ripe before the time ; 2. pre-dict, foretell ; 3. pre-pollency, superior power ; pre-ponderate, outweigh ; preside, to be set over ; pre-centor, head or leading singer.

Note.—*Pre* differs from *pro* its root, in necessarily implying motion in its two objects, and notes the relation which animated objects have to others following in the same path.

*eter.*—1. across the direction of, against ; 2. by or past ; as, 1, preter-natural, not according to the course of nature ; 2. preter-it, gone by ; preter-mit, put or pass by.

Note.—*Preter* differs from *pre* its root, in supposing that its object may or may not move, and that the correlative moves in a line across its path, or the line of its aspect, if it is at a.

*o.*—1. before ; 2. beforehand ; 3. forward ; 4. for ; 5. from ; 6. openly ; 7. instead of: as, 1. pro-tect, cover before, shield ; 2. pro-vide, look for beforehand ; 3 pro-ceed, go forward ; pro-late, extended forward ; 4. pro-pugn, fight for, before in defence of ; 5. pro-hibit, hold before, keep from ; 6. pro-claim, speak forward, openly ; 7. pro-consul, substitute for a consul, vice-consul.

Note.—*Pro* and *ante* are thus distinguished. *Ante* is more general than *pro*, applying to means as well as to things. The two objects of *ante* define each other mutually ; but though t governed object of *pro* necessarily defines the correlative, the latter has no reciprocal influ-ce ; that is, it is not *considered* that the governed object is *before* the correlative. (See note ider *re*,)

.—1. again ; 2. back, or contrariety ; perhaps, for retro-; 4. intension, as if again and again: as, 1. re-assert, assert again ; 2. re-cant, say back, unsay ; re-tection, uncovering, bringing again to view ; 3. re-linquish, leave behind ; 4. re-mote, moved afar off.

Note.—*A, re, pro, se*, insert sometimes *d* and *pre, s*, before a vowel ; as, a-d-emption, re-tem, re-d-undance, pro-d-ition, se-d-ition, pre-s-ent.

*tro.*—Backwards or behind: as, retro-spect, looking behind or backwards.

.—Aside, apart: as, se-clude, shut apart ; se-duce, lead aside ; se-lect, choose out (See note under *re*.)

*ne.*—Without, (opposed to with:) as, sine-cure, office (with revenue, but) without care or employment.

*b,* (suc, suf, sug, sum, sup, sur, sus.)—1. under, beneath ; 2. for super, over ; 3. down, under ; 4. privacy, underhand, unawares ; 5. in place of, or substitute - 6. diminution, or lower degree ; 7. below, after ; 8. one part of ; 9. root: as, 1 sub-ject, cast or put under ; 2 suffuse, flow over ; 3. sub-side, settle down under, 4. sub-orn, instruct privately ; subreption, creeping slily upon ; sur prise, take by stealth ; 5. sub-stitute, put in place of or for ; sub-dean, vice dean ; 6. sub-acid, acid in a low degree ; sub-divide, divide into less parts ; 7 sub-sequent, following after or under ; 8. sub-duple, sub-triple, &c., one part o two three &c. ; 9. sub-duplicate, sub-triplicate, &c., square, cube, root, &c.

Note.—Before c. l. g. m. p. r. b becomes the same, and sometimes s before c. It loses b before sp, st

*subter.*—Beneath, under: as, subter-fluent, flowing under; subter-fuge, plea to escape under, evasion.

Note.—*Subter* differs from *sub* its root, in supposing that no contiguity takes place between the inferior and superior body.

*super.*— above; 2. upon; 3. over; 4. excess; 5. besides; 6. after: as, 1. super-natural, above nature; 2. super-crescence, growing on; 3. super-visor, overseer; 4. super-abundance, excessive abundance; 5. super-add, add beside; 6. super-conception, after conception.

*supra.*—1. 2. 3. 4. of *super*; as, 1. 2. or 3. supra-position, placing above, upon, over; 4. supra-lapsary, before the fall.

Note.—*Supra* originally bore the same relation, it is likely, to *super*, that *subter* does to *sub*, meaning *above*, whether objects intervened or not; as *subter* means *beneath*, in the same respect.

*trans.*—1. from one side to the other, over or through; 2. from one to another; 3. across; 4. beyond; 5. interchange: as, 1. trans-pierce, pierce through; 2. tran-substantiation, changing one substance into another; 3. trans-verse, turned across; 4. trans-atlantic, beyond the atlantic; 5. trans-location, making two things change places.

Note.—*Trans*, primarily respects interval between the two points at which the motion of a body begins and ends.

*ultra.*—1. beyond; 2. excess: as, ultra-montane, beyond the mountain; ultra-marine, beyond the sea; 2. ultra-royal, excessively attached to the king.

Note.—*Ultra* is opposed to *cis* or *citra*. It is opposed to *trans* in being applied in its simple state to time, number, and measure, and to objects not in motion. In English words, *cis* and *trans* are opposed; as, trans-alpine, cis-alpine, on the other side, on this side, the Alps

# TABLE IV

## *Greek Prepositions.*

*a.*—Negation: as, a-methodical, not methodical, a-pathy, without feeling; an onymous, without name; a-theism, disbelief in a God.

Note.—*A* is a negative particle. It inserts *n* before a vowel.

*ana.*—1. re- or back; 2. backwards; 3. upwards: as, 1. ana-camptic, bending back, re-flecting; ana-strophe, turning backwards, postponing words that usually precede; ana-diplosis, reduplication; ana-clatics, doctrine of refracted light; ana-lyze, resolve into first principles; ana-cathartic, cleansing upwards.

Note.—The original meaning was the line of direction of any thing traced backwards. becomes *am* before *b, p*.

*amphi.*—1. on both sides; 2. from one side to the other; 3. on either side; 4. on all sides or round: as, 1. amphi-brach, a foot having a short syllable on both sides of a long; 2. amphi-bolus, tossed from one to another; 3. amphi-bious, living in either element, (air or water;) 4 amphi-theatre, a round theatre.

*ti*, (ant, anth.)—1. against; 2. reverse; 3. instead of; 4. interchange; 5. alternation; 6. counterpart: as, 1. anti-monarchical, against monarchy; 2. anti-climax, reversed climax; anti-pope, one holding the place of the true pope; 4. anti-ptosis, putting one case for another; 5. anthem (for ant-hymn) a hymn sung in alternate parts; 6. anti-type, thing represented by the type.

Note.—The primary meaning is *facing*, fronting, set opposite to.

*o*, (ap, aph.)—1. from; 2. forth; 3. out; 4. contrariety; 5. farthest point from: as, 1. apo-strophe, turning from; aph-œresis, taking from (the beginning of a word; apo-cope, cutting from (the end of a word;) 2. apo-stle, one sent forth; 3. apo-physis, a growing prominent; 4. apo-calypse, revelation; 5. apo-gee, farthest point from the earth; aph-elion, farthest point from the sun.

Note.—The Latin *ab* is derived from *ap* by changing *p* into its cognate *b*.

*ta*, (cat, cath.)—1. against; 2. over: as, 1. cata-chresis, misuse of a trope; 2. cata-clysm, a washing over, inundation, deluge.

Note.—The primary meaning was, the line of direction along which a thing tends or is stated.

*ia*, (di.)—1. through; 2. distinction: as, 1. dia-meter, measure through; dia-gonal, line through the coners; 2. dia-gnostic, symptoms by which a disease is distinguished.

Note.—*Dia* must not be confounded with *dis* signifying the same as the Latin *bis* twice, in *æresis* dialogue, &c.

*n*, (el, em.)—1. in; 2. among: as, 1. en-cysted, in a vesicle; emblem, inlay, enamel; 2. en-demial, among the people.

*vi*, (eph)—1. upon; 2. over; 3. outer: as, 1. epidemic, upon the people; 2. epi-scopate, overseership, bishoprick; 3. epi-dermis, scarfskin.

*c. ex.*—1. from; 2. out: as, 1. ec-centric, deviating from the centre; 2. el-lipsis, a leaving out; ec-phonesis, a crying out.

Note.—*Ec* before consonants, *ex* before vowels.

*yper*.—1. above, over; 2 excess: as, 1. hyper-bole, above the truth; hyperbola, line thrown or passing *right* over a cone; 2. hyper-critical, over critical.

Note.—The primary meaning was *higher*. It corresponds to the Latin *super* or *supra*.

*ypo*, (hyp.)—1. under; 2. disguise; 3. interchange: as, 1. hypo-thesis, supposition or placing under; 2. hypo-crisy, simulation, disguise of the real character; 3. hyp-allage, interchange of cases.

Note.—The primary meaning was *high* relatively to another object, which therefore must be *ne* or *under* in respect to the other. It corresponds to *sub*.

*ueta*, (met, meth.)—1. trans, or change; 2. after, beyond: as, 1. meta-morphose, to change the form; meta-phor, transferring a name to another object; met-onymy, change of names; 2. meta-physics, science beyond physics.

*Note.*—The original meaning was *with*, in its various senses. It is thus contrasted with *syn*. The latter was applied to objects concurring to produce one action or event, *meta* to objects simply accompanying one another, though not so concurring.

*para*, (par.)—1. beside, from beside or not coincident with; 2. at the side: as, 1. para-centric, not coincident with the centre; para-dox, assertion not agreeing with appearances, or deviating from received opinion; 2. par-helion, a false sun aside of the true; parallel, one at the side of the other.

*peri.*—1. around; 2. nearest point to; as, 1. peri-meter, measure round; peri-phrasis, circumlocution; peri-phery, circumference or line round; peri-cardium, membrane round the heart; 2. perigee, peri-helion, nearest point to the earth, and sun.

*pro.*—Before: as, pro-gnosticate, perceive beforehand, foretell; pro-lepsis, anticipation, pro-phesy, foretell.

*syn*, (syl, sym, svs, syr.)—1. with, or together; 2. coincidence: as, 1. syn-thesis, placing together; sym-pathy, feeling with; syl-lable, letters taken together in one sound; sym-phony, sounds together; syn-agogue, congregation; syn-opsis, view together; syn-tax, placing together, construction; 2. syn-chronism, concurrence of times.

*General Remark.*—There are other Greek and Latin Prepositions, but they very rarely enter into the composition of English words.

# TABLE V

*French and English Prefixes.*

*a.*—1. at; 2. on or in; 3. to or for; 4. article *a* or *one*; 5. -ing, -or, -ed; 6. in verbs from nouns, means bring or give to; from adjectives to make; 7 with adjectives making adverbs, means -ly, manner, or state; 8. with some words expletive: as, 1. a-work; 2. a-shore, a-bed; 3. a-field, a-vouch, vouch to or for, a-wait, a-vow; 4. a-piece, a-par or one piece; 5. a-float, floating; a-drift, a-live, a-broach, broached, a-sunder; 6 a-maze, a-muse, a-feared, put in amaze, muse, fear; ac-company, bear company; ap-praise, set a price on; af-forest, to reduce to a forest; as-sort, reduce to sorts; ad-just, make right; ag-grandize, make great; 7. a-new, newly; a-lone, in a lone state; a-right, a-fresh; 8. a-wake, wake; a-rise, a-rouse, a-ware, ware, or wary.

*be.*—1. be or by; 2. to be; 3. at or for; 4 to; 5 in verbs derived from adjectives, to make; from nouns, to act like, by or upon; 6. intensive or expletive; 7. privative: as, 1. be-cause, be or by the cause; be-side, by the side; be-ware, be wary; be-fore, by the fore place; be-hind, by the hind place, below; 2. become, come to be; 3. be-wail, wail at or for; be-speak, be-weep, be-moan; 4. be-take, to take to; be-fall, be chance; 5. be-dim, make dim; benumb, befriend, act the friend by; be-witch, act the witch upon; besot, to make a fool of; be-dew, wet with dew; be-grime; 6. be-spatter, spatter, or spatter much; be-sprinkle; 7. be-head, deprive of the head.

*ounter.*—1. (The French *contre*, Latin *contra*) against; 2. contrariety; 3. reciprocal; 4. correspondent: 5. equal opposition: as, 1. counter-act; 2. counter mand, retract a command; counter-evidence, counter-march, back; 3. counterchange; 4 counter-part; 5. counter-vail, avail equally in opposition; counter-balance, exactly balance.

*e.*—1. from; 2 decrease; 3. contrariety; 4. intensive or expletive: as, 1. de-bar; 2. de-face, de-fame, detract from the appearance, reputation; de-grade, lower in grade; de-base, lower; de-compound, to compound still lower; 3. debark, disembark; de-compose, dissolve; de-camp, disencamp; decipher, unravel the meaning of ciphers; 4. de-paint, de-pasture, despoil, devoid.

*is.*—1. contrariety; 2. privation; 3. apart, diversily; 4. expletively; as, 1. dis-honest, not honest; dis-incline, dis-inter, unbury; disjoin, separate; 2. dis-arm, deprive of arms; dis-spirit, dis-passion, dis-honour; discredit; 3. spread, dis-spread diversely; dis-part, part asunder; 4. dis-annul.

*n*, (em.)—1. with nouns, put in or into, make into, give to; 2. with adjectives, to make; 3. with verbs *in*, intensive or expletive; as, 1. em-bark, go into a ship; en-circle, put in a circle; en-camp, en-cage, em-power, give power to en-courage, en-force, put in force; 2. en-dear, make dear; en-noble, enlarge en-marble, make into marble; en-slave, make a slave of; 3. en-wrap, en-chafe, en-grave, en-gender, en-glut, make to chafe, to grave, &c.

*or.*—1. forth, from, out, or away; as, 1. for-swear, for-bid, for-get, for-sake, for-bear, for-give.

*ore.*—1. before; 2. beforehand; 3. forth or from; 4. forepart of; 5. forward: as, 1. foregoing; 2. fore-see; 3. fore-close; 4. fore-head; 5. fore-land.

*rain.*—against; as, gainsay.

*n*, (il, im, in.—1. all the meanings of *en*; 2. negation; 3. contrariety, rarely; as, 1 im-body, put into a body; im-bosom, im-bower, im-brute, make into a brute; in-spirit, give spirit to; in-law, restore to the rights of law, opposed to out-law; im-brown, in-graft, in-weave, im-plant, in-born, in-bred, in-wrought, in-sight, make brown, graft in, weave in, &c.; 2. in-com-plete, il-legal, im-pure, ir-rational, not complete, &c.; in-capacity, il-legality, ir-religion, want of capacity, &c.; 3. in-dispose, disincline.

Note.—Both *en* and *in* being used to verbalize, are commonly joined with nouns, rarely with adjectives, and more rarely with verbs; in which last, as they are not wanted, they may be expletive, unless they make a neuter verb active.

*male.*—Ill; as, male-administration, male-content.

*mis.*—1. wrong; 2. ill: as, 1. mis-con-ceive; 2. mis-trust.

*won.*—1. French or Latin for *not*, sign of negation; 2. privation; as, 1. non-juring, not swearing; non-existence, want of existence; non-age; 2. non-plus, deprived of the power of saying more; non-suit.

*mer.*—1. over; beyond; 3. too much; 4. down; 5. more than; 6. to outdo by; 7. at too high a price: as, 1. over-arch; 2. over-go; 3. over-load; 4. over-throw; 5. over-balance; 6. over-power; 7. over-buy.

*nut.*—1. out; 2. outside; 3. abroad; 4. beyond, in distance, time, size, and number, weight, price, &c.; 5. to excel in acting the part of; 6. privitive; 7. intensive, or out of bounds: as, 1. out-bar; 2. out-line; 3. out-born; 4. out-go, out-live, out-grow, out-number, out-weigh, out-sell, out-bid; 5. out-knave; 6. out-law; 7. out-rage.

*un*,—1. undoes; 2. deprives; 3. negative; 4. expletive: as, 1. un-do, un-bury; 2. un-man; 3. un-able, unbelief; 4. un-loose.

Note.—*Un* and *dis* may be thus distinguished; *un* generally takes away a positive quality, *dis* reverses it. Thus, *unbelief* is simply a want of belief, and may be predicated even of those who are ignorant of its object; but *disbelief* is believing to be false, and can only be predicated of those who know the object of belief. *Un* sometimes occasions ambiguity; thus undeceivable, undeceiving, undeceived, are either derivatives of the negative verb *undeceive*, or negatives of the simple word *deceive*. Un is prefixed to all words originally English, and to all participles made privitive adjectives, as, *unfeeling*; and to most substantives having an English termination, as, *unfertileness*; which, if they have a borrowed termination, take *in*, as, *infertility*. If we borrow adjectives we retain the prefix *im*, as, *impolite*; but if we borrow and form, we use *un*, as, *unpolite*.

*up*.—1. up; 2. high; 3. over: as, 1. up-hold, up-lift; 2. up-land; 3. up-set.

# TABLE VI.

*Terminations.*

## NOUNS.

### 1. *Diminutive and Augmentative Nouns.*

*ock, ard, et* or *let, el* or *le, ing* or *ling, kin, y, eon, ion, oon*; rarely, *ila, lle, llo, tla, tte, llo, ot, in, oid, age, cce, aster, ow, ern,* and the sole *ah*; which denote a diminishing of the size, age, goodness, or dignity, as, hillock, a little hill; bullock, a young bull; park paddock; staggard, slow or sluggard; tower turret; ant emmet; crown coronet; eyelet, rivulet; home hamlet; nozle, sack satchel, particle; globule, yacht yawl, sanding, whiting; gosling, lordling; lambkin, (man or) monkey, baby; rascallion, lump luncheon, noon muncheon; ball ballot balloon; galley galleot galleon, gallon; spike spiggot; viol violin violincello; fortin; spadille, Drusus Drusilla, Priscilla; lunette, brown brunette, palmetto; Charlotte, Henrietta, Harriet (for Harriette;) sylphid, Nereus nereid; spheroid; fortilage; populace; poetaster; shadow, hollow; cavern; postern; sirrah.

Note.—Some nouns are diminished by abbreviation; as, in history story, rivulet rill, citizen cit, mistress miss, mobility mob, brigantine brig.

Note 2.—Names of persons are variously diminished by abbreviation and otherwise; as, Francis Frank, Henry Harry Hal, Walter Wat Watty, Alexander Aleck or Sander, whence Sawney, Sanderson Sanders, Peter Perkins, Thomas Tom, (Tomkinson) Tomkins, (Tomling) Tomlinson, Elizabeth Eliza Betsey, Sarah Sally, Esther Hester Hetty, Jane Jenny, Catharine Kitty, Margaret Peggy, &c.

Note 3.—*Let* is a contraction of little, *kin* of kind, a child: *and* means genius or natural disposition: *ling*, little or little one. All words in *ling* seem to be participles of frequentative verbs in *le* or *el*. *Oid* implies rather imperfection than diminution, signifying resemblance or tendency to the form of.

Note 4.—Some of these terminations, especially *y*, in proper names, besides diminishing, denote sometimes endearment, and sometimes contempt.

### 2. *Terminations of Agents, joined with verbs, nouns, and adjectives.*

*er*, or, *ant*, *ist*, *ent*, *ary*; (rarely *ust*, *iff*, *loin*, *tain*, *ion*, *on*, *o'*, *ard*, *zen*, *ness*;) the adjective and participial terminations *ate*, *tory*, *ac* or *ic*, *al*, *ar*, *ain*,, (for *ane*;

frequently *can, ian, ene, ine, esc ite;* and in the plural *ch, ish,* denoting 1. the occasional actor, and 2. the habitual and professional actor; 3. maker; 4. worker; 5. dealer; 6. keeper; 7. driver; 8. governor; 9. professor; 10. adherent; 11. inhabitant or native; 12. descendant; 13. one armed with; 14. possessor of a thing or quality; 15. user; 16. one charged with; 17. one of; 18. expletive, &c. But *ier* or *yer,* generally denotes dealer; *ian,* professor; *ite,* descendant; *an,* with the last six, inhabitant or native: as, 1. 2. acter, he that acts occasionally; actor, he that acts professionally; saver saviour, begger beggar, catechiser catechist, paraphraser paraphrast, informer informant, assister assistant, presider president, doter dotard, glutton, witness, spinner spinster; 3. hatter, sonnetteer, clothier, punster, dialist, economist, statuary, historian; 4. tinner, glazier, gardener, collier; 5. grocer, hosier, malster, tobacconist; (5. 4.) lapidist, lapidary; 6. jailer, cashier, chamberlain, librarian, publican, wharfinger, castellain; 7. drover, charioteer, muleteer; 8. shire sheriff, bailiff, brigadier; 9. necromancer, lawyer, warrior, methodist, artisan, musician, puritan; 10. sectary, partisan, (deism) deist, Calvinist, Christian; 11. villager, Londoner, carmelite, bedlamite, courtier, mountaineer, stagirite, citizen, Norwegian, American, Tarentine, Nazarene, Chinese; (plural) French, (Dane) Danish; 12. Levite; 13. musketeer, grenadier; 14. annuitant, captain, chieftain, holder of the head, chief piece; chaplain, favourite, zealot, maniac, demoniac; barbarian, barbarous person; youngster, potentate, (rough) ruffian, drunkard, (wise) wizard; 15. sworder, sawyer, drummer; 16. officer, messenger, almoner, cellarist, tapster, criminal, centurion, decurion; 17. chorister, trooper, scholar; 18. sophister.
To these add some irregularly derived agents, instruments, &c., work wright, tribe tribune, smite smith, pinch pinchers pincers, hand hammer, hale or haul halter, tie tether, sauce saucer, plate platter, fry fritter, bough bower, sun summer, wind winter window, garb garment, array raiment, hold hilt, gird girth girdle, shoot shutile, horn hornet, &c.

Note.—Dealers, insert *y* after *w,* and *i* after *l, r, th, s; age* runs into *enger* in passage, message, wharfage; *er* becomes *eer* diminutive in several, as, sonnetteer, &c., *st* is sometimes inserted before *er,* as, songster; and *i* before *st* in chorister, barrister; or follows *s* or *t* in all verbal agents except governor, conqueror, sailor; verbs in double *ss* have agents in *or,* except engross, discuss. Agents in *ator* are 150, while those in *ater* are but relater, idolater, slater, prayer, conservator, exasperater, regrater. Agents in *ctor* are 36, those in *cter* are detracter, protracter, exacter, perfecter, neglecter, expecter, directer, detecter, contradicter, afflicter, inflicter, obstructer. Agents derived from nouns without change, take *er,* except escheator, assignator, suitor, preceptor: and some contrasted words; as, debtor, creditor, grantor, &c.

### 3. *Receivers of the act of the verb, or of a thing.*

*ee, t, te;* as, endorsee, mortgagee, assignee, referee, legatee, patentee, licentiatereceiver of an endorsement, mortgage, assignment, &c., obligee, grandee, relict, bankrupt, saint, adult, graduate, delegate, person obliged, made great, left, convicted, with bank broken, made holy, grown up, graduated, delegated. To these add *end, and, andum,* denoting *that which ought or is to receive the act of the verb;* as, reverend, multiplicand, subtrahend, minuend, dividend, memorandum, that which ought or is to be revered, multiplied, divided, subtracted, diminished, remembered.

Note—*Ee* is varied from *é* the termination of French perfect participles; *t, te,* from the Latin

### 4. *Official Terminations.*

*ship*, *dom*, *age*, *hood*, *ate*, *alty*, *ure*, *cry*, *cy*, signifying with official persons; 1. office; 2. jurisdiction, or that over which they preside; 3. title of respect; 4 (with other persons) character, quality; 5. state or condition; 6. duration of the state; 7. art, trade, wares, place: as, 1. stewardship, kingdom, captaincy, agency, (bishop,) episcopate, consulate, baronage, prelacy, mayoralty, priesthood, prelature; 2. tetrarchate, marquisate, electorate, bishoprick, bailiwick, deanery, county, dutchy; 3. lordship; 4. friendship, soldiership, infancy, idiocy, folly, sophistry, bigotry, surgery, prudery, mocker mockery; 5. noviciate, pupillage; 6. apprenticeship; 7. carpentry, surgery, housewifery, archery, pedlery.

### 5. *Collective Terminations.*

*ry*; very rarely *y*, *ity*, *alty*, *age*, *ate*, *ing*, *hood*, *red*; to be rendered by the plural of the nouns collected: as, yeomanry, imagery, spicery, finery, drapery, clergy, ancestry, nobility, commonalty, herbage, foliage, triumvirate, shipping, clothing, sisterhood, kindred.

### 6. *Terminations of Abstract Qualities joined with Adjectives*

*ness*, *ity*, *tude*, *nce*, *ncy*, *ty*, *sy*, *ism*, *ion*, *ure*, *th*, *ht*, *men dom*; to be rendered quality or state: as, goodness, quietude, excellence, decency, silence, safety, solidity, sobriety, gravity, courtesy, bondage, parallelism, imperfection, contrition, temperature, truth, breadth, length, (whole heal hale) health, slow sloth, dearth, young youth, merry mirth, foul filth, height, sly slight, acute acumen, wise wisdom, freedom; with hot heat, proud, pride, sorry, sorrow, &c.

Note.—*Age, ism, ion, ure*, though properly verbal terminations denoting action or its effects, are classed here, because the words to which they are joined are used no longer as verbs, but participles or adjectives. *Ness* and *ity*, are the most frequent, there being about 1350 nouns in *ness*, and 600 in *ity*. The rest are very uncommon

### 7. *Terminations of actions, or verbal and participial Nouns.*

*ing*, *ion*, *ment*, *ure nce*, *age*, *l*; and very rarely *ade*, *ism*, *se*, *ss*, *x*, *al*, *th*, *ht*, *ice*, *y*, *cry*, *or*, *our*, *ter*, *der*, *ship*, *ledge*, *red*, *ison*; denoting, 1. the act of the verb; 2. its effect or the thing produced by that act; 3. actor; 4. faculty of acting; as, 1. a producing, coercion, cohesion, redemption, confirmation; amendment: defiance, abhorrence; repulse, applause; (1. 2.) lapse, concourse; offence; egress; contempt, complaint, conquest, assault, desert; flow, flux; trial, burial; inquiry, mockery, bribery; evangelism; (1. 3.) stoppage; death, growth; flight; notice; behaviour; laughter, slaughter; attainder; blockade; courtship, (analogically courtiership;) knowledge; hatred, comparison, disinherison; enthusiasm, acting like an enthusiast; 2. an offering, thing offered; horror, error; provision, thing provided; ornament; creature; freightage, draught, weight, gift, feint, blossom, from blow; 4. understanding; imagination; judgment; intellect. Other verbals are formed by a change of the final consonants into their cognates and otherwise, or without any change; as, life, belief, batch, breach, speech, expense, loss, choice, race, practice, prophecy, gap, tale, sale, loan, bliss, song, wreath, food, gait, deed, &c.

Note.—Verbs in *de, nd, nt, rt, rge, rse,* change *se, d, t, ge, se,* into *sion,* except *in- con-, at tend; sert, -tort,* which have *tion,* while *tend, ob-, pre-, in-, por-, ex-tend,* and the simple *-tort* have *sion ; -pel, -vel,* become *pul,* vul-sion, mane, mansion; cline, clension; fuse, fusion; cede, cession; *mit. cide,* mission, cession; and *cur* ends the list of those which take *sion.* Stringe takes striction; join, junction; stinguish, stinction; punge, punction; duce, duction; tain, tention; vene, vention; monish, monition; minish, minution; quire, (*y*) quisition; pone, pose, position; ceive, ception; move, motion; scribe, ecription, sume, sumption; reedeem, redemption; sorb, sorption; solve, volve, solution, volution. Verbals in *cion* are coercion, suspicion, internecion. Of 1630 in *tion,* 1200 ends in *ation.* Of 240 in *ure* 200 in each of *ance, ence,* or *ncy* and *cze,* 30, in *ure,* 120 in *ance,* 130 in *ence,* (of which 30 are inceptives in *scence,*) and but 8 or 10 in *age* are strictly verbal. Nineteen verbs in *fy* (mostly in *efy,* from Latin verbs in *eo*) change *fy* into faction, factive, factory. About 50 others (which end in *efy*) change *fy* into fication, ficative, ficatory.

### S. *Local Terminations.*

*ton,* (town,) *ham, wick* or *wich,* (village,) *ness,* (promontory,) *bury,* (borough,) &c. the collective *ry, ery ;* the adjective and participial *ary, ory :* as, Charleston, Charles' town; Peacham; Berwick, Norwich; Sheerness; Newbury, Newburgh, Petersborough; heronry, coalery, collier colliery, ropery, foundry, fishery, aviary, dispensary, armory, observatory.

### 2. *ADJECTIVE TERMINATIONS.*

1.—*ish.*—Tendency: as, foolish, churlish, girlish, swinish, apt to be like a fool, &c.; feverish, brinish, tending to fever, &c.; freakish, bookish, whitish, reddish, inclined to freaks, books, to be white, &c.; snappish, apt to snap, ticklish, easy to be tickled.

Note.—This termination has nearly the effect of *esco* of Latin inceptive verbs.

2.—*some.*—Tendency: as, quarrelsome, inclined or apt to quarrel, &c.; toothsome, handsome, fit or agreeable to the tooth, &c.; gamesome, wholesome, loathsome, tending to make game, &c.; blithesome, dark-, lightsome, tending or apt to be blithe, &c.

3 *Of Plenty—y, ful, ous, ose, acious.*—To be rendered, full of, or filled with, or the like: as, gritty, healthy, wealthy, stony; fearful, peaceful, vicious, hazardous, dangerous; operose, crinose, tumulose, verbose, full of, or filled with health, &c.; labour, hair, hills, words; bibacious, pugnacious, apt to drink, fight; minacious, loquacious, full of threats, talk.

Note.—Y is derived from *e,* the termination of the French participle perfect, and *ous* and *ose* form that of the Latin. Therefore adjectives with these terminations may be translated by participles of English verbalized nouns, with little or no variation of meaning; as, knotty knotted, cloudy clouded, veiny veined, sandy sanded, rugose wrinkled, &c. With containers, *ful* makes nouns and means the quantity they will hold; as, handful, spoonful, what the hand will hold, &c.

4.—*Of Want.*—*less.*—to be rendered without, or not to be: as, heartless, staunchless, resistless, exhaustless, trustless, not to be quenched, &c.; which are scarcely used but in poetry.

5. *Matter or Substance.—en*, and perhaps *eous*.—To be rendered made or consisting of: as, golden, brazen, woollen, silken, leathern, made of gold, brass, &c.; vitreous, ligneous, ferreous, made or consisting of glass, wood, iron.

Note.—Adjectives of the termination *en*, seem to be the participles of nouns verbalized; as of golded, brazed, &c., made gold, &c.

6.—*Of Property or Likeness.—ly, ic* or *ical, al, an, ar, ary, ne, ous, se, ac* or *acal, ese, isch, ch, ite;* to be rendered like, belonging, having, &c.: as, marly, heroic, heroical, national, presbyterian, American, Herculean, consular, customary, mundane (the world,) terrene (the earth,) serpentine, Alexandrine, Nicene, wit wise, fail false, globose, prosodial, prosodiacal, Chinese, French, Romish, Swedish, Muscovite, Israelitish; lenten.

7.—*Multiplicatives.—fold, ple.*—To be rendered, together, &c.; as, twofold, threefold, &c., double, (from duple,) triple, quadruple, &c.

8.—*Direction.—ward.*—which means looking; as, toward, froward, forward, looking to, from, before.

9.—*Order.—th.*—fourth, fifth, &c.

10.—*Participial Active.—ing, ant, ent, sory, tory, id, und, bund:* as, lasting, pleasant, different, promissory, prohibitory, excusatory, that which lasts; pleasing, differing, &c.; vagrant, indignant, existent, illusory, wandering, disdaining, &c.; lucid, valid, liquid, fluid, shining, availing, melting, flowing, jocund, joking, vagabond, wandering.

Note.—*Ate, ation, atory, atire, ary, able, ant, ance,* are kindred terminations; also, *ion, sion, tion, to y, sory, ible, ent, ence.*

11.—*Potential Active.—ive, ic.*—provocative, palliative motive, analytic, caustic that which may (or does) provoke, palliate, move, analyze, burn.

12.—*Potential Passive.—ile, ible, able.*—as, productile, producible, facile, docile, provocable, that which may be produced, done, taught, provoked.

Note.—English derivatives have *able;* except descend, extend, rend, elude, discern, press, fuse, contract, effect, collect, divert, revert, manifest, digest, resist, exhaust, solve; and the doubtful, commit, praise, infer, reverse, which have *ible.*

12.—*Participial Passive.—ed, en, ate, ete, ite, ote, ute, t, se, ss, x:* as, fledged feathered, drunken made drunk, inviolate not violated, prolate extended forward (along the axis,) oblate extended in the way of the motion (across the axis,) complete filled up in all the parts, definite bounded, remote removed, resolute resolved, exact performed, perfect done throughout, strict bound, exempt bought off, adverse turned towards (against,) recluse shut back, apart, remiss, remitted, complex woven together, convex raised; sainted made a saint, winged, forked, furnished with wings, forks; chalybeate, impregnated with iron, vitriolate; passionate guided by passion, laureate crowned with laurel, complicate complicated, reprobate reprobated.

### 3. Terminations of Verbs.

1.—*Inceptive.—en, ise* or *ize, fy, ate, er.*—denoting a beginning and growing action, gradually communicating or acquiring a quality, thing, or person;* and may be rendered to make, become, grow, give, receive, &c.: as, shorten, weaken, lengthen, strengthen, heighten, frighten, Christ christen, chaste chasten, chastise, civilize, humanize, criticise, apostatize, philosophize, methodize, to turn critic, apostate, philosopher, or to turn dealer in criticism, apostacy, philosophy, method or methodism; vilify, amplify, stupid stupify, falsify, grateful gratify, petrify (stone,) ossify (bone,) brute or brutal brutify, sanguify (blood,) ramify (branches,) certain certify, testify (witness,) deify (God;) sublime sublimate, validate, compassionate, capacitate; birth burthen burden; food fodder, (dominus, a master,) domineer.

Other verbs of the same kind are formed by changing consonants into their cognates lengthening the vowel, &c.; as, glass glaze, bath bathe, breath breathe, cloth clothe, grief grieve, half halve, shelf shelve, loth lothe loath, wry writhe, ten tithe, secret secrete, holy hollow, wind winnow, gold gild, part parse, dry drain.

2.—*Frequentative, or diminutive.*—*le,* rarely *el, l, er,* or *r.*—denoting frequency and consequently diminution of action; as, talk tattle, wade waddle, drip dribble drivel, shove shuffle, crack crackle, draw drawl, grose grovel, chat chatter, spit spatter sputter, gild glitter, smile simper, sing simmer, mould moulder, climb clamber, sleep slumber, wave waver, low lower lour, out utter, fail falter, hiss whiz whisper, whine whimper, stand stammer, stick stutter.

3.—Intensive or augmentative verbs, are variously formed without rule; as, snore snort, yell yelp, wave waft, twine twist, break burst, clean cleanse, bound bounce, crack crash crush, lick lash, gnaw gnash, gape gasp, gripe grasp, chime chink, sit set, full fill, swell swill, lie lay, rise raise, prize praise, &c.

### 4. *Other Terminations and peculiar meanings of the foregoing*

*ly.*—Adverbial.—To be rendered manner; as, wisely, in a wise manner.
*iad.*—Fate of; as, Iliad, Columbiad, Dunciad, fate of Ilion, Columbia, Dunces.
*age.*—tax, allowance, dwelling room; as, wharfage, leakage, personage, stow age.
*ism.*—worship, doctrine or creed, and idiom; as, paganism, Calvanism, Grecism
*ing.*—district; as, a *riding* of Yorkshire, a tithing; &c.
*y.*—country; as, Germany, Gascony, Italy.
*th.*—period; as, moon month.
*ic.*—is sometimes a contraction of the participial *icate,* and sometimes denotes *art;* as, fabric from fabricate, i. e. fabricated; rhetoric, logic.

---

*Exercises explaining the use of the foregoing Tables.*

1.—Read Art. 1. Table 6. with the notes 1. 2. explaining each word as it occurs: thus, hillock, a little hill; bullock, a young bull, &c. Try to mention other words of similar terminations.

* Any word or phrase may become a verb by prefixing *to* as hand to hand, long to long, thee and thou to thee and thou.

2.—Reverse this exercise: thus, What word signifies a little hill, a young bull, &c., a short or a false history? Address Francis familiarly, endearingly, contemptuously, or with vulgar familiarity, &c.
3.—What terminations denote diminution or augmentation?
4.—What is the meaning of each in note 3?
5.—Mention all the terms in *aid*; in *aster*; in *ard*.
6.—Read Art. 2. explaining each word as it occurs: thus, acter, one who occasionally acts; actor, one who acts professionally or habitually; hatter, a maker of hats, &c.
7.—Reverse this exercise: thus, What word signifies one who occasionally acts &c. &c.?
8.—Recite the terminations of agents.
9.—What termination denotes dealer?
10.—What words insert *i* and *y* before *er* to form them? See *Note*.
11.—What terminations denote professor, descendant, inhabitant, or native?
12.—What are the meanings of *ier, yer, ian, ite*?
13—What agents end in *or*, in *ater*, in *er*? What letter does *or* follow, with the exceptions?
14.—Perform similar exercises on articles 3, 4, 5, 6, 7, 8.
15.—Recite the rules and observations in note under 7.
16—Illustrate the remaining articles in the same manner.
17.—What are the first meanings of *a, ab, abs, ad, am,* &c., through the Latin, Greek, French, and English prefixes?
18.—To which is each opposed?
19.—What is the difference of *ob, ex, de*; of *ante, pre,* and *pro; contra, ob,* and *preter;* of *di* and *se;* of *trans* and *ultra*?
20.—What are the rules for repeating the prepositions after words compounded with them?
21.—What are the signs of contrariety? of intension?
22.—Form and explain the derivatives of *cumb,* to lie; *turb,* to confound, &c.&c.
23.—Reverse this exercise, i. e., what word signifies *to lie at, to lie under, lying back,* &c. &c.

Note.—In hearing the daily spelling or parsing lessons, cause the classes to derive the words, &c. as directed in the Advertisement.

---

*cumb,* } to lie,
*cubate,* } to brood.
*turb,* confound like a crowd.
*epi* } *demic,* the people.
*en* }
*fic,* fical, making, causing, producing.
*lucid,* receiving } light.
*lucent,* giving }
*luminous,* light.
*lumine-ate,* to give light.
*scend,* to climb.
*fend,* to strike.

*prehend,* to hold, seize.
*pend,* to hang, to weigh.
*send,* to stretch.
*scind,* to cut, tear.
*spond,* to promise.
*ound,* to rise in waves, boil, flow.
*found,* } to pour.
*fuse,* }
*tund,* to smite.
*cord,* heart, or chord.
*plaud,* to clap.
*srcibe,* to write.

*script*, written.
*prove*, to make good.
*place*, to put.
*balance*, to poise.
*vince,* } to conquer
*vict,* }
*nounce*, to tell.
*duce,* } to lead, draw
*duct,* }
*rade*, to rub.
*grade*, to step, degree.
*gress*, to step.
*vade*, to march, go.
*suade*, to advise.
*cede*, to depart, resign.
*sede*, to sit.
*side*, to settle.
*cide*, to cut, slay, killing, killer.
*cide*, to fall, or happen.
*fide*, to trust.
*lide*, to strike.
*ride*, to laugh.
*vide,* } to see.
*vise,* }
*rode*, to gnaw, eat.
*clude,* } to shut.
*close,* }
*clause,* } to shut, closed.
*cluse,* }
*lude*, to play.
*trude*, to thrust, push.
*sude*, to sweat, ooze.
*quiet*, rest, repose.
*quiescent*, resting, tending to rest.
*gage*, pledge.
*judge*, to declare the law.
*cour-age*, heart-iness.
*lect*, to choose, gather.
*legate*, to despatch.
*lige*, to bind.
*change*, to alter.
*fringe*, to break.
*stringe,* } to grasp, bind.
*strict,* }
*charge*, to load, enjoin.
*merge,* } to sink.
*merse,* }
*sperge,* } to scatter.
*sparse,* }

*terge,* } to cleanse.
*terse,* }
*verge*, to bend, incline.
*fuge*, to fly.
*fugacious*, apt to fly.
*gorge*, the throat.
*apo* }
*ana* } -*strophe*, turning.
*cata* }
*be, re, par,* } -take
*under, over, mis-* }
*voke,* } to call.
*vocale,* }
*ex, in,* -hale, to breathe.
*sume*, to take.
*mundane*, of the world.
*fine*, end, bound, limit.
*finite*, bounded.
*finish*, to end.
*termine, -ate,* to limit.
*vene,* } to come.
*vent,* }
*a re,* -venuo.
*venture*, to be about to come.
*cline*, to bend, incline.
*marine*, of the sea.
*pone,* }
*pose,* } to place, put.
*posite,* }
*position*.
*de, en, in, un,* throne.
*ad, in, co,* -here, to stick.
*spire*, to breathe.
*quire,* }
*quest,* } to seek.
*quisite,* }
*plore*, to wail, weep.
*centre*, (middle,) point.
*ec* }
*para* } -centric.
*figure*, fashion, shape, form.
*jure*, to swear.
*mure*, a wall.
*base*, foot (of a column.)
*crease*, to grow.
*crescive*, growing.
*crescent, crescence*, tending to grow
*crement*, growth.
*crete*, grown.

*phrase,*
*phrasis,* } speech.
*preciate,*
*praise,* } to put a price.
*prise,* to take.
*lapse,* to slip.
*burse,* a purse.
*ab, dis, -use,*
*ce, ex, -cuse,* a trial.
*bate,* to beat.
*locate,* to place.
*date,* to mark the time.
*add,* give to.
*create,* to make, produce.
*gregate,* to flock.
*navigate,* to sail a ship.
*naval,* of a ship.
*nary,* collection of ships.
*fable,* may be spoken, or told.
*jugate,* to yoke
*sociate,* to couple.
*mediate,* to come in the middle.
*radiate,* to throw rays.
*foliate,* to leaf.
*viate,* way.
*colate,* to drip.
*ambulate,* to walk.
*animate,* life.
*nominate,* to name.
*umbrate,* to shadow.
*literate,* lettered.
*migrate,* to remove.
*monstrate,* to show.
*state,* to stand, place.
*stant,* standing.
*substantiate,* give substance to.
*sist,* to stand.
*stitute,* to put, place.
*tenuate,* to make slender.
*novate,* to make new.
*novel,* new.
*novice, -ate,*
*plete,* to fill, filled.
*cite,* to move, stir, call.
*tribute,* to give, grant, bestow.
*secute,* to follow.
*mute,* to change.
*pute,* to reckon, cut.
*rogate,* to ask, beg, demand.

*cave,*
*cept,* } to take hold.
*cipient,* holding.
*vive,* to live.
*solve,* to loose.
*volve,* to roll.
*move,*
*serve,* to keep.
*struc,*
*struct,* } to build.
*story,*
*tach,* to touch.
*stinguish,*
*stinct,* } to put out, mark
*anti,*
*amphi,* } *scii,* shadows.
*pel,* to drive.
*sail,*
*sult,* } to leap.
*vail,* to be strong
*stil,* to drop.
*dia*
*ana* } -gram, writing.
*epi*
*claim,* to cry, call.
*firm.*
*form.*
*ante*
*post* } -meridian, mid-day
*sign,* to mark.
*pugn,* to fight
*tain,* to hold, to keep.
*join.*
*locate,* to place.
*peal,* to call.
*pellation.*
*agon,* angle.
*cern,* to see
*crete,*
*creet,* } seen.
*orn,* deck.
*journ,* a day
*similar,* like
*lunar, y,* of the moon.
*fer,* to bring, bear.
*late,* borne, extended.
*dia*
*peri* } -meter, measurer
*hyper*

*pare,*  
*pair,* } to make ready, procure.  
*cur,* to run.  
*anti*  
*hypo*  
*meta* } *-thesis,* a placing.  
*par-en*  
*syn*  
*fess,* to own.  
*ferous,*  
*gerous,* } bearing.  
*parous,* bringing forth.  
*vorous,* devouring.  
*press.*  
*act,* to do  
*fract,* to break.  
*tract,* to draw.  
*fect,*  
*fice,* } to make, or do.  
*ject,* to cast.  
*flect,* to bend.  
*spect,* to look.  
*sect,* to cut.  
*secant,* cutting.

*dict,* to say.  
*cinct,* to bind, bound.  
*habit,*  
*hibit,* } to have, hold.  
*it,* a going.  
*jacent,* lying.  
*sent,* to feel, think.  
*rupt,* to break, broken.  
*sert,* to sow.  
*vert,* to turn.  
*verse,* turned.  
*port,* to bear.  
*tort,* to twist.  
*gest,* to bear.  
*past,* a taste.  
*test,* to witness.  
*sist,* to stand, (see state.)  
*fix,* to fasten.  
*flux,* a flowing.  
*cracy,* government.  
*tomy,* cutting.  
*logy,* speaking, description.  
*graphy,* writing, description.  
*metry,* measure.  
*meter,* measurer.

**THE END.**

www.ingramcontent.com/pod-product-compliance
Lightning Source LLC
Chambersburg PA
CBHW030335170426
43202CB00010B/1137